IMAGINING TOMBSTONE

CultureAmerica

Erika Doss
Philip J. Deloria
Series Editors

Karal Ann Marling
Editor Emerita

Imagining Tombstone

The Town Too Tough to Die

KARA L. MCCORMACK

University Press of Kansas

Published by the University Press of Kansas (Lawrence, Kansas 66045), which was organized
by the Kansas Board of Regents and is operated and funded by Emporia State University,
Fort Hays State University, Kansas State University, Pittsburg State University, the University
of Kansas, and Wichita State University.

Library of Congress Cataloging-in-Publication Data
Names: McCormack, Kara L., author.
Title: Imagining Tombstone : the town too tough to die / Kara L. McCormack.
Description: Lawrence, Kansas : University Press of Kansas, 2016. | Series:
   CultureAmerica | Includes bibliographical references and index.
Identifiers: LCCN 2016000657 | ISBN 9780700622238 (cloth : alk. paper) |
   ISBN 9780700622740 (ebook)
Subjects: LCSH: Tombstone (Ariz.)—History. | Popular culture—Arizona—
   Tombstone. | Popular culture—West (U.S.)
Classification: LCC F819.T6 M43 2016 | DDC 979.1/53—dc23
LC record available at http://lccn.loc.gov/2016000657.

British Library Cataloguing-in-Publication Data is available.

Printed in the United States of America

10 9 8 7 6 5 4 3 2 1

The paper used in this publication is recycled and contains 30 percent postconsumer waste.
It is acid free and meets the minimum requirements of the American National Standard for
Permanence of Paper for Printed Library Materials Z39.48-1992.

For Finian David and Elijah Dawit,
who may walk into their own legend one day . . .

CONTENTS

ACKNOWLEDGMENTS

I have been "living" with Tombstone for a number of years now, and I am indebted to many for helping bring this project to fruition. At the University of New Mexico, my academic adviser and committee chair, Dr. A. Gabriel Meléndez, was a tremendous influence on and supporter of my work. His work in film and critical regionalism studies greatly affected my own academic endeavor, and his encouragement on this work helped make my arguments stronger and clearer. Dr. Rebecca Schreiber imparted her expertise in popular culture and cultural studies to me, an eager and willing student who realized after a number of meetings about this project that I will always be awed by her knowledge and approach to scholarship. Dr. Paul Andrew Hutton had been an integral part of my studies at the University of New Mexico and continues to be a mentor and wellspring of advice. I thank him for his support and inspiration. My friends and colleagues at the *New Mexico Historical Review*, most notably Dr. Durwood Ball, were amazingly supportive and encouraging. Dr. Ball continues to offer guidance as I navigate the seas of academia after graduate school, for which I am very grateful.

I want to thank everyone at the University Press of Kansas, especially Michael Briggs for his advice and guidance. I am deeply and forever grateful to Michael Elliott of Emory University and David Wrobel of the University of Oklahoma for their careful reading of my manuscript and thoughtful suggestions for improvement. I would also like to doubly thank David Wrobel for his availability and advice whenever I have needed it. An early version of one of these chapters was published by the *Journal of Arizona History*, and I thank Bruce Dinges for being so welcoming of my work. I'd also like to thank Caitlin Lampman at the Arizona Historical Society. The research for this work was partly funded and fully supported by Stanford University and the Thinking Matters Program, and I would like to thank them for giving me the opportunity to make that last visit to Tombstone, as well as giving me the time and space to finalize this manuscript. I would especially like to thank Ellen Woods, Parna Sengupta, Shelley Fisher Fishkin, Eric Roberts,

Allyson Hobbs, and all my friends and colleagues for offering advice, support, and guidance in research and all other academic endeavors.

I would like to thank my family. My sisters Suzanne and Beth helped me study for the GRE all those years ago and have supported me ever since. Suzanne has also been completely willing and available to help me with TIF files and other image questions, making time for me no matter what she had on the grill. My nephews Finian and Elijah have brought such joy to all of us, and I thank them for warming our hearts. I thank my mother, Anne, and my father, Robert, for being so supportive of this endeavor since I came up with the idea years ago. My father's love for all things western was an early influence on my choice of field, and his continued interest in my work has been a gift to me. I would also like to thank all of my family and friends in New Mexico, Massachusetts, and California who have supported me through time and space, and for that I am forever grateful.

Lastly, I would like to thank the people of Tombstone, both locals and visitors, all of whom opened up to me in ways I could not have imagined before I began. Specifically I would like to thank "Bronco Bill" Pakinkis, Nancy Sosa, Janice Hendricks, the wonderful people at the beautiful Tombstone Monument Ranch, and all the people I met throughout this journey. You all shared your passion for Tombstone and the Old West and helped me craft a deeper, much more thoughtful exploration into the efforts to sustain this great town.

I cannot thank you enough.

Introduction

The Tombstone Mystique

In 1877 mine prospector Edward Lawrence "Ed" Schieffelin set out from Fort Huachuca in the Dragoon Mountains in southeast Arizona Territory in search of silver, encouraged by stories of a previous prospector named Frederick Brunckow, a German émigré who found silver in the same area decades earlier.[1] As Schieffelin headed east into dangerous Apache territory, he was told by skeptics that all he would find would be his own tombstone. Instead, he found silver. He called the strike Tombstone in response to his critics, and the area went on to become one of the fastest-growing silver mining towns in the West. So it begins.

Of course, the story of the area starts long before this moment. Apaches had been living on this land for centuries before Ed Schieffelin made his discovery. Francisco Vásquez de Coronado brought his expedition through the San Pedro Valley in 1540, and Spanish settlers resided there for close to three hundred years before Arizona came under Mexican rule in 1821. Most of modern-day Arizona was acquired by the United States as part of the Treaty of Guadalupe Hidalgo in 1848, and the Gadsden Purchase pushed the US border to its current limits in the Southwest in 1853. But the official story begins with Schieffelin staking his claim and naming the place Tombstone. Considered the origin story of the city, the founding of Tombstone by Schieffelin is as important to the Tombstone legend as what would become known as the "Gunfight at the OK Corral."[2] With the Schieffelin story, Tombstone finds its place among the legends of riches and romance that continue to circulate about the broader West.

Portrait of Edward Schieffelin, founder of Tombstone, ca. 1880. (Courtesy of Sharlot Hall Museum, SHM Photographs, #14573)

After christening the Tombstone Mine and the Grave Yard Mine in August 1877, Ed joined forces with his brother Al and their associate Richard Gird to stake more claims. The Tombstone Mining District was formally organized on 5 April 1878. Situated thirty miles from the Mexico border and sixty miles from the New Mexico line, Tombstone became famous in those

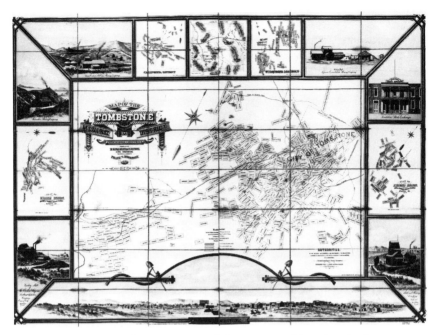

Color lithograph map showing mining claim names and locations in the Tombstone Mining District, Cochise County, Arizona Territory, 1881. Compiled by M. Kelleher and M. R. Peel, designed and drawn by Frank S. Ingoldsby. (Photograph courtesy of Library of Congress, Geography and Map Division)

days because of the millions of dollars in silver that were being extracted from its mines. Unlike Dodge City or Wichita, Kansas, which were cowboy and cattle towns, Tombstone was populated by hundreds and then thousands of men seeking their fortune from silver mining. From its modest beginnings as a camp where "a few hundred fortune hunters" slept in tents and wagons, Tombstone quickly "leaped upon the map as a full-fledged town." Its population soared from two thousand in 1878 to six thousand a year later, rivaling Tucson, the largest city in the territory and the Pima County seat.[3]

In November 1878, five months prior to Tombstone's official founding, a stage line called the Tucson and Tombstone Express started carrying travelers between these two bustling towns for ten dollars (fifteen dollars round trip).[4] In addition to miners, the promise of riches and a growing population attracted lumber companies, real estate moguls, lawyers, doctors, and merchants. Soon lavish hotels, high-end restaurants, and textile shops that sold the best silks and satins were opening in the central business district

now known as Allen Street. Newcomers saw a town of paradoxes, teetering between ramshackle and refined, a town where wine, champagne,
and a variety of mixed drinks were as popular among patrons as beer and
"shots of red-eye." Visitors encountered beautifully crafted and appointed
saloons and gambling halls with long bars of polished brass and mahogany,
carpets from Europe, and live piano accompaniment.[5] Indeed, "the mining camp that four years earlier had consisted of canvas and adobe" now
had "French restaurants, oyster bars, tennis courts, a bowling alley, and ice
cream parlors."[6]

Fast-growing Tombstone had its problems, too. Mining towns like
Tombstone had a large number of male citizens whose pursuits after work
were dubious. Saloons, gambling halls, burlesque shows, and prostitution
were all hallmarks of this burgeoning town. The prevalence of drinking establishments and the pace at which the town expanded led to some alterca-
tions early on in Tombstone's history. By the time Wyatt Earp, his brothers
James and Virgil, and their wives arrived in Tombstone at the end of 1879,
attracted by the promise of riches and opportunity, Tombstone already had
a rowdy reputation. But this was not unusual for a frontier town. In fact,
writer Casey Tefertiller suggests that Tombstone was "no wilder than most
mining towns and certainly not as wicked as Dodge with its city-of-sin atmosphere."[7] Typical as Tombstone was, law and order were hard to come
by in this newly founded town. In an effort to curb crime, the city council
passed an ordinance in April 1880 prohibiting anyone from carrying firearms within city limits. Virgil Earp, who had already served as a deputy in
Yavapai County and constable in Prescott, Arizona, was appointed deputy
US marshal of southern Arizona when the brothers stopped in Tucson.
He was appointed acting town marshal of Tombstone in October 1880, a
position he held for two weeks until another man beat him out in a special
election in November. When the man who had won that election skipped
town without explanation, Virgil was appointed permanent town marshal
in June 1881.

Wyatt had hopes of starting a stagecoach business when he arrived in
Tombstone, but instead he took a job with Wells Fargo as an armed guard.
Because Wyatt had a history of being a lawman, in July 1880 the Democratic sheriff, Charlie Shibell, appointed him undersheriff for the eastern
part of Pima County, which included Tombstone at the time. Wyatt held
that position for only three months when Shibell selected John Behan, a
lawman and legislator in the area since 1866 and a fellow Democrat, as
undersheriff after Shibell's contentious and questionable reelection.[8] Soon
after, however, Pima County was cut in two, and Tombstone found itself

in the newly formed Cochise County, which was in need of a sheriff of its own. Both Behan and Wyatt were interested in that position, but, according to Wyatt, when Behan agreed to make Wyatt his deputy, Earp withdrew from the campaign. In a victory praised by the outlaw faction in the area, Behan won the election and, again according to Wyatt, promptly reneged on his promise. Instead, Wyatt became manager and peacekeeper at the Oriental Saloon. James tended bar. Their brother Morgan arrived in the summer of 1880, and all the brothers staked claims in hopes of profiting from the wealth of the mines.

Wyatt Earp, 1881.

While the Earps were making lives for themselves in Tombstone, a group of cattle rustlers and horse thieves was gaining traction in the southeast corner of the territory. Run out of the West Texas plains by the Texas Rangers, "the rootless ex-cowhands and saddle tramps" found themselves heading west toward small towns in Arizona where law enforcement was scarce or absent altogether. These rustlers came to be collectively known by their former profession, as cowboys or Cowboys. Within a short amount of time in this new country, the rustlers built alliances with local ranchers Newman Haynes Clanton and brothers Frank and Tom McLaury, all of whom were known to have illegal dealings in the area.[9] Here, then, are the Cowboys of the Earp legend, the men who would come to be linked with the outlaws in the popularized version of the battle near the OK Corral. Also apparent in the relationship among the Clantons, the McLaurys, and the Cowboys are the possible origins of the rift between the Earps on the one hand and the Cowboys and the Clanton clan on the other.

One theory of the antagonism points to the fact that the Earps were both lawmen and businessmen—at least they wanted to be, and in many ways they identified with the forces of incorporation that were transforming the Old West. They were, according to Earp biographer Allen Barra, "unabashed Republicans in Democratic country."[10] While the Cowboys—as cattle rustlers and outlaws—were not necessarily models of the Democratic ideal, they were opposed to northern Republican capitalism and affiliated with those who favored rural agrarianism, including the Clantons, McLaurys, and other ranchers in the territory. After the Civil War, the West saw incorporation and industrialization at a pace not seen before. The silver boom in Tombstone rapidly attracted small-time miners and big-time businessmen, bankers, merchants, and railroad moguls, many of whom brought their families and Victorian-era attitudes to this small Arizona town, causing a palpable tension between industry and agriculture, between the old ways and the new. Some have asserted that these differing political ideologies, or at least these different approaches to life in the West, may have fueled the enmity between the Earps (and their friend John "Doc" Holliday, who arrived in Tombstone in 1880) and the Clantons that engendered that now-famous gun battle. Cochise County sheriff John Behan (whom Wyatt called his "political rival and personal enemy"[11]) was also a Democrat who, by most accounts, overlooked the illegal acts for which the Cowboys, the Clantons, and the McLaurys were known. Some have also argued that Wyatt presumably having an affair with Josephine Marcus, Behan's mistress at the time, may have contributed to antagonisms between these two bands of men.

On the morning of 26 October 1881, citizens spotted Newman Clanton's son Ike—after a long night of drinking and rabble-rousing—on Tombstone's streets with a gun in violation of city ordinance, verbally and vocally threatening the Earp brothers and Doc Holliday. Ike did so to anyone who would listen to him, in the streets, at various saloons, and other establishments around town.[12] Ike had particular animosity toward Wyatt because of a deal they had struck in which Ike promised to supply Wyatt with the location of the suspects in a stagecoach robbery earlier that year that left the driver and a passenger dead. The deal would ensure that Wyatt would gain glory for finding the killers while Ike would get the reward money. The idea came to nothing, but this dangerous secret about Ike's plan to betray his friends made him increasingly paranoid, especially after a night of excessive alcohol consumption.[13] By the afternoon, Ike's brother Billy, Tom and Frank McLaury, and their friend Billy Claiborne were also spotted in the streets of Tombstone in a show of support. At around 2:45 p.m. that day, with the knowledge that the Cowboys were waiting in the lot behind the OK Corral and with dozens of townspeople watching, the Earps and Holliday began their walk—"one that would be imitated by so many movie and TV actors that it would become a ritual of Hollywood westerns"—in an apparent effort to defuse the situation.[14] Under imminent threat, Claiborne ran off first, then Ike. By their own account, the Earps intended only to disarm the Cowboys, but instead they ended up in a thirty-second bloody battle with the remaining gang members, killing Frank McLaury, Tom McLaury, and Billy Clanton (who died an hour after the fight). Morgan, Virgil, and Holliday were all wounded. Wyatt walked away from the incident unharmed.

After the street fight came the Earp hearing (known as the Spicer Hearing after the justice of the peace who heard the case, Wells Spicer) and more famously the Earp Vendetta Ride, during which Wyatt, Doc Holliday, and a number of deputized posse members sought revenge, at first for the attempted assassination of Wyatt's brother Virgil in December 1881 and later for the murder of his brother Morgan in March 1882. Led by Wyatt Earp, now a deputy US marshal, and funded by big businessmen, Wells Fargo, and the federal government, this group pursued known Cowboys throughout Cochise County. While Earp's efforts were governmentally sanctioned and privately supported, Sheriff Behan issued a warrant for Earp's arrest for the murder of Frank Stilwell, whom Wyatt suspected of killing Morgan. Now as both lawman and outlaw, Earp and his posse traveled the territory in search of his enemies. During this revenge ride, infamous Cowboys Johnny Ringo and Curly Bill Brocius were killed.[15]

Although it garnered some local publicity directly after the event, the gun battle was all but forgotten as larger issues threatened Tombstone. Wyatt Earp left Tombstone in March 1882, was later joined by Josephine Marcus, and headed to California, where he worked for decades to get his story told the way he wanted. In the meantime, two fires and floods struck Tombstone in the early 1880s to devastating effect. Add to this the falling price of silver and Tombstone's economy was on a downward spiral by 1890. Just about ten years after its initial boom, this silver mining camp busted, its population fell by two-thirds, and it became a shadow of its former glory.[16] The people left behind were compelled to keep Tombstone from becoming a ghost town like so many other mining districts in the West. In the ensuing decades they marketed Tombstone as a retirement community and later as a warm, dry place where tuberculosis sufferers could convalesce. But when the county seat was moved from Tombstone to Bisbee in 1929, townspeople were running out of options. Tourism seemed to offer some hope. Inspired by the national trend toward visiting the American West in the early decades of the twentieth century, Tombstone's townspeople began to consider how their past could be used to save their future.

Despite the colorful years and richness of Tombstone's history preceding the street fight in 1881, it and its aftermath have come to define Tombstone,

Arizona, in the present day; Wyatt Earp, Hollywood, and the people of Tombstone all saw to that. Western historian Richard Slotkin points out that it was an aged Earp himself who, in 1920, long after any great notoriety of the man or event died down, "appeared on a movie lot in Pasadena hoping to cash in on the enthusiasm for 'authentic' western figures." His quest for celebrity and recognition cast a new spotlight on the famed gunfight, one that would shine brightly for decades to come.[17] In fact, the story of Tombstone and Wyatt Earp has been constructed, retooled, romanticized, and challenged in the years long since either might have had any real viability. Earp's visit to that movie lot and the subsequent Hollywood productions that featured some version of Earp and the street fight ultimately went on to help the people of Tombstone save the town from bankruptcy by drawing visitors looking for glimpses of the Wild West. The preservation efforts made by townspeople from the mid-twentieth century into the twenty-first, the use of Wyatt Earp and the gunfight by Hollywood, and the ways the Earp myth and the mythic West more generally have flowed to nations around the world have contributed to the sustainability of the town of Tombstone for generations.

Most works about Tombstone focus on the Earps and the gunfight and on the subsequent trials and tribulations of the main characters involved. Some authors, in an effort to decenter that event, have focused on Tombstone's silver mining history instead. Few works have critically examined Tombstone as a tourist destination, and no full-length work has been written on modern-day Tombstone in the past forty years.[18] In those last four decades, Tombstone has ostensibly become ever more "Disneyfied" and is under steady scrutiny in its attempt to maintain its historical integrity while luring tourist dollars. In fact, many of the town's efforts to draw visitors endangered its designation as a National Historic Landmark District in 2004. All of the preservation efforts the town has taken on publicly express a commitment to safeguarding the "authentic" and historical. At the same time, however, preservationists also consciously work to commodify its past—based largely on western myth, or at least the abstraction of a singular event that fits well within the Wild West narrative—in an effort to entice visitors.

The tension between authentic integrity and the need to attract visitors is a constant in Tombstone. People visit in part because they want to understand the history and in part because they want to experience the Old West—a place and time (and at times, an idea) that is very much tied to conceptions of the national story of progress. The lasting images of Wyatt Earp as the quintessential western lawman and of Tombstone's sustainability are embedded in present notions of a romanticized past that undergirds imaginings of what makes America America: (white) masculinity, rugged individualism, opportunity, fortitude, and freedom. Indeed, after a number of fires and floods ravaged the town in the late nineteenth and early twentieth centuries, decay and disinterest left Tombstone on the verge of becoming a ghost town until the 1940s. As enthusiasts sought to reinvigorate their community and investors sought to profit from renewed interest in US history as constructed through images of the American West, Tombstone began to transform back into an old, wild mining town based on what many believed were the most important components of its own history. In this case, revelry and raucousness were highlighted; downplayed (though not entirely absent) were signifiers of a town as much on the cusp of civility as any other boomtown of the West.

Even as the centrality of Tombstone as a signifier of the Old West ebbs and flows, the town still remains dominant in imaginings of the West by visitors, and even by those who have never been there. In Tombstone we see the ways the real and imagined West are entangled as well as the relationship between history and myth—two components of the West that are inseparable in the public consciousness. Further, as a space that rests between the old, "savage" West and the new, "civilized" West, Tombstone represents an articulation of societal progress so central to modernist notions of the American nation. That it (mostly) succeeds in offering a construction of the themes embodied by the mythic West—similar to western films and television shows but more powerful in its ability to add an embodied experience to literary or Hollywood representations—adds to Tombstone's salience. When the Earp brothers, Doc Holliday, and the Clanton clan shot it out on the streets of Tombstone, the news of the event spread from San Francisco to New York City—evidence of the spectacular nature of the episode to those living both inside and outside the region. The resuscitation of this event by Hollywood and the townspeople of Tombstone necessitated a reversion to the gunfight as spectacle. By now, the history of the town and the ways the town is imagined are so enmeshed as to make disentangling the two not impossible per se, but perhaps irrelevant to the resonance of the town as both a tourist destination and a signifier of the Old West.

This project explores the ways the town of Tombstone has evolved in the twentieth century, how it reconstructed itself in the image of a Wild West town based as much on popular culture as on its own complex history, how popular culture and Tombstone are now inextricably linked, and how the town has been accused of sacrificing historic integrity for the sake of remaining a viable tourist destination that meets the expectations of its visitors. Writing in 1972, historian Odie B. Faulk laments, "Promoters have come to the city to cash in on the glories of the West that never was. . . . The tourist pays to see a plastic replica of Tombstone in 1881."[19] While Faulk seems to dismiss the idea that Tombstone was a violent mining town in the 1880s, which of course it was, the complexities of that violence, as well as the town's own history—which goes far beyond this one thirty-second event in 1881—remain secondary to that which is presented to tourists.

But the fact that people visit Tombstone at all means it offers them something beyond simplified history—and beyond pure entertainment. While Tombstone celebrates a violent as opposed to bucolic past, perhaps it nonetheless serves to assuage what David Wrobel calls "postfrontier anxiety," brought about by the realities of encroaching modernity and the loss of the "wilderness" that so riddle nostalgic imaginings of the West.[20] Or perhaps in its celebration of white masculine violence and wildness, we can explore ideas of ritual and redemption, of subversion and reification of law, authority, and the powers of incorporation. This analysis examines not only how preservation efforts in Tombstone and the re-creation of an imagined past highlight the competing interests of boosters, preservationists, and residents of the town, but also why this reconstructed, simplified history of Tombstone—as the epitome of the Wild West—resonates with both its own townspeople and its visitors.

Arizona has long been an attractive site for tourists looking to experience the natural beauty and wild environment of the Southwest. Not only is Arizona the Grand Canyon State, but it also is home to a number of other ecological wonders as well as old western towns preserved or restored to their former glorious selves. Jerome, Arizona, for example, a once thriving copper mining town, reemerged as an art community in the 1970s, but it still offers visitors a taste of the Old West through museums, saloons, and period decor. In the southeast corner of the state, Benson boasts proximity to Kartchner Caverns, with the longest stalactite formation in the world, and Cochise Stronghold, the area that once protected Apache war chief Cochise, for whom the county is now named. Tombstone rests almost exactly between Benson and the copper mining town of Bisbee, which also became an art community in the 1970s and offers visitors access to historical structures like the Copper Queen Hotel, Victorian homes, and the Copper Queen Mine, and modern features such as art galleries, wineries, and breweries. Tombstone benefits from its historical and natural surroundings and all of Arizona's attractions, which draw millions of visitors annually.[21] But Tombstone does something different from these other areas of interest: a total public commitment to and immersion in its late nineteenth-century Wild West history.

Somewhere between two and five hundred thousand people visit Tombstone every year, demonstrating the powerful relationship the present has with the past.[22] In addition to the quest for fun, visitors hope to "experience" history in this Old West town. At the same time, with such a strong link between the town and its portrayal by Hollywood, Tombstone's authenticity as a historic space has been in constant question. Many visitors believe Tombstone offers an authentic representation of its own past and that of the American West as a whole. Others see Tombstone as inauthentic and superficial, offering only a performative version of a more profound history that is lost in the translation. Still others do not seem to care, at least not consciously. But part of Tombstone's success lies in the fact that its historic buildings, historic reenactments, and newly constructed façades and signage built to replicate historic Tombstone align with tourists' imaginings of the Old West encountered through a century of movie and television westerns. As Dydia DeLyser demonstrates in her study of the concept of authenticity at Bodie State Historic Park, a California ghost town, perceived authenticity in towns such as Tombstone is a powerful tool in attracting tourists, and that perception depends on how well the town meets the expectations of its visitors based on their understanding of a constructed western past.[23]

DeLyser's analysis focuses on the ways the landscape of Bodie abets notions of authenticity. She argues that "in Bodie's provocative landscape, visitors and staff use authenticity as a vehicle to engage popularly held notions about the mythic West and American virtues, fantasies about the past that hold meaning for those who indulge them."[24] In Tombstone the experience of authenticity is constructed through an amalgam of western landscape, preservation, performance, and movie references. Indeed, the blending of these components is so seamless that it becomes imperceptible, rendered visible only if any one element were not aligned with visitor expectations. This is interesting in a couple of ways. First, Tombstone is continually described as both authentically historic and like a theme park. In fact, the Arizona Office of Tourism says that the town is "equal parts Deadwood and Disney" and that its faithfully preserved and restored buildings are "straight out of a Clint Eastwood movie."[25] It seems that being both authentic and somehow inauthentic—if we can claim that Hollywood and Disney are not purveyors of "authentic history"—is pivotal to Tombstone's success as a tourist destination. Second, through the cross-pollination of Hollywood and history, Tombstone's authenticity is both reified and contestable. The negotiation is ongoing. Interrogating how townspeople and visitors manage the concept and the experience of authenticity is vital to understanding the Tombstone allure.

As DeLyser reminds us, authenticity as experienced by tourists and staged by the spaces hoping to entice them has received much attention by scholars in the past thirty years: "Some have been critical of tourists, seeing them as easily lured in by glossy confections" of the hyperreal and ascribing legitimacy to those places and experiences that are manufactured and synthetic.[26] Umberto Eco believes Americans are so seduced by the simulated that though "the American imagination demands the real thing," it "must fabricate the absolute fake" to attain it.[27] According to Eco and others, in fact, "in hyperreality, the reproduction is better than the original."[28] Anthropologist Edward Bruner takes a different approach. He and other scholars have sought to explore the concept of authenticity more fully, understanding it as constructed within a social context, carrying with it a variety of meanings.[29] Writing about Lincoln's New Salem, a heritage site in Illinois that celebrates the life of Abraham Lincoln, Bruner explores the concept of authenticity as encompassing the many ways in which visitors to New Salem develop meaning from the site. Bruner argues that all culture is continually invented and reinvented and that we need to transcend "such dichotomies as original/copy and authentic/inauthentic," especially since in such constructions, one term is privileged over the other. He identifies four ways the term *authenticity* can be defined: verisimilitude, whereby the site gives the appearance to modern-day visitors of the historical moment claimed; genuineness, whereby the site is a "complete and immaculate simulation, one that is historically accurate and true," and a person from the time period represented would believe it to be real; original, as opposed to a copy, in which case a reproduction could not be authentic but perhaps a few original items could lend authenticity to a reproduction; and duly authorized, certified, or legitimized, by the state or the nation.[30] All of these conceptions of authenticity converge, interact, and overlap in modern-day Tombstone.

Authenticity figures heavily in the success of Tombstone as a tourist destination, but what makes it authentic is fluid. While many challenge the site's realness (Is Boothill Graveyard "real"? Does the dirtless Allen Street make the site inauthentic? Do tongue-in-cheek performances minimize the seriousness of the site and render it less authentic?), others are interested in learning about their past and accept the site as authentic in that it is a historical site—one authorized by the National Park Service as historically significant—even as they enjoy its entertainment value. Still others do not visit Tombstone in search of this idea called authenticity but are more interested in "having fun" by participating somehow in the pageantry of the Wild West. Here authenticity lies in how closely Tombstone meets the imaginings of these visitors, whose ideas have been fortified through popular culture. In other words, while authenticity in expectation and experience are important—the town must meet tourists' expectations of what a real Old West town is—historic authenticity seems less so, even as assessments about the site's "realness" continually circulate within and around Tombstone.

Even as—or perhaps because—the historic authenticity of Tombstone is persistently questioned, the concept of authenticity acts as an imperative marketing tool for the owners of the historic sites, attractions, and even motels in Tombstone. For example, Tombstone's information website calls Tombstone "the most authentic Western Town left in the United States." The Birdcage Theatre advertises itself as "Tombstone's most authentic attraction" while the Tombstone County Courthouse Museum is widely considered the space that exhibits the most "authentic history of Tombstone."[31] The Larian Motel states that "visitors to Tombstone, Arizona are rewarded with a host of many original buildings and authenticity that others can only try to recreate." Other sites invoke the power of history as legitimizer, like the Gunfight Palace, which states, "We give you a magnificent history lesson and reenact actual shootings and killings that took place here back in the wild days." Of course, while performing history, the Gunfight Palace is not an original to Old Tombstone; it was built in 2011 and is only suggestive of original sites in town.[32]

The appearance of authenticity—verisimilitude—seems to be the most important component leading to an "authentic" experience for tourists, and townspeople play on this appearance of authenticity in their representation of the town. In many ways, the commercialism in Tombstone has become part of its appeal—performance, entertainment, and sepia-toned souvenir photographs are all part of the show and have been part of Tombstone for so long that if anyone tried to eradicate them in the name of authenticity, tourists might no longer be interested. Authenticity of the space is greatly if not entirely constructed through visitors' and townspeople's knowledge of the Old West based on their encounters with the West in popular culture. Ironically, restoration can often lead to accusations of inauthenticity, as demonstrated through Tombstone's continual assertion that this is a real town, not a movie set—even if it looks like one and despite what the Arizona Office of Tourism might claim.[33] The fact that the language used by the

Arizona Office of Tourism arguably serves to delegitimize the historicity of Tombstone demonstrates a tension within the region of how best to attract tourist dollars and keep people coming back. It is important to keep these notions of authenticity present as we travel through Tombstone. While it is impossible to grasp the extent to which each visitor believes Tombstone to be authentic—that is, original or plausible, suggestive of authenticity or a realistic replication—the concept is continually enacted on its streets and in its buildings, whether historic or merely evocative of history.

A number of overarching questions have guided this study. First, it was important to investigate how Tombstone, in its quest for revitalization, has negotiated between historic preservation/historic integrity and meeting the expectations of tourists. Here there is tension between what is authentic according to the National Park Service and the meaning authenticity has for townspeople and for sightseers. In what ways has popular culture influenced both the ways Tombstone has constructed and maintains itself and the expectations of its visitors? How have the expectations of tourists been translated into the public image of Tombstone? It is also imperative to look at the relationship historically between civic leaders/boosters and townspeople. How have varying motivations and competing interests played out in the preservation of the historic district? What is the relationship among these various groups today? We must be able to situate Tombstone within wider trends in historic preservation efforts and heritage sites that are central to an analysis of the power of narratives of the past, the importance and strength of tourist dollars, and the link between the manipulation of history and place. We must also ask, Why does it work? Why do people visit Tombstone, and what prompts some of them to move there? Further, has Tombstone maintained its popularity throughout the twentieth century or has it ebbed and flowed, and in relation to what external processes? And finally, how has Tombstone managed to distinguish itself as unique among other mining towns in the region?

Beginning with Frederick Jackson Turner's *The Significance of the Frontier in American History* in 1893 and continuing through the 1950s with Henry Nash Smith's *Virgin Land* and into the 1980s with Patricia Nelson Limerick's *The Legacy of Conquest*, inquiries into the significance of the American West to US culture have been the principal enterprise of the western historical profession for well over a century. Turner's vision of the settlement of the American West was romanticized and popularized at the time by Buffalo Bill Cody and Theodore Roosevelt, dime novelists, fiction writers, and artists, and later by film and television producers. Despite the challenges to this romantic vision by scholars, efforts to include voices that had been left out of Turner's narrative, and attempts to downplay or even disparage the significance of the mythic West, popular culture and collective memory have ensured that Buffalo Bill's and Roosevelt's romantic versions of the West stand as the most widely accepted account of the nation's frontier history.

The reason the myth of the American West resonates is that it does particular ideological work, reinforcing and reacting to certain power dynamics—reflecting, perpetuating, and responding to shifting political, cultural, and social values and principles, as ideas about American history, the American experience, and American identity change. The mythic West is the focus of many scholars who are trying to tease out its function and significance to audiences and consumers, what it has meant to them over time and under different political and social circumstances, and why it has been so resilient. Tombstone's viability as a tourist destination means it is as wrapped up in notions of the mythic West as Monument Valley and Buffalo Bill. Part of the goal of this project has been to explore the ways Tombstone caters to that myth, offering visitors a glimpse at both the romance and the violence that constitute conceptions of the western frontier.[34]

This study involves a number of research methodologies. Archival material helped shed light on the ways preservation efforts have been discussed and debated from the 1950s right up to the present day. Issues of the *Tombstone Epitaph*—Tombstone's oldest continuously running newspaper, established in 1880—and issues of the *Tombstone News*, Tombstone's current daily newspaper, illuminate the ways tourism and the concept of history continue to inform and affect the town. Newspapers were and still are an essential element in promoting particular political and cultural agendas. By discussing, dissecting, and defending different social issues, newspaper editors have been important agents in shaping the opinion of their constituencies. In Tombstone, editors of the *Epitaph* have used their position to encourage—among other things—civic boosterism that would be realized in the form of preservation and tourism. Newspaper archives offer a glimpse into the ways editors and readers discussed the necessities of crafting and marketing a public identity—and what that identity would constitute—in a public forum. Newspaper articles, editorials, and letters offer an understanding of the exigencies that prompted such a move, the debates between civic boosters and townspeople that ensued, and the decisions that were made and by whom to pursue historic preservation and heritage tourism as the primary means to prevent economic collapse.

In addition to archival research to understand the history of preservation and the importance of narrativizing the past in this old mining town, I used the anthropological method of participant observation as a tool for examining the meaning that visitors and townspeople make of the built environment, performances, and landscape surrounding Tombstone. My numerous visits to Tombstone enabled me to experience the site as a tourist: visit museums, tourist attractions, saloons, and restaurants; view performances and reenactments; take photographs; and purchase souvenirs. It also allowed me to observe the ways other visitors engage with the space and the ways those who live and work there engage these visitors. Throughout the course of this project, I found that visitors and residents freely discussed their connection to Tombstone with me, offering their opinion on the attractions, leisure activities (like sitting at the Crystal Palace Saloon for a beer), reenactments, historical significance, political tensions, and general attitude of the town. The conversations I had at various restaurants, saloons, shops, and entertainment venues with a number of visitors and townspeople gave me even further insight into the motivations for journeying to and living in Tombstone. Many visited more than once, some every year. Others visited, then moved their families there. Epistemologically, my analyses are very much entrenched in my own conceptions of the space, of the ways visitors' responses to what they were experiencing could be read based on my own responses, and of what numerous tourism and cultural studies scholars have said about tourists and meaning making through the consumption of cultural productions and public space.

In addition, this project calls on extensive analysis of film and television and theories of the dialog that takes place between producer and audience to grasp the power and resonance of the mythic West as an articulation of those values seen as essential to the American character. Tombstone is in many ways the realization of Hollywood fantasies, where residents and tourists can take part in the West of the imagination as seen in popular films and other productions of popular culture. Hollywood, in other words, is key and central to Tombstone's success. If Tombstone constructed itself as a frontier town based on popular culture representations of itself, and if tourists' expectations of Tombstone are formulated through representations of Tombstone in popular culture such as films, television series, and literature, then it is necessary to see how the town has been imagined within the realm of popular culture. It also seems fair to assume that western films as a genre (not just those films about Tombstone) serve to inform the ways Tombstone maintains itself as a Wild West town and set the expectations of visitors. An analysis of films about Tombstone and Wyatt Earp prior to 1951, such as *My Darling Clementine* (1946), and more recent films, such as *Tombstone* (1993) and *Wyatt Earp* (1994), as well as a survey of western films as a group—especially those films that perpetuate notions of the Wild West—heavily inform this project.

In thinking about the significance of Tombstone to our understanding of the relevance and resonance of the mythic West, I wanted to explore not only the site but also the way that the space is imagined both nationally and globally. As a local-to-global story, the flow of the chapters reflects this idea. I start with the local, touristic experience in the town (chapter 1); move into the history of and continued preservation efforts at the site (chapter 2); discuss Hollywood's version of the man, the event, and the town, which has a much broader reach (chapter 3); then explore the global consumption and retooling of the imagined Tombstone (chapter 4). Chapter 4 also circles back to the local to Tombstone Monument Ranch, formerly known as Apache Spirit Ranch, the German-opened-and-operated ranch located just two miles from Tombstone's historic district. This return to the local continues with a discussion of the historians and biographers who remain impassioned about the man and the event (chapter 5), and of course a discussion of the problems at the border. The piece itself mimics a touristic experience, taking the reader on a journey through the history of Tombstone, through its streets and historic buildings, through reenactments and representations on screen, to the far reaches of the world, and to its own backyard.

Chapter 1 maps out the touristic experience in Tombstone, focusing specifically on the importance and centrality of the concept of history to Tombstone's sustainability. Using the Tombstone Courthouse Museum as a metaphor for the ways history is enacted and utilized in the town, its location off the main street of the historic district seems to help define this building as the space in which "true" history wins out over the "performative" history beyond its walls. The history of the courthouse museum underscores the imperatives of economics and heritage history to Tombstone. In the historic district, history and entertainment are coconstitutive, inextricably linked to the narrative that has come to define Tombstone and the Old West in the popular imagination. This chapter also explores the ways that historical authenticity is continually called on and called into question in this space.

Chapter 2 traces the history of preservation efforts in Tombstone from the late 1940s to the present day, demonstrating how boosters marketed the town based on popular versions of itself, sometimes at the expense of its own historic integrity. The chapter also explores the ways that performance is essential to the preservation of the town: without performance, Tombstone would not have the same allure. In its constant quest to meet the expectations of tourists, Tombstone must also meet the demands of its own citizens as well as follow the rules set out by the National Park Service. This negotiation has seen constant struggle since the Tombstone Restoration Commission was established in 1949 and has attracted almost constant criticism. But it also has resulted in Tombstone's continued resonance to hundreds of thousands of visitors, who help maintain a special place for Tombstone in the popular imagination. Historic integrity seems continually belied by entertainment, and the two have had a precarious relationship throughout their cohabitation in the city. This negotiation and their centrality to Tombstone's sustainability are also examined in this chapter.

Chapter 3 explores the ways Wyatt Earp and the famous showdown in October 1881 have been represented in film and television throughout the twentieth and twenty-first centuries. The films chosen for analysis represent the different iterations of Wyatt Earp through the last sixty-nine years and the broad appeal and power he as symbol has had in both expressing and shaping perceptions of the West, law and authority, and the nation itself. Wyatt Earp and his place in the mythic West hold different meanings for different people. He has been both continually reinvented and steadfast to specific attitudes and beliefs of American culture. This chapter seeks to expose how, as a contested figure, he has been able to maintain social significance over generations.

Chapter 4 focuses on the flow of cultural ideas wrapped up in the myth of the West from the United States to the world and back again, and the transformations that occur through that process. The chapter demonstrates how audiences/consumers around the world have made sense of the western myth generally and Tombstone, Arizona, more specifically through their consumption of popular culture and public space. The ways these films and spaces are consumed and recontextualized globally speak to the power and resilience of the Tombstone and western myths for worldwide audiences. Ultimately, the global circulation and consumption of the mythic West challenge traditional conceptions of the ways the US West informs American cultural identity.

Chapter 5 focuses on the historical frenzy that has built up around Wyatt Earp, the gunfight, and Tombstone's place in the Old West. As a contested figure, Earp and his life story have been written and rewritten numerous times since the late nineteenth century, with each professional or grassroots historian, each novelist and journalist exploring his actions and motivations from as many different angles as there are Earp experts. This field, known as Earpiana, might just as easily be referred to as Earpania, so impassioned are his biographers that they have themselves been involved in many "showdowns" over the details of the gunfight and the character of Earp, demonstrating the deep and prolonged power of his story and the central position he has held in popular and historic representations of the Old West.

In the early 1880s, Tombstone, Arizona, became the fastest-growing silver mining town in the West, luring thousands to its camp with hopes of a better future, one based on toughness, perseverance, and luck rather than on birthright. Two years after its founding, a thirty-second gunfight on its newly formed streets went on to define Tombstone and its history long after the last piece of silver was taken from the town's mines. Now Tombstone attracts hundreds of thousands of visitors hoping to recapture the wildness of its heyday, catch a glimpse of townspeople dressed as Wyatt Earp and Doc Holliday, and explore modern-day Tombstone through the lens of its carefully abstracted history. Tourist expectations of Tombstone have been cultivated through a stream of Hollywood films and television series, novels and photographs, history and legend, without which Tombstone would have become just another ghost town. Negotiating authenticity and economic exigencies, restoration and preservation of Tombstone has been a concerted effort by civic boosters, wealthy outsiders, Hollywood imaginings, a global fascination with the West, and tourism—the single biggest industry in town.

In many ways, Tombstone is like other former mining towns that dot the western landscape, so many of which have sought to commodify a past seen as vital to their survival. In other ways, Tombstone is unique, with its proximity to the Huachuca Mountains, its centrality in a county named for a Chiricahua Apache war chief, its noteworthy success as a silver mining town, its historic reputation as being part of one of the deadliest regions in the West, a gunfight seemingly tailor-made for Hollywood, and a ready-made hero in the still-contested figure of Wyatt Earp.

This small town has managed to remain relevant through the ebbs and flows of attitudes about the West at different moments. We can better understand the significance and salience of the mythic West by exploring the ways Tombstone has self-commodified; the symbiosis between Tombstone and Hollywood; and the ways Tombstone, Wyatt Earp, and the "Gunfight at the OK Corral" continue to circulate domestically and around the world. But Tombstone's public identity did not just happen. It is the result of a concerted and prolonged effort to commodify a past that many have seen as the most tangible way to ensure Tombstone's survival. Hollywood and the global fascination with the West have actively (if not deliberately) assisted and supported Tombstone's efforts to remain relevant. All of these avenues of sponsorship (preservation, tourism, popular culture, the circulation and consumption of images of the West worldwide, and the continued contest to tell the story) have cultivated a western town still vital (if not always central) to our understandings of the significance of the West in American (and global) mythology.

In Tombstone, the dominant narrative of its past demonstrates which part of the past is worth saving, worth promoting, and worth consuming. The dialogic relationship that has developed between the keepers of history in Tombstone, the producers of the pop culture West in Hollywood and worldwide, and the consumers of these productions—whether film viewers, travelers to Tombstone, or visitors to western-themed towns in countries around the globe—is central to the sustainability of the place as fundamental to imaginings of the mythic West; as a tourist destination; and as a living, breathing town.

I

Making History

Modern-day Tombstone, Arizona, seems like a contradiction in terms. Billing itself as a town stopped in time—in 1881, the most famous, and many would argue most important, year of the town's past—the town acts out its history on a daily basis to tourists who come to the historic district to experience and relive the fantasy of the Wild West. Make-believe shoot-'em-ups, barroom brawls, and public drunkenness keep the tourists entertained, as do the reenactments of the "Gunfight at the OK Corral" and other street performances that go on each day. There is history there—after all, the battle outside the OK Corral is an actual historic event, and the town is a historic landmark district, designated by the US Department of the Interior in 1961 as a "nationally significant historic place," one "possess[ing] exceptional value or quality in illustrating or interpreting the heritage of the United States."[1] But history in and of itself appears almost secondary. While it is important to tourists and residents alike—acting to legitimize the town's very existence—the performance, the entertainment, seems to trump history at least partially, if not altogether. As one cowboy performer outside the OK Corral remarked to a tourist walking by: "This is Tombstone, there's no history here!"[2]

Indeed, though fashioned after itself in the 1880s, Tombstone has the feel of a western movie set, one in which performances and reenactments draw thousands of visitors on an annual basis. But Tombstone's history and its performance are contingent on each other, and the two must coexist to ensure that the town survives. Tombstone is only 4.3 square miles, with the Tombstone historic landmark district occupying only forty-two acres of that land at the town's center. But the historic landmark district is also the central business district, one that promotes tchotchkes as enthusiastically as it does historic spaces. Gunfights and brawls, performances of public drunkenness and subversion define the streets of Tombstone, both within the popular imagination and in this living monument to the Old West.

One block from the main street of Tombstone's historic district stands a building that many believe is one of the few places that present the town's "true" history to visitors: the Tombstone Courthouse State Historic Park. Through preservation efforts in the 1950s, the building was salvaged from destruction, turned into a museum, and designated a state park in 1959. In 2010 the Arizona State Parks Board voted to close the courthouse due to state budget shortfalls. Acknowledging that this site represents what many in town believe is the most authentic articulation of Tombstone's history, and with a keen understanding of the importance of that history to the town's existence, Tombstone officials worked diligently with the state to prevent the closing of the museum, and operations were transferred to the town in April of that year.

The courthouse museum is the site of decades-long efforts to preserve and tell Tombstone's history and, more recently, is central in debates around the importance of heritage tourism in Arizona. The museum also symbolizes the durability of Tombstone and its efforts to tell its history to visitors, while its location off the main street of the historic district also represents the peripheral yet imperative role "authentic" history plays in the town's survival. The history of the courthouse museum—as both courthouse and museum, as vendor of "true" history within its walls while performative history goes on without—underscores the imperatives of economics and heritage history to Tombstone. It is important to explore the different ways Tombstone's history is told both inside the museum and outside on the town's streets, with performance, romance, and museumification. Through this discussion, we begin to understand the ways the different approaches to representing the historical narrative are important to the visitors, to townspeople, and to the town itself.

This chapter will first take us on a tour of the historic district, pointing to the main tourist attractions as one drives southeast along Arizona State Route 80 and walks onto Allen Street, Tombstone's central business, historic, and tourist district, where performances and souvenir shops charm visitors. It will then take us to the Tombstone Courthouse State Historic Park, the site many believe offers the most neutral and accurate representation of Tombstone's past. The tension that exists between what is deemed "authentic" history and entertainment and the centrality of both to Tombstone's ongoing survival are also the focus of this chapter.

Tombstone's Historic Landmark District

Called "a living testament to the Old West" and known as "the Town Too Tough to Die," Tombstone, Arizona, is off the beaten path: visitors must drive twenty-five miles south of I-10 from Benson, Arizona, on Arizona State Route 80 through the small town of St. David and the vast beauty of the desert landscape to get there. It is a destination—not merely a place one visits on the way to somewhere else (although many do go further south to Bisbee, another mining town that has marketed its past). Arriving in Tombstone is like being transported into another time, 1880s Tombstone— through a combination of history and kitsch, heritage site and entertainment. Tourists visit Tombstone to experience how life was in this Old West mining town, and Tombstone may be one of the best extant examples of that historical time period. Historic sites intermingle with performative displays, all of which serve to set such locations apart, as sociologist John Urry argues, to mark them as distinct from the modern and make real notions of the rustic and wild Old West.[3]

The brown sign on the outskirts of Tombstone declaring the town a historic landmark proclaims the site significant. Signs like this direct the tourist gaze to "features of landscape or townscape which separate them off from everyday experience."[4] Urry and Adrian Franklin both argue that part of the pleasure of the touristic experience is the encounter with something completely beyond or outside the familiar.[5] At the same time, tourists arrive at these spaces with some expectation "constructed and sustained through a variety of non-tourist practices," including television, film, literature, and magazines—all of which, as we will see, contribute to the atmosphere of Tombstone's historic district. Indeed, Tombstone is both out of the ordinary and the actualization of tourists' manufactured ideas about the late nineteenth-century Old West supplied by the popular media for generations.

Before arriving in the historic district, SR 80 passes Boothill Graveyard, one of the most popular places in Tombstone that blend the historic with the entertaining. As it says in the "Descriptive list of the more than 250 graves" brochure that they give out at the Boothill gift shop, "Because of the many violent deaths of the early days, the cemetery became known as

Boothill Graveyard. . . . Buried here are outlaws with their victims, suicides, and hangings, legal and otherwise, along with the hardy citizens and refined element of Tombstone's first days." Originally known as Tombstone Graveyard, the site was neglected after the town built the new Tombstone City Cemetery on West Allen Street in 1884. In the 1920s the city took on the project of restoring the graveyard to its original state. It was renamed Boothill Graveyard after Boot Hill Cemetery in Dodge City, Kansas, which had been attracting tourists for years.[6] While the cemetery was reconstructed and named in a conscious effort to bring tourists to Tombstone, the graveyard is real (on its website, it states "actual graveyard"), and many of the people who were buried there have marked graves. The original wooden grave markers were prone to deterioration because of the temperature and high winds, so the markers were replaced in the 1940s with steel replicas. In 2012 the city requested the markers be replaced again with replicas made of wood to make them seem more "authentic."[7] John Heith, lynched by an angry mob in 1884, is buried here, as is Marshal Fred White, killed by Curly Bill Brocius in 1880. The three men killed behind the OK Corral in 1881—Billy Clanton, Frank McLaury, and Tom McLaury—are also all buried at Boothill Graveyard. The fact that for decades the site was uncared for underscores how secondary the gunfight was to the history and public identity of the town prior to the 1930s.

Tourists pour into the cemetery grounds to roam among the graves. They follow the guidebook with names and descriptions of everyone in the cemetery, taking pictures of markers possibly of someone with the same last name or of all the "Unknowns" (which one visitor joked must be the "Smith" of the Southwest). In fact, despite the literal morbidity of the site, people pose and laugh as much as they do at any other attraction in town. Some of the gravesites are marked with small crosses with a name and a short description, such as "Miles Sweeney, Murdered" and "May Doody, Diphtheria." Others have full headstones, a few with unconventional descriptions that are the focus of many photographs. One marker reads, "Here lies George Johnson, hanged by mistake. 1882. He was right, we was wrong, but we strung him up and now he's gone." Another reads, "Here lies Lester Moore, four slugs from a .44. No Les, no more."[8] The Lester Moore headstone is by far the most popular, and has been commodified for purchase in the gift shop on the cemetery grounds as salt and pepper shakers, banks, sew-on patches, magnets, key chains, T-shirts, shot glasses, mugs, and baseball caps.

Boothill Graveyard received the Readers' Choice award from *True West* magazine for Best Historical Cemetery of the West in 2014.[9] But like other sites in Tombstone, and Tombstone in general, Boothill is variously viewed by visitors as authentic and inauthentic, as historical and artificial. One traveler commented that the site is "restored but less authentic." He went on to say that he expected the site would be run down with "broken tombstones and half dug graves" (perhaps like the suspended decay at Bodie State Park that DeLyser discusses) but instead found it "very clean and well organized," which took "some of the appeal away." In regard to the eccentric—and historically accurate—epitaphs, he wasn't sure "if these were authentic or not." Another visitor described the site as too commercial, asserting that the "rhymes on the grave markers" made it all seem "a little too 'touristy.'" While another sightseer wanted to "commend the folks who have done what they can to preserve this historic site and still make it available to the public," adding that her experience "felt as authentic as one could reasonably expect," yet another guest declared, "There was no hint of history left in this place."[10]

Further along SR 80 toward the historic district is the renovated Wyatt Earp House, outside of which stands an impressive bronze statue of Wyatt Earp that was commissioned by the house's owners and unveiled at a "major event" in November 2008. Sculpted by artist Tim Trask and called "Stepping into Legend," the statue, according to the press release of the event, "shows Wyatt Earp poised to take that first stride toward the notorious OK Corral, where the most famous Old West gun battle took place." Romance was used to both create the statue and describe it in the press release, which states that the bronze Wyatt's "steely eyes are sharply focused with courage and determination. No other depiction of Wyatt Earp is as haunting or as evocative as Trask's timeless bronze sculpture."[11] Ironically, because it is not situated within the historic district, the house is easy to miss. And while the interior has been renovated and some furnishings arranged for the appearance of authenticity, the space is used as an art gallery for local artists attempting to capture the allure and wildness of Old Tombstone and the events of the gunfight rather than as a museumized site highlighting the ways Wyatt Earp and his common-law wife, Celia Ann Mattie Blaylock, may have lived. The home does not get a lot of foot traffic according to its owner, and the statue of Wyatt was meant to draw more people to the site.[12] That objective has not yet been fully realized.

Just a few blocks away from the Wyatt Earp House is Tombstone's National Historic Landmark District, lying between Fremont Street and East Toughnut Street and South Third Street and South Sixth Street. Allen Street was closed off to drivers from Third Street to Sixth Street in 2004, again marking it as a tourist site, both historical and consumer-driven. There are

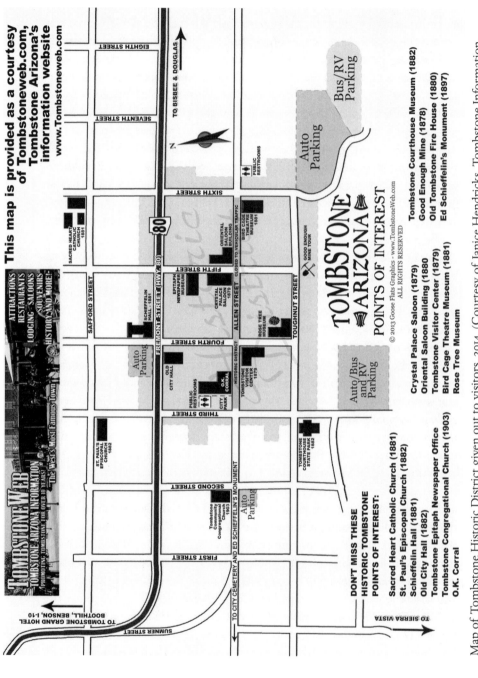

Map of Tombstone Historic District given out to visitors, 2014. (Courtesy of Janice Hendricks, Tombstone Information, Tombstoneweb.com)

horse-drawn carriages that provide tours to the town's landmarks and attractions and a lesson about their historical significance. On either side of Allen Street are wooden sidewalks and wooden and brick buildings reminiscent of the Old West. There are also metal markers erected in 2009 that offer brief histories of the buildings that line the streets. There are a number of saloons, some of which are historical, like Big Nose Kate's (originally the Grand Hotel), named for Mary Katherine Horony Cummings, the common-law wife of John "Doc" Holliday; and the Crystal Palace, rebuilt and named in July 1882 after the building saw total destruction by fire in May of that year. Others are modern, such as Doc Holliday's Saloon, opened in 2011 by the owner of Six Gun City, which burned down in 2010.[13] Visitors meander in and out of gun stores; smoke shops; photography studios where they can get sepia-toned photos of themselves dressed in period costume with "wanted" stamped across the top; and a plethora of shops selling turquoise and silver jewelry, "western" wear, and the typical tourist souvenirs (postcards, shot glasses, T-shirts, mugs, key chains, magnets, etc.). Depending on the day, the street is bustling with tourists clamoring for space along the wooden planks to people watch, eat ice cream and fudge, read the *Tombstone Epitaph* (a souvenir reprint of the original 1881 reports of the "Gunfight at the OK Corral"), and take pictures of the scene and of the locals dressed in period costume who walk among the visitors.

It is not unusual to see people dressed in period costume—as lawmen, gunslingers, maybe outlaws, or members of the ladies' auxiliary. In fact, one reenactor told me how imperative he feels it is that all the locals dress in period costume.[14] Casey, who works at the Visitors' Center, agrees. She says that people come to Tombstone with certain expectations, and it's up to the locals to oblige them. And most, it seems, do. Three men walking along the wooden sidewalk on Allen Street wearing black dusters, bow ties, and "gunfighter" hats said that while they volunteer as performers at the OK Corral, they dress this way because this is just how they dress. They claim that the people walking around town in 1880s costume are locals who actually dress and behave as though they live in 1880s Tombstone (although, of course, there is electricity and running water in twenty-first-century Tombstone). These men had all only recently moved to the city: one is a retired schoolteacher, one a recent high school graduate from Tucson, and one a New Englander who teaches at the local high school. All arrived within the previous three years.[15] All first visited as tourists and decided to stay, extending their touristic experiences, one might say, by actually *becoming part of* the touristic experience—representing sociologist Adrian Franklin's idea of

OK Corral, 2013. (Courtesy of Nancy Sosa, History Raiders Research and Consultation)

tourism being infused in the everyday. They also unreservedly exemplify Hal Rothman's conception of the neonative, those who come to a particular western place as tourists and then transform themselves into locals, even becoming the most vocal defenders of the touristic ideal and promoters of the space to future visitors.[16] Many Tombstonians were once tourists, and in many ways, they still are—at least in the way they continue to experience the site. Franklin argues that tourism is the space in which "fantasy has become an important social practice" and that "the everyday world is increasingly indistinguishable from the touristic world."[17] Indeed, tourism to a great extent is absorbed into the daily life of Tombstone. Former tourists reenact or perform events from Tombstone's past for other tourists. In Tombstone the public, touristic identity is in fact the identity of the city and the people themselves.

We see an interaction and intermingling of identities at the Crystal Palace Saloon, a historic site and favorite watering hole for tourists and locals alike. A man in a cowboy hat sidles up to the bar so he can ask one of the barmaids—who are dressed like showgirls and women of the evening, in feather boas, bustiers, and lots of lace—for a T-shirt that says "Crystal Palace: Good Whiskey and Tolerable Water." He and the barmaid exchange friendly banter before he heads out with his new shirt. It is easy to talk to people here, all strangers but known to each other somehow. Sociologist

Victor Turner's concept of *communitas*, whereby new sets of relationships, unmediated togetherness, and "normal" hierarchical structures are suspended and a community of shared experience develops, is demonstrated throughout the site.[18] Angela and Darren, truck drivers from Oregon, start a conversation with me without provocation, and they even buy a round of drinks. They say that they travel all over the United States, rarely having two days off at the same time. When they do, they come to Tombstone. This is the third time they've been here. They cannot articulate why they come back every year beyond saying that they "just love it here." They love the excitement, the carnivalesque, the historical.[19] While we are seated at the bar, a man dressed like an 1880s cowboy comes in and orders a drink after being stopped by tourists to pose for photographs. According to Angela, this happens all the time: tourists ask to take pictures, but "these people are just the locals. This is simply how they are." In other words, the residents both mark themselves and are marked as tourist attractions, and the tourists respond by capturing their image and the moment in photographs.

But performance is just one incentive to visit. I met Randy and Gail on their third visit to Tombstone. These "history buffs" travel from Iowa less for the entertainment and more because of what happened here 135 years ago. They insist that tourists need to "get over the commercialism part of Tombstone to really appreciate the true history behind it." Their advice to visitors is to "know your history before you come," and, like Angela and Darren, they believe the locals are the best resource when it comes to getting right the story of Tombstone's past. Randy's recommendation: "Once here, grab a local and ask questions." Kaapi, a first-time visitor from Washington State, remarks on how the town is both historic and entertaining. Like many others, she loves "how actual history blends with touristy fun!"[20]

The mixing of history and fun is seen in the gunfight reenactments, which are a standard in Tombstone and one of its greatest draws. During the day, dozens of tourists along Allen Street witness the accidental shooting of Marshal Fred White in 1880 by Cowboy Curly Bill Brocius. The reenactment is meant to be both historical (i.e., educational) and entertaining, with exaggerated movements and clownlike performances. When the outlaws are shot down, the crowd cheers and applauds. Then the performance shifts to one of a ladies' fashion show, and the crowd slowly disperses. It is interesting to note this relatively genteel demonstration of womanhood in the 1880s; the actual lives of women on the frontier were far more complex. As William Shillingberg explains, women found life in Tombstone particularly restrictive: "A caste system was rigidly based on their husbands' occupations. Wives of superintendents seldom mingled with those of common miners, and wives of gamblers and saloonkeepers enjoyed fewer contacts beyond their own circle." In addition to this regimented class structure, women were barred by custom from saloons and gambling halls, and the town offered few other amusements. To pass the time, "women formed clubs to discuss the latest eastern and California literary periodicals, helping break the cycle of work and boredom." But for some women, these activities offered no real comfort: "Saloonman Tom Corrigan's wife twice attempted suicide," writes Shillingberg. "A badly aimed pistol shot to the head forced surgeons to remove her right eye." Whether it was "the bleakness of frontier life or her husband's violent domestic habits [that] drove her to despair" is unknown.[21]

Perhaps this less pleasant picture of women in 1880s Tombstone would actually have held tourists' attention longer. While the fashions in this performance may have been historically accurate, women dressed in the "latest" trends of the time are clearly not what most people come to Tombstone to see. It is the gunfights, the outlaws, the "wildness" of Tombstone that is the major attraction. While found in the National Register of Historic Places, thereby marked as a place of national historic significance, Tombstone also is humorous and enjoyable, even antithetically "kid-friendly."[22] Old photographs around town reveal that the space looks like it did in the 1880s (and *not* how it looked in the first half of the twentieth century), but the performances lend a Disneyland quality to it. It is this blend that attracts tourists: one father brought his son to Tombstone in 2009 because he wanted him to get a sense of history; they came back the following year because his son had had so much fun.[23]

The most famous event in Tombstone's history is the street fight that has come to be known as the "Gunfight at the OK Corral." This event is reenacted three times daily for approximately 250 spectators. It is by far the most anticipated and well-attended event of the day. Before the actual show begins, people can journey into the corral to stake their place in what they believe will be the spot of the reenactment. Mannequins are automated to reenact the gun battle whenever a button off to the side is pushed. (The mannequins are actually on the spot recorded by Wyatt Earp as the participants' location during the shootout.) Someone pushes the button, and everyone watches the mannequin reenactment in silence, some reluctantly taking photos of this relatively unlively and unengaging event. When it ends, someone remarks, "Is that it?" expressing disappointment at paying $7.50 for a live show and being met with this. This situation exemplifies Urry's theory of anticipation as part of the tourist experience. Urry argues that "[people] seek to experience 'in reality' the pleasurable dramas they have already experienced in their imagination." But "since 'reality' rarely provides the perfected pleasures encountered in daydreams," people are often left dissatisfied.[24]

Fortunately, this mechanical reenactment is not what the audience has paid for; it is still fifteen minutes to showtime. The live event takes place in two parts: the first, a comedic performance of a "possible" fight between locals and interlopers in the 1880s West; the second, the "historical and award-winning reenactment" of the showdown outside the OK Corral. While the performance is a little clumsy at spots, the audience laughs along and continually shoots photographs of the players. When the Earps and Doc Holliday shoot their adversaries dead, the players freeze mid-action for a few moments, posing to allow tourists to snap even more pictures. At the end of the show, audience members are invited to join the players to take still more photographs. Clearly, capturing the moment at which law wins out over lawlessness through photography is seen by both the actors and the audience as imperative to the Tombstone experience.

Tombstone Courthouse Museum

According to a brochure produced by Tombstone's merchants and given out at various motels, the visitors' center, and other establishments around town, Tombstone is "The Town that is a Museum, A Museum that is a Town." The brochure goes on to say that the merchants of Tombstone "take pride in keeping their town as authentic as it was 100 years ago, giving the millions of visitors a real look back into the wild west as it really was."[25] To that end, all shops and businesses subscribe to the look and feel of the Old West through their signage and the overall rusticity of their spaces. Among the myriad souvenir shops and western-themed saloons are situated a number of museums, or at least sites that are just as interested in promoting history as they are consumer goods. The *Tombstone Epitaph* offices, the C. S. Fly Photography Studio at the OK Corral, and the Bird Cage Theatre all promote museumized representations of their own pasts. In addition, Schieffelin Hall, the Rose Tree Museum, the Pioneer Home Museum, and the Tombstone Western Heritage Museum are open as museums to visitors. Perhaps the most notable museum in Tombstone is the Tombstone Courthouse State Historic Park, which is not on Allen Street but on East Toughnut Street, a block outside the main tourist area. While most tourists spend their time wandering up and down Allen Street, some venture a little farther to get a taste of what some consider the most authentic history of Tombstone.

The courthouse in western lore is synonymous with stability and authority. It is where countless marshals, sheriffs, and judges in both the real and popular culture Wests have successfully saved towns and communities from the unruliness of renegades for decades. It is central to an understanding of the ways authority and order were utilized to eradicate lawlessness as the West became incorporated, more tame, and "civilized." It is synonymous with fictional western characters such as Marshal Will Kane (*High Noon*, 1954) and Sheriff John T. Chance (*Rio Bravo*, 1959). It lives in historic western figures such as Pat Garrett, Bat Masterson, and Wild Bill Hickok. And, of course, Wyatt Earp. As Scott Simmon argues, "The locale for the West's true power struggle was never the street, but the courthouse."[26]

The courthouse museum was originally the Cochise County Courthouse, built in 1882 to serve Cochise County, of which Tombstone was the seat at the time. After the county seat was moved to Bisbee in 1929 and the building sat empty for a time, the courthouse was sold to the city of Tombstone in 1942 for $1 and again sat idle and in disrepair for more than a decade. The structure was saved from impending destruction in 1955—a moment that marked a resurgence in historic preservation throughout the United States—by the Tombstone Restoration Commission, led by Edna Landin, president of the commission. Through a fund-raising campaign that drew national attention, Landin—also former president of the chamber of commerce—was instrumental in the renovation of the courthouse, its new life as a museum, and the campaign for the building to be accepted as an Arizona state park by the newly established Arizona State Parks Board.

The courthouse became a state park in 1959, only the second site to be named a state park in Arizona and the first to be opened to the public. It was placed on the National Register of Historic Places in 1972 and is one of the oldest courthouses still standing in the state. "If the county government was to be accorded the authority and respect that it needed to effectively govern," argues architectural historian Al Larson, "an impressive building was needed to help in that regard—to represent the authority and power of the state as well as those in authority in the county."[27] Indeed, the Cochise County Courthouse's red brick façade, heavy redwood frame, high ceilings, and large wood doors all serve to represent the supremacy and command bestowed on law enforcers in the late nineteenth century.

The museum offers visitors the opportunity to explore what seems like a relatively neutral historic narrative of Tombstone, with varying

Tombstone Courthouse State Historic Park, 2011. (Photograph by author)

interpretations of the events of the famous battle outside the OK Corral, favorable exhibits on Apache heroes Cochise and Geronimo, and even an exhibit in the old courtroom about water rights and the deportation of striking mine workers from Bisbee to New Mexico in 1917—narratives altogether absent from the performances outside. It is clear that history is revered in this space. The courthouse's own history, the history of the town, the history of the territory—which all come together under this one roof—demonstrate the importance of demythologized history to Tombstone, at least in this small corner of the historic district. Said to offer "tourists accurate, historical information on an Old West town as steeped in myth as it is history"[28] where visitors can "get a glimpse of the true old West," the courthouse is touted by townspeople, town administrators, and even the Arizona Park Commission as presenting the most authentic representation of Tombstone's past.[29] These claims of accurate and true history reinforce the courthouse's supremacy as both an institution of law and a vendor of the historical record.

Visitors to the museum wander through the courthouse offices, which not only are historical in themselves (the first room is that of the county sheriff, in which one can view the purchase deed for the building, among other artifacts) but also have now become purveyors of history. The sheriff's office leads into a larger room with a display of Wyatt Earp and his common-law wife, Mattie Blaylock. Tourists see photographs of Earp and Blaylock, his razor, and other personal effects. For a man whose life is vital to the existence and survival of Tombstone as a tourist destination, the exhibit is relatively small and unimposing. Among the other exhibits in this room—none of which seems to trump the other in importance—is a look at the history of Fort Huachuca, the camp turned fort whose proximity to silver mines allowed for the city of Tombstone to be established when Ed Schieffelin used the camp as a base from which to explore the surrounding area in the heart of Apache country. This Schieffelin founding story is repeated over and over throughout modern-day Tombstone, reminding visitors that the place was indeed forbidding for white prospectors and settlers, a public identity that has allowed the town of Tombstone to become inextricable from the very concept of the "Wild West."

Further along in this room of the museum, visitors are introduced to Chiricahua Apaches Cochise and Geronimo—given far more complimentary assessments than they are in other historic sites in town (the *Epitaph* offices, for example). There is a display on Native life as well, possibly the only one in the town that attempts to accurately illustrate life pre-Tombstone. The Historama site on Allen Street—a multimedia exhibit and film about the history of Tombstone that opened in 1964, is menacingly narrated by Vincent Price, and seemingly has not changed since—does begin with a look at Native life before Schieffelin. But the Historama, perhaps a product of its time, reproduces tired stereotypes of Apaches by perpetuating ideas of precivilized, hostile Native people in the area. Furthermore, inclusion of Native people in the Historama ends with the founding of Tombstone.

In fact, the representation of Native people in the presentation and performance of 1881 Tombstone is ambiguous at best. The Apache presence in the area is central to the founding narrative of Tombstone; after all, Ed

Schieffelin was meant to meet his doom in his search for silver because of the Apaches. The county in which Tombstone resides was established in 1881 and named for Cochise, the Chiricahua Apache war chief now buried in the Dragoon Mountains, northeast of town. It is interesting that the county would be named for such a formidable foe of white American settlers. Perhaps because his surrender in 1872 allowed for further white settlement in the area, naming the county for him was a celebration of "progress" and a demonstration of the triumph of manifest destiny. But Cochise's part in the narrative of Tombstone essentially ends at the naming of the county.

Geronimo, the Apache warrior who fought alongside Cochise (his father-in-law) against Mexican and US military forces, is also central to the history of Tombstone and the surrounding area. While often seen as a hero by his own people, he was labeled a terrorist by the United States for his resistance to white encroachment. He was captured in 1877 by John P. Clum—who would go on to become Tombstone's first mayor in 1881—and sent to the San Carlos Reservation, north of Tombstone, with thousands of other Apaches. Geronimo escaped four years later. By that time, Cochise County residents had already gathered in Tombstone to draft a resolution to the president demanding the complete removal of Apaches from the area. According to historian Katherine Benton-Cohen, "The resolution pointed to the Chiricahuas' continued raids and evasion of troops." The document also linked the Apaches to the Cowboys, those outlaws who had afflicted the town a few years prior. Geronimo eluded US troops until his capture in 1886, when white county residents got their wish and all remaining Apaches—including those who had been living peaceably at the San Carlos Reservation—were sent by train to "decrepit, dank facilities at Florida's Fort Mason and Fort Pickins."[30]

Geronimo gained some celebrity in his later years among white Americans, but he remained a prisoner of war for the rest of his life. The actual removal of Apaches from the area is little discussed in the small exhibit on Apache peoples at the courthouse museum, and not at all in Tombstone's historical production outside. Geronimo's capture by Clum is celebrated through photographs at the *Epitaph* office and somewhat at the courthouse museum. Some of the annual parades do include Native dancers in traditional dress. Otherwise, the Native presence seems almost entirely reduced to one man who plays the "drunken Indian" character at the end of festival parades.

While there is some acknowledgment at the courthouse museum of the Chinese population in Tombstone in the late nineteenth century, including an exhibit on Quong Gu Kee, proprietor of the Can Can restaurant on Allen

Street, and China Mary, who owned a general store and was heavily influential among the Chinese population, the historic Chinese presence is lacking in the performances in modern-day Tombstone. Approximately 4 percent of Tombstone's residents in 1882 were Chinese, many of whom had arrived in the United States to work on the construction of the Southern Pacific Railroad through Arizona.[31] Chinese residents in Tombstone even had their own Chinatown, called "Hoptown," which residents accessed through private tunnels, implying that the population was significant enough to warrant its own space. In the early and mid-1880s, Tombstone townspeople experienced what Eric Clements calls a "fit of nativism" and, similar to their cries for the removal of the Apaches, started an anti-Chinese movement that called for white citizens to force the Chinese out of the city.[32] In 1880 John Clum organized the Anti-Chinese League, and the fervor again gained traction in 1886, a year that saw the creation of the "Anti-Chinese Political Party" and a boycott of Chinese laundries. This anti-Chinese sentiment was reflected on the national stage with the passage of the Chinese Exclusion Act of 1882, which banned Chinese immigration to the United States. So in the late nineteenth century, the Chinese became the focus of anti-immigration campaigns in the West. As the nation's first "illegal immigrants," the Chinese were the focus of border patrol agents who attempted to prevent Chinese—not Mexicans—from entering the United States at the Mexican border.[33] All of these events suggest that the Chinese population in Tombstone was highly visible. Though the city has recently begun to acknowledge its historic Chinese residents outside the courthouse with a new sign indicating where Hoptown had once been located and a marker and sign for the old Can Can restaurant on Allen Street, the complexity of their presence in Tombstone and the tensions under which they lived have been relatively silenced.

While the Native and Chinese presence is downplayed in modern-day Tombstone, the town has held an annual Salute to Buffalo Soldiers Days since 2009, sponsored by the Wild West Detachment Marine Corps League of Tombstone. The event is fitting for Tombstone because of its proximity and relationship to Fort Huachuca, headquarters of the Tenth Cavalry—the "Buffalo Soldiers"—and a national historic landmark in its own right. Even with this annual event, Tombstone's diversity remains on the periphery of, if not entirely absent from, the dominant narrative of the town's history. The lack of diversity in modern performances and representations of Tombstone highlights the notion that there can be little to no incorporation of Native and other people of color in a "civilized" town. The narrative has been simplified and narrowed down to such a degree that there is little space for the deep inclusion of different cultures into the story. But as we see in how Geronimo is typically represented, as well as in the drunken Indian in the parade, the old antagonisms still get played out, just in new and different ways.

Whiteness is celebrated in new and different ways as well. Back at the courthouse museum, the first main exhibit room once housed a large display on German western writer Karl May (1842–1912). This exhibit underscored the strong link between Germany and the mythic West in the German imaginary. As the most widely read German author of all time, May's novels about life in the mid- to late nineteenth-century American West greatly influenced the ways American cowboys and Indians have been conceived in the German imagination. As interesting as this is, there were no exhibits on the ways the mythic West has been consumed or appropriated elsewhere in the world—at the Wild West Show at Disneyland in Paris, for example; or in western films (either based in the American West or similar in structure to American westerns) produced in Italy, Poland, East Germany, Russia, India, Australia, and other nations; or the ways Wyatt Earp, Doc Holliday, and the "Gunfight at the OK Corral" have resonated internationally.

Perhaps the display was to show the currency of the mythic West, in which Tombstone is so central. In this way, tourists might have found it interesting that the stories they themselves grew up with had their counterparts in a foreign land, written by a man who had never even visited the American West but wrote purely based on the legends he himself was exposed to as a child. They might have been interested in discovering that much of German national identity resides in the myth of the American West, especially through a deeply romantic fascination with Native peoples—a phenomenon called *Indianthusiasm* by Hartmut Lutz.[34] Perhaps then too, tourists would have been fascinated that the town in which May grew up and where the Karl May Museum currently resides—Radebeul, Germany, near Dresden—is known as "Little Tombstone." The May exhibit was actually crafted in Radebeul at the Karl May Museum specifically for the courthouse museum in Tombstone, while a Tombstone exhibit was crafted by the courthouse museum specifically for the Karl May Museum in Radebeul. There was even a link to the Karl May Museum on the courthouse museum's website. Again, none of this was mentioned in the exhibit, demonstrating that simplified versions of history and biography offer only glimpses into the real stories without the messiness of depth and density.

While this exhibit was temporary and is no longer featured at the museum, this intriguing link between Tombstone and Germany continues, as

German visitors will soon have the opportunity to tour the museum with a German interpreter.[35] The May exhibit has been replaced with a large display about John Heith (sometimes spelled "Heath"), the only man who was sentenced to life in prison rather than death by hanging for his part in the Bisbee Massacre in 1883.[36] Not satisfied with the sentence, a mob of men from Cochise County broke into the county jail where Heith was being held, took him at gunpoint, and hanged him from a telephone pole at the corner of First and Toughnut Streets in downtown Tombstone. So, the celebration of the mythic West as an international space (the exhibit about Karl May) has been replaced by a monument to frontier justice that perhaps more typifies the Wild West to visitors.

The same room offers displays about the street fight between the Earps and the Clantons, but this gets less space than expected at the museum. There is a small display on Doc Holliday and an exhibit of sketches giving different perspectives of the street fight behind the OK Corral, an exhibit that takes up only one small corner of the entire room. It is possible that in its efforts to offer a neutral history of Tombstone, the museum chooses to downplay this central event. While the fight is vital to the ways the town is conceived in the popular imagination and fundamental to the site as a tourist destination, it had less impact on the town at the time than one might have thought.

Other exhibits in the courthouse offer a glimpse into the lives of miners, ranchers, and pioneers, as well as the ways law and order were maintained in late-nineteenth-century Tombstone. The treasurer's office, sheriff's office, and even the gallows outside have been reconceived to render Tombstone's history even more exciting for visitors. Despite the museum's (and others') assertions of neutrality and authenticity, an "invitation to a hanging" that lures tourists to the gallows erected in the jail yard behind the courthouse firmly entrenches this space within the overall "wildness" the town of Tombstone seeks to promulgate. Indeed, the hanging to which visitors are invited is one of only two hangings that occurred at the courthouse.[37] While these hangings did happen at the courthouse, and the gallows are accurate reproductions, the museum is as invested in perpetuating certain notions of the Wild West as is the rest of the town in attempts to entice tourists, demonstrating how economic imperatives often render the exaggerated truth a potentially more profitable enterprise.

In this town that is in many ways itself a museum, it is not entirely ironic that the courthouse museum is integral to the historicity of Tombstone. Tombstone's entire reputation as a wild western town relies on the juxtaposition of the courthouse to the outlawry for which it is known. To that end the museum offers a glimpse into the lives of Tombstone's genteel citizenry—including the material culture of pioneering white families, such as china tea sets, needlepoint, bonnets, hairpins, fans, and a bible; displays on less controversial leisure activities, such as athletic and sporting events, lectures, theater, socials, and so on; exhibits pointing to endeavors considered more "wholesome fun" than "rowdy amusements," such as parades and the Tombstone City Band; and exhibits on those profit-making enterprises that were firmly planted inside the law: ranching and mining. At the same time, however, the museum makes good use of Tombstone's status as the quintessence of the Wild West, dedicating as much space to those "rowdy amusements" as to those considered more respectable.

This is not to say that the Tombstone Courthouse State Historic Park is not displaying actual history. Tombstone is a town of contrasts. It was, in fact, both rowdy and civilized. It is to say, however, that the museum, in an effort to entice those tourists who have made their way to Tombstone based on very specific expectations of the space, is—like the rest of the town—celebrating and making good use of its raucous past. But it also maintains its seeming neutrality by showing a side of the town that is not necessarily explored outside its walls. To Tombstone residents and tourists alike, the Tombstone Courthouse Museum has become known as "the place to go to discover the facts behind the legends."[38]

* * *

Of course, no museum is "neutral" in its representation of events and people that shape a space. The Tombstone Courthouse Museum is no exception, and visitors might be surprised to learn of the recent struggles that surrounded the museum as a site. On 15 January 2010, in an effort to close gaps in the state budget, the Arizona State Parks Board voted to close the Tombstone Courthouse Museum, along with twelve other parks.[39] The state "swept" money from the state parks' operating budgets to cover general government expenses, deciding to keep open only those parks deemed most economically viable. With this decision, operations were handed over to the city of Tombstone, and the courthouse museum became central to discussions about not only the narratives that are important to Tombstone's history but also the importance of history itself.

Art Austin had been the park supervisor at the courthouse for twenty-eight years, until the state of Arizona stopped funding the park at the end of March 2010. Prior to operations for the museum being transferred to the town of Tombstone, Austin expressed his concern over Tombstone being responsible for the preservation and representation of its own history. Not trusting in the ability of the town to maintain the historic integrity of the space, Austin scoffed at the idea of authenticity anywhere in Tombstone beyond the walls of the courthouse. He said that after the release of the movies *Tombstone* in 1993 and *Wyatt Earp* in 1994, it became imperative for reenactors outside to dress and act like the people in the movies, claiming that that is what tourists now expect.[40]

Indeed, even more than twenty years later, the films *Tombstone* and *Wyatt Earp* largely influence the ways tourists and performers understand the town. Both movies are continuously shown on flat screen televisions at the Crystal Palace and Big Nose Kate's on Allen Street, played throughout the day and into the evening with the sound down, to remind tourists what brought them to Tombstone in the first place. *Tombstone* and *Wyatt Earp* movie posters, hot plates with the image of Val Kilmer's Doc Holliday, and T-shirts with the line "Justice is coming," the tagline from the 1993 film, or "I'm your huckleberry," Kilmer's most famous line, are available at many of the souvenir shops. A number of tourists cite the films as their only knowledge of Tombstone and its history, many claiming it as the main reason for their visit. Barb, a server at the old Russ House (now a Mexican and Italian restaurant), says she knew the movies and "that was about it" before she decided to spend her winters there. Big Nose Kate's patrons Shelly and Georgia both say they came to Tombstone because of the movies. Rodney, who was stationed at Fort Huachuca and visits Tombstone on a regular basis, goes so far as to say it is time that Hollywood produce another movie to reinvigorate interest in the town.[41]

Historian David Wrobel reminds us that "this phenomenon of visiting places that have been seen on the big screen is sometimes so pronounced that a historic site becomes significant as a tourist attraction largely because it has been depicted in a movie." Wrobel discusses Librarian of Congress Daniel Boorstin's contention that "the modern tourist was . . . merely searching after that which he/she was expected to experience" and that "the tourist even visited sites depicted in movies and matched the actual reality of the site against the hyperreality of its celluloid presentation."[42] While Boorstin lamented the transition of "traveler" to "tourist," a transition that he felt signaled a loss in cultural aesthetics and taste, his argument about the influence of popular culture on tourism in the creation of simulated environments is fitting. *Tombstone* and *Wyatt Earp*, as well as the many other films that crowd the history of the western genre in the twentieth century, certainly have affected tourists' expectations and help set the tone for the gunfights played out on the street and at the OK Corral. The films dictate the speech, swagger, and costume—from sashes to hats to dusters to mustaches to bolo ties—of the performers and many of the townspeople as well.

But—as Boorstin and other scholars of tourism have argued—using these films to guide historic accuracy can be problematic. Austin pointed, for example, to the use of color in both the painting of buildings and the clothing used by performers. Red, the color used in the movie *Tombstone* for sashes worn by the Cowboys, was not a widely used color for clothing in the 1880s, according to Austin.[43] The same is true for paints. In the 1880s, white, light gray, and buff were the most dominant colors because colorful paint was expensive and hard to come by. This had not stopped buildings in the historic district from using red and other bright colors, however, a fact that made Austin bristle. But the continuing negotiation between tourist expectations and historic accuracy brings into stark relief how history is important but also secondary. Franklin argues that "the so-called 'post-tourist' no longer needed authentic objects to confirm their gaze but enjoyed the fakery, the games of simulation and the virtual imaginary that the thematised tourism 'worlds' of the 1990s provided."[44] The intertextual impact of *Tombstone* and *Wyatt Earp* on the way the town's performers present themselves to tourists also underscores the significant impact that the popular culture West has had on the preservation of the town of Tombstone.

Other historical incongruences have caused some local strife in Tombstone, as well as endangered its designation as a National Historic Landmark District. In 2004 the National Park Service (NPS) declared the designation threatened, seeking to work with the city to develop an appropriate program of oversight and management. Its status has since been upgraded to "watch," but it is an ongoing process. Former Historic District Commission (HDC) chair Patrick Greene, who had also served as executive director of the chamber of commerce, complained about businesses in the historic district using neon signs, which, he said, keep appearing "like tribbles" (a reference to an original *Star Trek* episode, "The Trouble with Tribbles," from 1967).[45] Heated discussions went on as recently as May 2010 regarding this problem. Greene believed that "if neon can be seen from the historic district then the HDC does have jurisdiction. . . . Tourism is our main economy here and people come here to see the Old West."[46]

Greene was correct in emphasizing the importance of the appearance of historic authenticity to tourism and to the local economy. Sustained interest in the town via history and heritage, preservation, and Hollywood has continued to bring much-needed tourist dollars into Tombstone and managed to keep the town afloat for decades. According to the Southeastern Arizona Economic Development District (SAEDD), Tombstone is the most-visited attraction in Cochise County, and the Tucson and Southern Region, which includes Cochise County, is the second-most-visited region in the state of Arizona. Total travel-related spending in Cochise County reached $331.2 million in 2009. Again, according to the SAEDD, travel-related spending accounted for approximately $82.3 million in direct earnings in the county and generated approximately $11.5 million in direct local government tax revenue in 2009. Because this money represents taxes that are levied on visitors rather than residents, more money is left in the hands of residents, increasing their purchasing power and, as a result, generating higher levels of local spending that may also contribute to local area job growth.[47] It is not necessarily a thriving community, and certainly monies flowing into the town have not done so evenly throughout the last sixty years. But tourism is indeed their biggest money-making enterprise.[48] In fact, Tombstone has survived far longer as a tourist destination than as a silver mining town. While there would be no tourism if not for its history, maintaining the tourism industry is central to all discussions about the economy, preservation, restoration, reproduction, and business there.

Some attempts to remain historically authentic remain contentious. While Allen Street had been resurfaced—the pavement covered—in 2006 "in a manner that is appropriate for its period of historic significance (1880–1931)," that is, to look like a dirt road as requested by the NPS, this measure provoked controversy among visitors and townspeople alike.[49] Tombstone's windy days meant dirt went everywhere, into shops and eyes, all over merchandise, countertops, and artifacts. Some people claimed the dirt was a public health risk. Efforts were made to control the dust, mostly by covering the dirt with an oily substance that was supposed to dry overnight and be reapplied on a regular basis, but to no avail: "Instead, the streets stayed oily, and customers brought the mess from the streets to the stores."[50] Cries from business owners along Allen Street to remove the dirt included suggestions to paint the asphalt to look like dirt. Some cited the fact that Tombstone's streets had been paved for decades before the town received its historic status and that a dirt street, while it "'looks' fun and 'historic,'" has "nothing to do with the true history of the town." One merchant proclaimed, "Students on field trips and people in wheelchairs used to go right down the middle of the road. Now, without pavement, they no longer do so. 'Tourist-friendly'? I don't think so."[51] Under increased pressure, the town removed the dirt in 2009 and continues to seek ways to comply with the NPS order. More recently, dirt has now been placed on either edge of the paved road, but the debate rages on. Touristic expectation prompted one visitor to Tombstone to remark on a recent visit to the historic district, "They need to put the dirt back on the street! [Removing it] was a big mistake!"[52]

The closing off of Allen Street to car traffic in 2004 also came under fire by locals who no longer had the convenience of being able to get from point A to point B in their cars to conduct their daily lives. Then in 2009, Mayor Dusty Escapule (who was born and raised in Tombstone) pushed to extend the area closed off to car traffic to Fourth and Fifth Streets between Allen and Toughnut, "to preserve the historic feel" of the district. Many local business owners thought that he was only looking after his own interests rather than being concerned with the authenticity of the historic district. Escapule owns a stagecoach company called Old Tombstone Tours, which would have been unaffected by the closing. Tombstone Trolley Tours, on the other hand, would be unable to travel up and down Toughnut Street as it had done for years.[53] At a meeting on 26 February 2010, councilpeople and local residents spoke publicly on their support of the closure, although one councilperson and at least one member of the community expressed opposition to the measure. Tombstone resident Tom Anderson articulated concerns that some locals have had when it comes to meeting the needs of those who live there: "You have already taken away Allen Street for driving and parking and now you want to take away more." Councilwoman Stacy Korbeck-Reeder vocalized her concern that Tombstone Trolley Tours would be rerouted, stating, "At this point I can't vote yes, because they are part of Tombstone." Despite the resistance, the council approved the measure by a vote of four to one.[54]

At the time of all these controversies, Greene asserted that people in the town needed to "understand where their bread is buttered" and do all they could to maintain an "authentic" experience for visitors.[55] Attempts to define what is historical and what is not while addressing the needs of both locals and tourists in this living history town sometimes result in compromises or a lack of accuracy altogether, for which keepers of Tombstone's history must be constantly vigilant.

These notions of authenticity and accuracy and the constant negotiation between those invested in the town caused some to oppose the idea of Tombstone taking over operations of the courthouse museum. They feared that once Tombstone took over the site, the integrity of what they believed was the last vestige of true history in the entire town would be compromised. The town did in fact take over the museum in April 2010 and is still responsible for its operation. Changes were made at the start: the price of admission was raised from four to five dollars per adult, hours were extended from five to seven days a week, and volunteers traded in their state park uniforms for period costumes—although some volunteers still opt for street clothes. There had been a hope to create "living history" within the museum, such as trial reenactments, a tactic that has successfully attracted tourists to other sites in Tombstone for generations, but that idea has not yet been realized.[56] The original charter for the museum is still in effect, which means the town is prohibited from modifying anything on display or in storage in the building.

By all accounts, the transfer of operations went smoothly. The Tombstone City Council voted unanimously to enter negotiations with the state. The state entered into an agreement with the city, and the city entered into an agreement with the chamber of commerce, which now is sole operator of the site. The museum is self-sustaining, so all monies garnered from donations and entrance fees go directly back into the operations of the museum. In fact, Patricia Moreno, the park's manager in 2010, said the transfer was seamless and the running of the museum has gone so well with the Tombstone Chamber of Commerce at the helm that she did not see why anyone would be pessimistic about the transfer in the first place—perhaps a reference to Art Austin's cynicism.[57] Moreno's thoughts about the transfer reveal the ways that "history" as a concept served to motivate the town's citizens to maintain this museum for the good of Tombstone's own survival.

It took some campaigning on the part of the HDC and the chamber of commerce to get the locals' support to keep the museum open and running, clearly marking the museum as telling "authentic" and "true" history. Performances on Allen Street are *entertainment,* while the museum is *history.* Of course, other sites in Tombstone tend toward promotion of what has been termed "authentic history," including the Birdcage Theatre. But the courthouse is the most dominant example of this idea. The consensus is summed up well in an article about the courthouse museum in the *Tucson Sentinel:* "The loss of the Courthouse is more than economic. In a town where cowboys walk the streets, gunfighters draw their weapons, and madams flirt around corners, it's easy to step into Tombstone and get lost in the lore."[58] The museum, according to the citizens of Tombstone, is an escape from the fake or exaggerated, and the loss of this site would have a tremendous impact on the legitimacy of the town as a historic landmark. "Visitors from the world over have made the iconic venue a central part of their time in Tombstone," said Frederick Schoemehl, editor of the *Tombstone Epitaph National Edition,* a historical journal. "It is a sad and sorry state of affairs when a decision is made to close a facility so central to Western history."[59]

In fact, the importance of the museum seems more metaphorical than literal. The closing of the courthouse might not in fact have had an impact on the ways tourists understand Tombstone altogether, or on their visiting the town at all. But the discourse around the closing very much elicited the notion that shutting down the museum meant the loss of true history, and that struck a chord with the town's residents. After the agreement between Tombstone and the Arizona State Parks Board, the museum was reopened in May 2010 with a public celebration. At the grand reopening ceremony, Reese Woodling, president of the Arizona State Parks Board at the time, made clear the importance of keeping the courthouse open to visitors: "Without people like you [those attending the ceremony], we could not keep the past alive," stated Woodling. "Kids need this type of place because without history we are missing so much."[60]

The cries to keep the courthouse open were saturated with language about the value of history to Tombstone's existence. More recently, however, the Tombstone Archives, operated by Tombstone's historical records manager Nancy Sosa and funded through grants and private donations, packed up all of its historic documents and moved everything to Bisbee. Though she was hired by the city in 2008, budgetary restrictions prompted the establishment of the Foundation for the Tombstone Archives and an agreement for the foundation to reimburse the city for Sosa's salary and expenses. "I am the only city employee who has to raise the funds to pay herself," Sosa said in the face of a dispute over the foundation not paying what the city said it was owed. In addition to disagreements over keeping the archives active, the city would also have to build a temperature-controlled storage area to house documents that had already been damaged by mold. Sosa's final appeal included the argument that "in a town that has thrived through myth and legend, the history is the truth." Regardless, Tombstone was not willing to fund the endeavor. Everything was moved to the Archives and Public Records Division of the Arizona State Library, and Sosa lost her job.[61] Although there was some protest, in general the archives were closed without much fanfare, indicating that they were not seen as vital to the purveying of Tombstone's history, as many believe the courthouse is. This may partly be because there was no performance or period costume at the archives. More than that, though, the courthouse is not only a museum with artifacts within it but also a historic site of great significance. While celebrating Tombstone's "lawless" past—and while promoting itself as the epitome of the Wild West of the 1880s—the reconstructed Tombstone of 1955, 2010, and 2015 also operates to reproduce notions of power and political and cultural dominance. In Tombstone's historic district, both inside and outside the courthouse, law always wins. This may explain the importance of the county courthouse to Tombstone's legitimacy and its centrality in the idea of maintaining law and authority as hegemonic. This makes the museum essential to the town's ongoing validity. The closing of the courthouse, then, seemed to represent, at least to some, the utter removal of history altogether from the city of Tombstone.

The "overwhelming support" by locals (as represented by those in positions of authority) of the transfer of operations to Tombstone is an example of how important history is to the town—at least to those who have been appointed the custodians of history. Being removed from the "threatened" list by the Department of the Interior in 2009 and maintaining its status as a historic district is vital. As Mayor Escapule stated, "By being a historic district, it is nationally and internationally advertised as a landmark place to visit. It shows it's not a movie set or a theme park, but a real old town."[62] "Bronco" Bill Pakinkis, board member on the chamber of commerce, member of the HDC, and organizer of Tombstone's Wild West Days, believes that when it comes down to it, history is the most important component of Tombstone's success: "If it were not for Tombstone's historic past, we would not have tourism, [and] without tourism, the merchants would not have customers. [These] same merchants and business owners hire the locals to work in their businesses. So everyone works for the same successful goals."[63] While the phrase "historic past" implies that the past is only "historic" when an event of (reinvented) significance is a part of it, Pakinkis articulates a commonly held opinion in Tombstone that the past is imperative to the present. Not only does Tombstone see both the history of Tombstone and history itself as imperative to its survival; its official history has been sanctioned by the state and the nation as well, evidence that the West as a metaphor for American national identity still holds immense power and credibility even as many doubt its continued salience.

At the same time, however, "true" history remains on the periphery of both the main street of the historic district and many tourists' imagination. On the one hand, the past is crucial to the town's existence. But because the "past" in Tombstone essentially means that abstracted moment in its history around which the town has constructed its public identity—26 October 1881, the date of the "Gunfight at the OK Corral"—visitors encounter a carefully selected history, one that celebrates Tombstone as a Wild West town through sound bites and performance. As a museum, the Tombstone Courthouse State Historic Park organizes the past in ways that celebrate Tombstone and make sense to visitors. Now, under the auspices of the town itself, the museum is beholden to engage in official narratives because of economic imperatives, but also because of an identity that has been purchased wholesale by those officially charged with keeping that identity alive (many of whom, not coincidentally, are recent settlers in the community).

While it may be less performative than what lies outside its doors and offers insight into those elements of the town's history that perhaps are considered less entertaining than what is celebrated in the streets and saloons on Allen Street, the Tombstone courthouse is turning to those same devices of costume and entertainment to attract more people inside its doors. Further, the museum depends on what John Dorst calls "traditionalization": "the selective reduction of a complex history to a simple, readily comprehensible set of linkages that establish legitimizing connections between present institutions and an imagined past."[64] Such selectivity is inherent in museum setup. In order to tell a story to visitors, one that will elicit certain responses, emotions, and understandings depending on the mission and motives of the creators, the story must, by design, be uncomplicated.

So the Tombstone Courthouse State Historic Park is not neutral, as it may appear at first glance to visitors. While it may be offering a seemingly "authentic" version of the town's history—with displays about labor disputes and Native peoples as well as those about the Earp gun battle and Ed Schieffelin—the courthouse is as much engaged in a performance of history as the entertainers on Allen Street are. All are churning out versions of Tombstone's history that sustain a public identity that is most attractive to tourists, as well as themselves. In fact, in many ways—while there are economic reasons for keeping Tombstone's past alive in terms of tourist dollars—this history seems to be of dire importance to those who live there. Tombstone's ("historic") past and public identity are its people's past and identity. The past has become the key to Tombstone's future, and the town has been working with the understanding of that fact ever since.

2

Preservation and Performance

In 1951 Clayton A. Smith, editor of the *Tombstone Epitaph*, set about to convince the citizens of Tombstone, Arizona, that restoring the fronts of buildings on Allen Street in the center of town would help make Tombstone the tourist attraction in the West that Colonial Williamsburg, Virginia, had become in the East.[1] At his urging within the pages of the *Epitaph*, civic-minded boosters and townspeople began to reconstruct Tombstone in the image of what was popularly seen as its former glory and based on representations that had been popularized in novels, movies, and television series for decades. The town was already drawing tourists every October to its Helldorado Days, named after the 1928 book of the same name by Earp-era deputy sheriff Billy Breakenridge. Started in 1929, Helldorado Days is Tombstone's oldest festival celebrating the town's "wild" western history.[2] While considered a success in 1929, the festival lost its luster after only a few years and was discontinued in 1932.[3] The celebration had a resurgence in the late 1940s, along with a swell in domestic tourism, especially in the US West, giving Smith and other promoters in 1951 reason to seek to commodify and market Tombstone's public identity year-round by transforming the town to best fit the traditional narrative of the Wild West.

As Smith's nod to Colonial Williamsburg indicates, preservation of the nation's history was well under way by 1951. Tombstone's own efforts reflect a national trend midcentury to preserve heritage for touristic consumption. After years of struggle, Tombstone was hungry for the monies promised by the surge in domestic tourism after World War II, and the town began a decades-long endeavor to

Fremont Street buildings in decay with Dragoon Mountains in the distance, ca. 1930s. (Courtesy of Arizona Historical Society, http://arizonahistoricalsociety.org, AHS 52090)

present the Tombstone of the 1880s to visitors. In its quest to meet the expectations of tourists, Tombstone has also had to meet the demands of its own citizens as well as follow the rules set out by the National Park Service (NPS) in order to maintain the historic district designation it worked so hard to gain. This negotiation has seen continuous struggle ever since the Tombstone Restoration Commission was established in 1949 and has garnered almost constant criticism. But it also has resulted in building a tenacious and unwavering commitment on the part of townspeople to see Tombstone survive, for travelers and for themselves, for years to come.

Preservation in the United States

The preservation of America's past has been a continuing endeavor since as early as the mid-nineteenth century. Beginning with efforts to preserve George Washington's Revolutionary War headquarters in Newburgh, New York—which became the nation's first publicly operated historic site in 1850—and Ann Pamela Cunningham's efforts in Virginia to preserve Mount Vernon in 1853, elite white Americans have a long history of attempting to preserve the nation's heritage. "Like other historical disciplines," architectural historian Mitchell Schwarzer contends, "historic preservation emerged in the United States during the nineteenth century as an attempt to establish national identity through cultural affiliation to past events, sites, and buildings."[4] These early efforts focused on those buildings that symbolized the "birth of the nation" based on the American Revolution and the ideologies of independence and individual liberty essential to the ways that cause was remembered. Historic preservation was typically the concern of wealthy private citizens and societies, usually composed of and headed up by women. While the federal government had already set aside public lands as reserves or national parks, such as Yellowstone National Park in 1872, it was not until the passage of the Antiquities Act in 1906 that it became involved with preserving what were interpreted as important sites and artifacts of the nation's history. Through the Department of the Interior, the federal government started preserving sites and buildings that were considered most valuable to the development of the American nation. While these efforts first focused on archaeological ruins and military sites, the Historic Sites Act of 1935 included under its auspices historic buildings and sites on private property as well.[5] As symbols of American ideals, these historic sites and buildings were deemed worthy of preservation by those interested in safeguarding "shrines of transcendent significance to the nation."[6] These places were seen as foundational to the nation's heritage, acting as tangible incarnations of the so-called traditions and customs that undergird the ways the nation is popularly imagined.

Notions of what constitutes *heritage* are as flexible and fluid as what that heritage itself entails. *Heritage* can be defined both as something that is transmitted from the past and handed down by tradition, as in *legacy*, and as something inherited as a result of one's *birthright*. It is important to highlight the notion of "birthright" in this definition, as though historical events, people, and places both are the result of and result in American exceptionalism, the qualities of which are passed on from one generation to the next. The terms *heritage* and *history* are often used interchangeably, indicating the common conception that the nation's history is entirely intertwined with the national, official story—its heritage—promoting romanticized notions of the American character. What is considered the nation's heritage speaks greatly not only to the ways Americans and history keepers understand, construct, and make use of the past in contemporary society but also to how these history keepers wish to define themselves, their region, and their country based on that past. What is understood as significant or valuable is preserved; what is preserved is understood as significant or valuable. Heritage, in other words, by the very fact that it is being preserved, is considered valuable and worthy of being preserved. What is "valuable," "worthy," and "significant," of course, is subjective. And those who get to decide occupy an elite position within certain communities.

Pierre Bourdieu (among others) argues that the taste of a society is the taste of the ruling class, that it is learned and not innate, and that the value of an object is imposed on it rather than emanating from within.[7] How historical objects are imbued with local, regional, or national value has everything to do with those citizens who declare themselves the arbiters of local, regional, or national history. Economist Randall Mason proposes that the number of people invested in a particular object of heritage is directly related to the importance that object seems to demand. He also claims that what is considered a particular community's heritage must be upheld by that community: "Though heritage is certainly valued by individuals, its *raison d'être* is, by definition, to sustain a sphere of public interest and public good."[8] Cultural theorist Stuart Hall suggests that heritage is completely dependent on the idea that what is conserved is of value and authorized as valuable relative to "the unfolding of the 'national story' whose terms we already know."[9] The idea of heritage as embodying the spirit of the nation is still the foundation for the National Historic Landmarks Program, which designates certain sites as national historic landmarks "because they possess exceptional value or quality in illustrating or interpreting the heritage of the United States." The NPS also claims that designated sites must "possess a high, not simply a good, level of historic integrity" in order to be labeled historically significant and that the label in turn helps "ensure the preservation of historic places." In other words, sites must already be preserved in order to be designated historically significant, while the designation is necessary to guarantee preservation.[10]

Early genteel activists fought to preserve sites associated with great events and men such as the American Revolution or the nation's forefathers. Later efforts focused on preserving sites on a broader—if not always more quotidian—scale that celebrated the tenacity of larger segments of the public, leading to historic districts and "open-air" museum towns. These spaces were still considered fundamental to understandings of the nation, but by the 1920s business leaders were the new keepers of history, becoming increasingly central in the effort to bring history to the general public and making money in the process.[11] Automobile mogul Henry Ford, for example, funded the construction of Greenfield Village in Michigan, opened in 1929, a hodgepodge of historic structures that included a little red schoolhouse, slave cabins, a courthouse, a windmill from Cape Cod, an old inn, a New Hampshire firehouse, a Massachusetts shoe shop, and further symbols of early American life. Greenfield Village still markets itself as "a celebration of people—people whose unbridled optimism came to define modern-day America."[12] Greenfield Village "paid homage to blacksmiths, machinists, and frontier farmers, celebrated craft skills and domestic labor, recalled old social customs like square dancing and folk fiddling, and praised the 'timeless and dateless' pioneer virtues of hard work, discipline, frugality, and self-reliance." Ford's celebration of the common man over those considered "great" was a rejection of the "approach of exalting famous patriots and patrician elites." In fact, "he banished upper class homes, lawyers' offices, and banks from his village" altogether.[13] Similar commemorations to the folk can be seen at Old Sturbridge Village in Massachusetts and the Heritage Village Museum in Sharonville, Ohio.

Around the same time Ford was investing in Greenfield Village, in 1926 American industrialist John D. Rockefeller started funding the rebuilding of Colonial Williamsburg, which opened in 1934. Unlike Ford, Rockefeller was not interested in merely assembling historic structures that did not necessarily share a common space in history; rather, he wanted to restore a specific area to its "historic" character and purge it from its anachronistic (modern) setting. Rockefeller believed that "to undertake to preserve a single building when its environment has changed and is no longer in keeping, has always seemed to me unsatisfactory—much less worthwhile." He was interested in constructing a comprehensive vision of Old Williamsburg that did not simply give the impression of history but was what he imagined to be a complete replication of that history.[14] To that end, Colonial Williamsburg offered not a(n) (e)motionless historical museumized site—a place of quiet and staid reverence for historical and cultural artifacts—but a fully immersive and interactive "living history" space where visitors could "fully experience lifestyles and social patterns of the Colonial era" and link those lifestyles with the broader principles of America.[15] Even today, these ideals remain the backbone of the site's mission: "The Colonial Williamsburg story of a revolutionary city tells how diverse peoples, having different and sometimes conflicting ambitions, evolved into a society that valued liberty and equality. Americans cherish these values as a birthright, even when their promise remains unfulfilled."[16]

The phenomenological component to Colonial Williamsburg set it apart in the early decades of the twentieth century from other open-air museums. Since at least the 1940s, Colonial Williamsburg has not only displayed artifacts and reconstructed buildings but also reenacted (performed) the ways people lived in Virginia in the eighteenth century through "interpreters" who dress in period costume, tell stories, and demonstrate everyday activities. How the past is understood, translated, and explained directly influences how the space has been and is appreciated by visitors, and this encompassing learning experience proved entertaining, popular, and profitable. Soon Colonial Williamsburg "exemplified the economic potential of historic preservation," demonstrating the attraction of history to tourists whose vacation dollars spent in Colonial Williamsburg "became the main support for the real town of Williamsburg," a result that many other towns around the country were eager to emulate.[17] Of course, Williamsburg might not have been the most reliable model for historic accuracy in preservation. Rockefeller's conception of the historic town did not include representations of the working class, and there was no reference to the large number of slaves that made up nearly half of eighteenth-century Williamsburg's population. Unlike Ford's Greenfield Village, Colonial Williamsburg "commemorated the planter elite, portrayed as the progenitors of timeless ideas and values, the cradle of the Americanism that Rockefeller and the corporate elite inherited and guarded." Williamsburg presented a sterile version of the eighteenth century, free not only from the odors of an actual colonial town but all the cultural and social messiness that defined the era as well.[18]

The construction of Colonial Williamsburg fits nicely within the context of the nation's fascination and preoccupation with history and heritage. As public historian Mike Wallace demonstrates, it also highlights where history and ahistory collide, where an obsession with heritage and an utterly cavalier attitude toward fact and multivocality meet within American popular historical culture. It seems that Americans have been more interested in the romanticized legacy of their past than in the past itself. As Americans have flocked to constructed heritage sites, they participate in a wider contestation about what constitutes history and who gets to decide. Popular history allows consumers to maintain distance from actual events, glossing over the parts of the story that do not align with the ways people had wished life had been. "Historicide" is Wallace's term for the killing of "true" history and replacing it with a history that is neither true nor complete.[19] Living history museums and historical sites promote themselves as more extraordinary vendors of history than what can be learned from the printed page. In fact, historical sites depend on the marketability of experiential learning: "Hands-on heritage-as-history guarantees enjoyment," historian Michael Kammen argues, "unlike the deadly dull sort of history that is dispensed in the classroom, the library, and via the medium of print."[20] Indeed, the website for Greenfield Village boasts that, in addition to the "83 authentic, historic structures" on the grounds, "there's the fun stuff, too," while Colonial Williamsburg claims it is "full of fun for the whole family."[21] History as experienced entertainment has become the cornerstone of heritage sites nationwide.

Exposing the underlying factors that instill certain beliefs in the American public and that lead to particular histories to be told and retold—including contests for power, reification of hegemony, challenges to dominant narratives, and debates over who gets to be what Kammen calls "custodians of tradition"—is the primary objective of the field of cultural memory. Kammen explains, "Memory is more likely to be activated by contestation and amnesia is more likely to be induced by the desire for reconciliation." Memory and amnesia shape the ways simple stories replace complex events and circumstances in popular history. Kammen also offers some insight into the ways "tradition" functions, arguing that a certain amount of tradition "can supply the basis for social cohesion, especially in a nation so heterogeneous as the United States." However, if we are to look at the use of traditions more critically, we find that they "are commonly relied upon by those who possess the power to achieve an illusion of social consensus. Such people invoke legitimacy of an artificially constructed past in order to buttress presentist assumptions and the authority of regime."[22] Again, we are faced with contests for the power to tell the nation's history. By exposing the underlying ideologies that form the foundation for much historical narrative, these scholars are very much entrenched in the same sort of debunking that new western historians and, some would argue, producers of revisionist westerns participate in. In fact, the exploration into cultural memory coincides with the advent of new western history beginning in the 1980s, slightly later than the popular revisionist westerns of the 1960s and 1970s. These groups were reacting to older, less inclusive modes of narrativizing history and attempting to broaden the way we understand the nation's past. New western historians reject more positive and triumphalist interpretations of the West to stress the multiplicity and multivocality of experiences on the frontier, involving the convergence of diverse people—women as well as men; Asians, Native Americans, African Americans, and Latin Americans as well as European Americans. How these groups interacted on the frontier, whether in cooperation or in struggle, constitutes much of the focus of this brand of academic endeavor. These scholars emphasize that the West can be viewed within the framework of colonialism and explore the ways capitalist ideologies defined and transformed the region. Environmental scholars have also inserted a far less sanguine idea of the West into the current scholarship (a perspective, not coincidentally, that has also spilled over into popular culture, as seen in such films as *Blade*

Runner [1982] and *Escape from L.A.* [1996], and even in remakes of western films such as *3:10 to Yuma* [2007]). Scholars of cultural memory also reveal the ways the myth of the West and popular culture have clouded public perception about certain events and circumstances of the actual West, both historically and in the current moment. They also reveal how visitors call on those popular culture productions concerned with the nation's history to make sense of their interaction with memorials and heritage sites in simple and indiscriminate ways.

Cultural historian Marita Sturken labels those who participate in "distanced experiences" at heritage sites "tourists of history," people who both feel a connection to and maintain a distance from an actual event—a position that she defines as touristic and uncritical.[23] The distance maintained by consumers has also allowed for large gaps or even distortions in the "history" that is presented—a condition that applies to heritage sites throughout the West. The ways the Alamo, for example, has been interpreted at the site seem inextricable from the ways it has been represented in popular culture. In other words, it is not solely the actual site that serves as a site of contestation and struggle. Edward Tabor Linenthal traces the struggle over not only what the Alamo has meant to twentieth-century Americans but also who "owns" the right and power to make that determination. From the Daughters of the Republic of Texas to the League of United Latin American Citizens, Linenthal demonstrates the contestation over the official history of the battle of the Alamo—with the DRT holding the reins and only reluctantly incorporating the Tejano presence into the story. In this same tradition, cultural historian Richard Flores seeks to unravel the dominant narratives that circulate around the story of the Alamo, not only to expose alternative accounts but also to explore the history of those enlisted to guard the Alamo's heritage and represent that heritage to the world. Official histories and cultural memory fuel much of the debate around the Alamo, as Flores demonstrates. The Alamo's transformation into an American cultural icon helped shape social, economic, and political relations between Anglo and Mexican Texans from the late nineteenth to the mid-twentieth centuries. Attempts by heritage society members (what Linenthal calls "guardians of patriotic orthodoxy") and political leaders to define the Alamo as a place reflected struggles within Texas society over the place and status of Tejanos and Anglos. Flores's analysis sheds new light on the ways "Remember the Alamo" has been summoned to incite certain ideas of the history of Texas. This trajectory can be traced in films about the battle as well, including *Martyrs of the Alamo* (1915), *The Alamo* (1960), *Seguin* (1982), and *The Alamo* (2004).[24]

The contestations and debates circulating around heritage sites did not prevent these spaces of public history from finding numerous benefactors eager to contribute to the preservation of local histories for both the maintenance of a cultural patrimony and the injection of much-needed tourist dollars into local economies. In fact, the sites' lack of historical accuracy might be the very reason for their popularity—for, as with all cultural productions, consumers/audiences respond to those messages that resonate with them and oppose or dismiss outright those that do not. If tourists are looking for spaces that reproduce how they already understand the history of their nation, then the spaces themselves must deliver these messages to be successful. Possibly the largest attraction to these sites is their appeal to nostalgia.[25] Historical spaces offer visitors who romanticize a supposed simpler past a means of escape from the ills of the modern world. And if these sites could do so while also entertaining their visitors, then they would be even more prosperous. Colonial Williamsburg became central to understandings by other communities throughout the country of how to meld preservation, romance, and enjoyment into a marketable package. Indeed, Colonial Williamsburg (along with Charleston, South Carolina, and New Orleans, Louisiana) became the model for economically beneficial preservation efforts nationwide as other cities and towns established zoning ordinances for the creation of historic districts with the goal of attracting travelers. As Clayton Smith's reference at the beginning of this chapter demonstrates, Colonial Williamsburg served as the inspiration for Tombstone's historic preservation efforts in the early 1950s, along with its bid to attract more visitors to the town on a regular basis, an objective shared with other communities across the country.

It is fortunate, then, that most of these twentieth-century preservation efforts in the United States coincided with—or indeed contributed to—a surge in domestic tourism, especially in the West. With war in Europe disrupting travel overseas, Americans were seeking to spend their leisure time and money closer to home. Improved roadways, greater availability of automobiles, acceptance of the five-day workweek, and the promotion of national parks contributed to an ever more profitable tourist industry. Of course, it would not be an American pastime without being steeped in nationalistic meaning: President Franklin D. Roosevelt declared 1940 "Travel America Year." And in 1941 the Department of the Interior's US Travel Bureau claimed that "the defense of democracy" could be one of the benefits of traveling in America.[26] The desire to escape the modern world propelled many, mostly white, middle-class Americans westward. In fact, in the early decades of the twentieth century, "one of the fastest-growing industries in the West was tourism."[27] At a time when Americans were celebrating progress, they were also wistfully nostalgic about America's past and struggling to define the American experience. They looked toward the West, to the region that had pulled them for decades, the region that signified adventure, progress, and triumph, to find the meaning of American culture. With the marking of the closing of the frontier in 1890, the turn of the twentieth century brought with it "a nervous alertness as to what that event portended."[28] The feeling became what David Wrobel calls "post-frontier anxiety," by which Americans were becoming increasingly critical of the urban industrial complex and nostalgic for the lost "wilderness."[29]

While the natural wonders of the region were popular destinations, the federal government's initiation of protecting and preserving sites and structures related to westward expansion, such as log cabins, river crossings, sites of the Indian Wars, and mining towns "denoted the permanence of the epic American quest for territorial growth" and verified the importance of the West to American identity on the national level. By the 1950s travelers were seeking something they considered "distinctively western."[30] What was thought to be "distinctively western" had everything to do with the ways the "Old West" was presented in productions of popular culture, and soon "western city councils, tourist bureaus, private developers, and businesspeople happily obliged, creating tourist destinations to cater to people seeking the 'authentic' Wild West."[31]

This moment in the history of historic preservation and of tourism in the United States—and on the heels of the popular Hollywood production of the Earp tale *My Darling Clementine* (1946)—marks the beginning of Tombstone's own historic preservation efforts, an attempt to benefit from tourists' desire to experience the Wild West and spend the money Tombstone desperately needed to survive. Heavily involved in the makeover were the members of the Tombstone Restoration Commission, which was established in 1949. The commission was central to Tombstone's renewal as a wild western town. As Billy G. Garrett and James W. Garrison state in their *Plan for the Creation of a Historic Environment in Tombstone, Arizona*, "Organization of [the Tombstone Restoration Commission] symbolized the beginning of a third major growth period in the city's history. But this time silver ore was not being sought." Like so many other towns throughout the western United States in this time period, "Tombstone's businessmen and women were in search of tourist dollars." In an effort to take advantage of the growing interest in the West in general and their city's past in particular, they began to preserve and protect Tombstone's oldest buildings.[32]

Preserving Tombstone's Past

Tombstone's restoration commission began this endeavor with fervor and clear intent. Despite the passage of sixty years since Tombstone's prosperity as a mining town, the commission concentrated its efforts on re-creating the Tombstone of the early 1880s, including highlighting 1881, the year of the gunfight behind the OK Corral. Among the objectives set out by the commission in its articles of incorporation in 1949 was to restore the exteriors of buildings in what is now the historic district "to the style and architecture prevalent in and around Tombstone, Arizona, in the 1880's so that the City of Tombstone may become a monument to the Old West." In addition, the commission set out to oversee and control the construction of new buildings in Tombstone so that they would be built to look like or evoke the architecture of the 1880s, an objective that points to the restrictive nature of restoration and preservation efforts in the twentieth century. Ultimately, the commission was intent on "promot[ing] and advanc[ing] a western atmosphere in keeping with the 1880's and the general idea of restoration of the City of Tombstone to those times."[33] By March 1951, under the leadership of the restoration commission's first president, Clarence Mortimer Palmer Jr., the restoration of Tombstone's historic places and its marketing as the quintessential example of the Old West were under way. Publicity came fast: "The town claims the distinction of being the first and last of the American frontiers," states an article in *Desert* magazine that year. "Barely more than a half a century ago Tombstone helped close the last of the lawless frontier when it tamed the Apaches and renegade white men. Many of its original buildings still stand. Tourists visit Tombstone to see the old west."[34] The claim that Tombstone helped "tame the Apaches and renegade white men" plays neatly into fantasies about the movement westward, and this news item illustrates the centrality of Tombstone to notions of the Wild West by that time.

The restoration commission was responsible for drafting City Ordinance No. 146 to establish a restoration zone and a zoning commission that required new buildings to conform to the city atmosphere that prevailed in 1883, one year after a devastating fire destroyed many of the buildings in Old Tombstone. The ordinance was passed on 10 April 1954 and amended in 1964 and again in 1972, as notions of what constituted "restoration" and "preservation" shifted with each new attempt to capitalize on Tombstone's history. Under the leadership of the next commission president, Edna Landin (1955–1960), the commission also raised the funds necessary to purchase the Cochise County Courthouse, which was turned over to the Arizona State Parks

OK Corral, ca. 1920s. (Courtesy of Arizona Historical Society, http://arizona
historicalsociety.org, AHS 27218)

Board and opened as Arizona's first operational state park on 1 August 1959,
with the state taking over full operation on 1 July 1960. The commission
then went to work to preserve the area surrounding the courthouse. On 4
July 1961 the Department of the Interior declared the streets and buildings
surrounding the courthouse a National Historic Landmark District.

While it seems that the commission had been interested in preserving
the integrity of the town as the epitome of the Old West, emphasizing
rowdiness as much as law, authority, and gentility, the Department of the
Interior noted Tombstone's "lawlessness" in its proclamation, reifying and
perpetuating the idea that Tombstone's constructed image typified the
"Wild West": "Tombstone is one of the best preserved specimens of the
rugged frontier town of the 1870s and '80s. Site of one of the West's richest
silver strikes and the 'gunfight at the OK Corral,' Tombstone epitomizes
the legendary reputation of the 'Wild West' and lawlessness of the 19th
century mining camps."[35] Despite firsthand accounts of the town being as
much on the verge of civility as any other town in the West, with churches,
schools, libraries, and "other refinements of civilization" dotting the landscape almost since the town's founding, violence and unruliness are the
focus of the myth surrounding Old Tombstone.[36]

Palmer and Landin have parallel trajectories in Tombstone. Palmer and his wife moved to Tombstone from Brooklyn, New York, in 1948 for health reasons. He became fully immersed in Tombstone city life within a short time, becoming the restoration commission's first president in 1949 and acting as editor of the *Tombstone Epitaph* for a few months in the early 1950s. He also served as Tombstone's postmaster from 1954 to 1968.[37] Despite settling in Tombstone just one year prior to becoming commission president, Palmer's role gave him the authority to decide which components of Tombstone's past were worth preserving and promoting. Similarly, Landin moved to Tombstone from Ohio with her husband, Ted, in 1947, just five years before being appointed president of the chamber of commerce by the mayor in 1952. She became president of the commission in 1955. In these positions, Landin was one of those given the responsibility of determining the public identity of Tombstone—an identity that would, if successfully established, bring financial stability and growth to the town. Like so many civic boosters in the United States in the 1950s, Landin understood the currency that history could hold for Tombstone, and she spent her entire tenure as president of the commission committed to demonstrating the historical legitimacy of the Cochise County Courthouse and the town more generally. She is remembered as a "prolific correspondent and fundraiser establishing a friendly working relationship with the Governor and many state legislators." She also served on the Tombstone City Council from 1958 to 1960. She was honored in 1956 as "Woman of the Year of Tombstone," and she even has a city park named in her honor. In 2010 she was inducted into the Tombstone Founders' Day Hall of Fame.[38]

Like Palmer, Landin's eastern roots situate her within the wider trend of Hal Rothman's "neonatives." Imagining the West through nostalgia and romanticism, these newcomers hope to preserve the history of the region for the consumption of future tourists. Clearly attracted to the city as an adult, Landin, like other neonatives, became an expert and ardent defender of the culture and history of the region.[39] While Tombstone's reputation as a tourist destination and historic space had not yet been fully realized when Landin and her husband relocated there (despite Tombstone's success with its annual Helldorado Days), its identity was already well planted within the public imagination—an identity that not only attracted the Landins to Tombstone but also impelled Edna to perpetuate that identity through historic preservation, boosterism, and tourism. Landin wanted Tombstone to become the Tombstone of her fantasy, most likely based on popular culture representations of the town already widely known by the 1950s, and she worked tirelessly to have that fantasy become reality. Her story mirrors that of so many recent arrivals to Tombstone, including Patrick K. Greene, former chamber executive director and Historic District Commission chair from May 2009 to December 2010, who moved from Ohio to Tombstone with his family only a few years before being appointed to these positions by the mayor; former Tombstone city historian Ben Traywick, who moved to Tombstone from California in 1968; Andree DeJournett, who owns Big Nose Kate's Saloon and became mayor of Tombstone in 2004, just three years after moving there from Flint, Michigan; and countless others. In these roles, Greene, Traywick, and DeJournett, like Palmer and Landin, were required to continually negotiate the interests of the townspeople, local businesses, and tourists, privileging business and tourism as keys to the town's success.

Unlike Greene, Traywick, DeJournett, and Palmer, however, Landin was a woman working in what is considered to be a masculine space. These men followed in the tradition of so many before them, those who looked toward the West as a land of opportunity and romance, to perhaps, as Jane Tompkins argues, recapture (or discover) their masculinity, lost in the effete conditions of the modern era. As Tompkins states, "Fear of losing his identity drives a man west, where the harsh conditions of life force his manhood into being." The West, she asserts, "seems to offer escape from the conditions of life in modern industrial society. . . . The desert light and the desert space, the creak of saddle leather and the sun beating down, the horses' energy and force—these things promise a translation of the self into something purer and more authentic, more intense, more real."[40] While this "woman-less milieu" seems an unlikely place for Landin to stake a claim and make a difference, she was very much entrenched in what had widely been a women's endeavor—historic preservation efforts in the early to mid-twentieth century. And since the role of women in the settlement of the West has been rendered less visible or less significant in movies and television shows, Landin also shattered gender expectations that dictated to whom the ideologies of the Old West meant the most.

Landin had a tremendous impact on the refacing of Tombstone in the 1950s and helped put the town on the map for both tourists and historians. In 1950 she penned an ode to Tombstone, "Tombstone Arizona: The Town Too Tough to Die." Her romantic attitude toward her adopted home is clearly articulated in this sixty-line poem, which traces the tumultuous history of Tombstone while securing the moniker made famous by the 1942 film *Tombstone, the Town Too Tough to Die*:

Why is Tombstone Arizona called "The Town Too Tough to Die"?
Well Dear friends, if you will listen, we will tell you the reason why.
In '78 when it was founded, for its worth of silver ore,
People flocked here by the thousands, to partake in Nature's store.
. . . . .
That was the pioneer spirit that gave birth to this fair town,
But soon there followed others, like termites, to tear down.
All in quest of easy money, gamblers, harlots, outlaws rough,
Wrote their page in Tombstone's history, made its reputation tough.

Landin takes her readers through the floods and fires, the bust of the mines, the Great Depression, and the removal of the county seat to Bisbee in 1929.

With all the grief this town has had, and it surely is no lie;
It necessarily must be tough, or certainly, it would die.
But Tombstone is Americana, our heritage of the Old West;
For posterity it must be preserved as the LAST FRONTIER OF THE WEST.[41]

As part of the efforts referenced in the poem, Landin embarked on countless letter-writing campaigns, often, for example, petitioning studios to shoot their western films and television shows in Tombstone. She appealed to producers' nostalgia for the Old West as well as to their presumed interest in preserving its history. In a letter dated 11 February 1959 to Desilu Studios—where *The Life and Legend of Wyatt Earp* was filmed—Landin highlighted not only the "authenticity of locale" to be found in Tombstone but also that the studio would be helping restore "this 'Last Frontier of the Old West' as a part of our American heritage." She further pointed out that it would not be necessary for the studio to build sets specifically for the purposes of filming westerns, as they could use the buildings that were still intact in the town.[42]

In her attempts to attract Hollywood to Tombstone, Landin assumed historic preservation was one of the goals of western film and television show producers, an assumption that seemed to be proved false again and again. She also unironically promoted Tombstone as both "authentic" (or real or true) *and* like a movie set (or constructed, ersatz), playing into an idea explored by scholars and filmmakers in the latter decades of the twentieth century that critiqued popular images of the American West as two-dimensional and artificial. The tension between the notion of "authentic" or "true" history and "entertainment" or fluff has been and continues to be omnipresent in Tombstone. While it is difficult to pin down what these terms mean and how different or similar they are, Tombstone—like Landin—requires and makes use of both conceptions on the day-to-day level. Town historians and those on the Tombstone Historic District Commission promote Tombstone as an "authentic" western town, continuously attempting to thwart criticisms of being somehow artificial. Some entertainers may mock the idea of "history" being a part of the Tombstone experience at all. The chamber of commerce, in its effort to attract businesses to the area, may push "authentic" history as a way to highlight the seriousness and legitimacy of the town while also emphasizing that the "fun" aspect brings hundreds of thousands of people, and their money, to Tombstone annually. Indeed, efforts to separate these two concepts have proved futile, as both authenticity and entertainment are vital, even if Landin did not fully understand the tension.

The connection between authenticity and performance—perhaps not in films and television shows but on the streets of the town for the entertainment of visitors—became a reality less than a decade after Landin's efforts to make Tombstone a Hollywood movie set. Performance, in fact, is now central to the popularity and sustainability of Tombstone as a tourist destination. Landin may not have envisioned the extent to which performance would define the town; she did, however, imagine that Hollywood and popular culture would allow Tombstone to survive at a moment when the town could offer few other commodities besides the Wild West.

As late as 1965, years after stepping down as president of the Tombstone Restoration Commission, Landin was still championing Tombstone as "the Town Too Tough to Die." In *Desert* magazine in January of that year, Landin authored an article titled "The Legend Lives," which mirrors the poem she wrote earlier explaining the tenacity and temerity of this town—preserved and surviving "without Federal aid"—that had so many times been on the brink of extinction. Laying out Tombstone's history of silver mining, floods, and fires—and without mentioning Wyatt Earp or the OK Corral once—Landin describes Tombstone's many ups and downs, how it "almost died" by 1890, after the fires and the first flood; by 1909, after another fire and flood; by 1929, when the county seat was moved from Tombstone to Bisbee; and again by 1947, when Father Roger Aull, a retired priest who opened a clinic for respiratory ailments, died and the clinic was closed.[43] She credits "civic-minded citizens" and the Tombstone Restoration Commission with keeping the town afloat through their preservation efforts. "But," she says, "Tombstone does not live in the past alone. Located on U.S. Highway 80, it attracts motorists who wish to relive, in an authentic natural setting, a bit of the Old West. But most importantly, Western history here is still being made by self-sufficient citizens justly proud of their 'Town Too Tough To Die.'"[44]

Landin was also still active in ensuring the cooperation of local businesses in efforts to craft a Tombstone authentic to its 1880s appearance. In a "suggested letter to brewers in [the] restoration zoning area" dated 10 September 1965, Landin credits the Tombstone Restoration Commission for creating a "world-wide tourist attraction" as a result of their "preserving and restoring our historic land-marks as a 'Showcase of the Old West.'" To retain the town's status as a registered National Historic Landmark, a designation for which she had worked so hard a decade earlier, "we must continue to retain the flavor of the Old West." She goes on: "The purpose of this letter is to ask your cooperation by changing your local signs to conform with the types of lettering, etc. of the 1880s, so outlined in the enclosed copy of our Restoration Zoning Ordinance No. 146. . . . Just as we have had the support of other distributors, we feel sure we may count on yours too."[45] Her request for the support of local businesses in crafting this Old West town has been repeated by others in positions of power ever since.

Preservation efforts continued in the 1960s with a privately owned and funded preservation group in Tombstone, Historic Tombstone Adventures (HTA). HTA was organized in 1963 by "some strangers from the East" with "the fastest checkbooks around" to restore some of the buildings and sites in the city.[46] Harold O. Love, an affluent Detroit tax attorney, visited Tombstone in 1963 and, deciding that "Tombstone is choice-cut Americana," saw investment potential in this small western town. He rounded up some of his friends—"other non-boot-and-saddle types"—and began buying up famous landmarks around town with an eye toward recreating the Tombstone of 1881. By the time *Life* magazine was spotlighting Love's efforts in 1966, he and his friends had already spent more than $2 million on preservation and revitalization projects in Tombstone, purchasing the OK Corral, Schieffelin Hall, Fly's Photography Studio, and the Crystal Palace Saloon. "I would like to control all of Allen Street," he is quoted as saying by *Life* writer William S. Ellis, as he attempted to profit from Tombstone's history.[47] He also later bought the *Epitaph*, which he recrafted into a marketing vehicle highlighting the town's history to attract tourists.

In his restoration efforts, Love felt historic accuracy was imperative, which led him to hire John Gilchriese, then field historian at the University of Arizona and expert on Tombstone history. They used old photographs as guides for their projects, reconstructing the buildings' exteriors and interiors and even moving structures to "best approximate more closely" the

Birdcage Theatre, Allen Street, ca. 1920s. (Courtesy of Arizona Historical Society, http://arizonahistoricalsociety.org, AHS 28419)

ways the sites had been "when the Clantons ranged along the east wall [of Fly's Photo Studio] awaiting the Earps."[48] By this time, Hollywood had built up Wyatt Earp to be the singular western hero in a number of movies and the television show *The Life and Legend of Wyatt Earp*, one of the most popular portrayals of Wyatt to date. Love's vision for Tombstone was squarely focused on Earp and situated in the October 1881 gunfight (one year before a fire destroyed many of the structures in town), and he worked tirelessly, with the oversight and approval of the Tombstone Restoration Commission, to realize that vision. As with Edna Landin, Love recreated the town based on his notion of what Tombstone should be like—constructed based on a specific moment in history and, no doubt, on his interactions with popular culture. Love told *Life* writer Ellis that he would "like to see everything on Allen Street either restored or removed. Especially, he emphasized, *that*—and frowned out the window at a large neon sign across the street, screaming in multicolored mockery: PIZZA."[49] In 1983 Governor Bruce Babbitt named Love Arizona's ambassador of tourism. Like Landin, Love was inducted into the Founders' Day Hall of Fame in 2010. He was honored for his preservation efforts and his "enduring affection" for the town.[50]

Despite his attention to historic detail, Love's refacing of the Crystal Palace Saloon caused some controversy. His focus on crafting the town to

Crystal Palace Saloon, ca. 1930s. (Courtesy of Arizona Historical Society, http://arizonahistoricalsociety.org, AHS 45455)

look like it might have in Wyatt Earp's time resulted in his recreating and attaching to the saloon a façade that was based on photos taken before the structure burned down in May 1882. The structure to which the façade was affixed was built in the fall of 1882. It was, therefore, already a historic building without need for renovation, leading some to point out the obsession with this singular event rather than the entire historical time period in which Tombstone thrived. "If preservation of Tombstone's historic character is important to the community and the nation, why was it necessary to deface a genuine historic property?" ask Garrett and Garrison in their research report from 1972. "The answer is not to be found in the owner's purpose, but in a very limited interpretation of restoration work."[51]

A decade later, the Tombstone Restoration Commission was still hard at work securing Tombstone's place as a tourist destination for Wild West enthusiasts, as well as attempting to make sense of its own charter to preserve Tombstone's "1883 character." By this point, the president was another woman, Theda Medigovich, who owned and operated the Wagon Wheel Restaurant and the Silver Nugget Museum in Tombstone from the 1940s to the 1980s. She and her husband, Sam, were active in collecting, preserving, and recreating Tombstone's history.[52] As commission president, Medigovich felt it necessary to work with faculty at the College of Architecture at the University of Arizona to clarify the goals of the commission and the town itself. Billy G. Garrett and James W. Garrison's *Plan for the Creation of*

Crystal Palace Saloon, 2007. (Photo by Kathy Weiser-Alexander, courtesy of LegendsOfAmerica.com)

a Historic Environment in Tombstone, Arizona, published in December 1972, was the result of this endeavor. Even after twenty years of preservation and restoration work in Tombstone, the town's history keepers found it imperative to push further. In fact, the late 1960s and early 1970s had seen a dip in tourism along with a drop in the interest in the Old West. Films and television shows at this time were revising their formerly romantic fascination with the region that had for so many decades defined the nation's masculinist, individualist cowboy ideal. The trends of the 1960s and early 1970s necessitated the attempts to reinvigorate the lure of Tombstone, and the controversies of Love's efforts in the 1960s made it imperative to sharpen Tombstone's goals. Garrett and Garrison's work is an exhaustive look at Tombstone's history, its preservation efforts, and plans for future preservation. In it they ask two questions: "First, whether or not Tombstone's restoration is essential to the city's economy. Second, the extent to which restoration will affect development of other kinds of community activity." Their answer: "Every analysis which has been done on Tombstone's economy during the last ten years states that tourism is basic to the city's economy," an idea that continues to drive Tombstone today.[53]

Garrett and Garrison's "master plan" was an effort to define Tombstone's historic identity and determine ways to leverage that character. Similar to the ways John D. Rockefeller understood the connection between history and historical setting many decades earlier, Garrett and Garrison argued that "the documents of history acquire real meaning only when viewed in an informing context. Tombstone is uniquely fitted to provide such a context." Contributors to the report also contended with the entertainment/authentic history binary, encouraging Tombstonians to choose "the creation of an honest historic representation" over creating a western theme park "a la Walt Disney." Garrett and Garrison embarked on this mission because the Tombstone Restoration Commission realized that its purpose needed to be clearer, more focused, and better executed. "Vagueness and fragmentation had to be overcome if the importance of restoration work was to be honestly appraised by the community . . . [and] priorities needed to be set and coordinated in order to maximize efforts." The document contains a workbook on community policies, building appearance, and financial assistance. It also includes an analysis of the issues with the town's efforts to that point and what was necessary if Tombstone was to focus on becoming the epitome of an Old West mining town. "As every visitor has discovered," they pragmatically explained, "the city does not look like an 1880s mining town. It does have many old buildings, but the overall impression is ordinary, small, and rather run-down." With an acute understanding of the importance of popular culture in shaping tourist expectations, they asserted, "For the visitor who expects the Tombstone of the silver screen (or tube), it is just not there."[54]

Garrett and Garrison had numerous ideas for how to improve the authenticity of the town. Some of their recommendations included moving telephone and electric wires underground, installing gas lamps, restoring façades of buildings to the way they looked in 1885, restoring the firehouse, and putting dirt on Allen Street. The purpose of this drive was to *improve the experience* of tourists coming to Tombstone—in other words, to construct a town that better fit the expectations of the visitors. At the same time, historic preservationists were also impelled to ensure the continued livability of the town. Because Tombstone is unique in that it is a living community, the wider goal of Garrett and Garrison's report was to "suggest means not merely for the use and preservation of historic material, but means also for the integration of that material with the community's larger purposes." They knew that the future of Tombstone depended on continued interest in the city, and "although many may be disappointed, their visits are the single most essential contribution to any restoration process." In other words, tourism subsidizes restoration, and restoration feeds tourism. Further, because "for most people the accepted 'myth' of Tombstone is one of lynchings, gunfights, hangings, and a town 'too tough to die' in the face of enormous economic and social changes which in many cases have removed settlements from the southwestern desert," a strong focus on the town's raucous past had to remain a constant. In addition, the townspeople needed to work together to create a total experience for tourists. Garrett and Garrison point out that in 1972, "the expectations of most people are often unfulfilled because of the district's appearance. Tombstone does not quite look like a 'monument to the Old West.'"[55]

One of the biggest changes they brought to restoration efforts was to focus design decisions to a specific year—1885—rather than 1883 or "the 1880s" in general. They chose the year 1885 for a number of reasons, including the fact that many of Old Tombstone's structures were built after 1882, the year fires had destroyed much of the town. Further, since the town peaked prior to 1885, Garrett and Garrison concluded that no significant construction occurred after that year. And because so much of the restoration effort relied on photographic resource material, more photographs with enough detail to reference were found from around 1885 than any other time frame. They were also careful to point out that buildings erected after 1885 still have some purpose and could be part of overall efforts to restore the town: "Only if a structure seriously imposes on the overall district character, should thought be given to its demolition."[56]

Once the approach to preservation had been clarified, it was then necessary to double efforts to increase visitation. In 1974 Medigovich spearheaded a fund-raising and membership drive in preparation for the nation's bicentennial. She wrote a brochure as part of that effort that reiterated Tombstone's place in the lore of the Old West and the Old West's place in the history of the United States: "Tombstone is an integral part of the Nation's Bicentennial as the winning of the West was of fundamental importance to the United States in the years after the Civil War." In addition to drawing the link between the story of the West and the dominant narrative of the nation, she also appealed to Americans' romance with the West: "Stories of this saga are the myths of our culture. The characters are as legendary as any the world over. Cowboy or miner, sodbuster or frontier wife, the efforts of these men and women tempered the American character and left an impression which is felt in our time." Then, in all capitals: "TOMBSTONE IS A LIVING MONUMENT TO THIS PAST! IT IS THE BLOODSTAINED, POWDER-MARKED ORIGINAL! A REAL WESTERN TOWN WHOSE OLD STILL STANDING ADOBE BUILDINGS WATCHED A BYGONE ERA OF WESTERN HISTORY IN THE MAKING!"[57]

Clearly there was a tremendous push to bump up restoration in Tombstone in the early 1970s, an era that also saw the establishment of the first Tombstone Office of Tourism, originally called the Tombstone Businessmen's Association, whose sole purpose was to increase tourism and profits for business owners. The name of the association itself confirms the inextricable link between tourism and profit in Tombstone. In addition to the hopes of restoration lying heavily in the hands of businesspeople and investors, Garrett and Garrison, just as Landin and Medigovich had, argued that it was up to the local citizens to come together to create that environment for the sake of the town's survival. Shop owners were asked to change signage to conform to that of the 1880s; homeowners were asked to change paint colors; and, despite some criticism, more and more people started dressing in the style of 1880s clothing.

Performers of History

Citizens did heed the call to participate in protecting the historic and cultural integrity of the town, doing more than just dressing the part to attract tourists. Many joined performance troupes, reenactors interpreting and preserving Tombstone's history through theatrical display. The Tombstone Vigilantes (founded in 1948 and incorporated in 1954) and Tombstone's Wild Bunch (established in 1971) have had a hand in re-creating Tombstone in the image of its former glory—all with an eye toward attracting tourist dollars to ensure the town's ongoing survival. The vigilantes are still active in Tombstone, a town that has come to be known for the gunfights and other performances on its streets. Daily performance is the most exacting way Tombstone is set apart from other western heritage towns. It is the point at which Tombstone's authenticity is both reproduced and called into question. It has attracted visitors for decades but has also been the object of scorn and criticism from journalists, historians, and even tourists and townspeople, who feel it has somehow cheapened Tombstone's historic integrity.[58]

According to their website, the Tombstone Vigilantes "since their inception . . . have been dedicated to keeping the historical town of Tombstone
alive through reenacting events of the era." Volunteers "selflessly [give] of
their time to not only keep Tombstone's history alive but to raise funds
for worthy causes."[59] They were proclaimed the "Ambassadors of Tombstone" in 1994 by then-mayor Alex Gradillas because so much of their work
takes them to towns all around the West. This moniker is a point of honor
for the Vigilantes, who proudly display it on their website. The Vigilantes
were the first to perform history on a regular basis in Tombstone.[60] While
preservation efforts were part of a necessary drive to attract tourists to the
area, performance on Tombstone's streets has been disparaged since at
least as early as 1956. An article published that year in the literary journal
Prairie Schooner derides Tombstone for its use of performance to commem-
orate and celebrate its violent history. The author concedes that this violent
past is a "commodity to exploit" to attract tourists, but he also laments
the loss of Tombstone's former glorious self: "Of course, the vitality, the
elan, that sparked Tombstone in the 1880's is gone forever. In its place is
this warmed-over masquerade by service-club members who dress in the
garments of dead heroes, hoping to capture somehow the flavor of times
gone by." His comment that Tombstonians "keep alive the Earp-Clanton
mythology to attract tourists" seems both sneering and forlorn. Calling the
Vigilantes "the trigger-happy boys of Tombstone," the author scoffs at the
troupe for its nostalgic enthusiasm for the Old West: "At the drop of a
ten-gallon Stetson or less, the Vigilantes will drop all their business chores
and re-enact the Earp-Clanton gunfight at the old OK corral, using, to be
sure, blanks in their Frontier-type Colts."[61] The article was written before
Edna Landin succeeded in revitalizing the courthouse and other historic
sites, efforts lauded by the author. But his distaste in the performative element of Tombstone—even at that early date—is obvious.

The Tombstone Vigilantes are still very much a part of the landscape of
Tombstone. They perform mock hangings and historical shootouts on the
second, fourth, and fifth Sundays of every month (each Sunday known as
"Vigilante Sunday") on Allen Street. According to their website, "the mock
hangings are especially fun for the tourists. An unsuspecting victim is tried,
convicted and then hung [*sic*] by one of the Vigilante members within seconds of them meeting and, for a donation the victim can get a picture taken
while in the noose surrounded by their [*sic*] captors."[62] That visitors enjoy
being convicted and hanged for a crime is particularly interesting in light of
theories surrounding the power of ritualized violence and the carnivalesque

in the narrative of the Wild West, conceptions to which Tombstone is central. Violence and wildness are fundamental to Tombstone's existence and viability as a tourist destination. Performances of violence—gunfight reenactments, public hangings, and barroom brawls—serve to deprivilege the authoritative voice of hegemony on the one hand while reinscribing the importance and centrality of authority and law on the other; in Tombstone, lawmen always triumph. Even the name of this troupe is telling: vigilantes occupy the periphery of organized society, stepping in to impart justice when the institutions of law are too inept to do so. But in Tombstone, not only do these Vigilantes work inside the parameters of society; they also privilege the tenets and principles of that society. Indeed, the Vigilantes are very much involved in civic pride. In addition to helping organize Ed Schieffelin Days, Wyatt Earp Days, and Helldorado Days every year, as well as their own event known as Vigilante Days, they also donate monies collected during private events to "worthy causes throughout Tombstone."[63]

The Vigilantes are not universally revered by townspeople in Tombstone. A number of locals who perform at some of the inside theaters complain that the Vigilantes steal their business. They give free shows on Allen Street, collect donations, and make it difficult for other businesses that charge admission to compete. "We're just trying to make a living," bemoans one performer. It is a tension, many say, that has been around since the town was founded, between big business Democrats and Republican ranchers, between the powers of incorporation and those holding on to the old ways, now between those in positions of power (mostly those with extensive business holdings in town) and those who "just live here."[64] These performers feel that the local government cares more about the big events and less about the people who live and work in the town on a daily basis. Ironically, the Vigilantes offer the wild Tombstone popularly imagined by visitors, and their annual Vigilante Days celebration is one of the busiest weekends for Tombstone's tourism industry. More people visit—but they spend their money in specific ways. Those reenacting at indoor theaters are both dependent on and choused out of earnings by the Vigilantes and other groups performing only for donations on the streets.

That business owners and politicians benefit from town policies more than those who work and live there, and that this tension is not visible to tourists, seems to be a well-worn sentiment. One performer moved to Tombstone a few years ago from Pennsylvania and works at one of the theaters on a side road in the historic district. He has a lot to say about corruption in town and how those who make the decisions seem to not want Tombstone to be a tourist destination, or seem at least not to care about promoting the town's history for which it is famous. He says that too much of the tension has to do with money, that the wealthy people get what they want at the expense of those actually working to support their families. Two other reenactors seem angry with the local government, which they feel does not support them enough, and at the visitors who complain that the individual attractions are too expensive. "This isn't an amusement park," one exclaims, pointing to the ongoing debate around authenticity and entertainment that is central to Tombstone's identity and to the tension that has arisen regarding tourist expectations.[65] People who live in Tombstone and perform Tombstone's history for visitors must manage a conflation of identities that often are at odds. The fact that performers are trying to survive the exigencies of the present by performing the past may be lost on tourists, who, some complain, only see Tombstonians as props in their Wild West fantasy. Visitors remain oblivious to this conflict as they stop and watch reenactments on Allen Street while overlooking or bypassing the indoor performances for which there is an admission fee.

Another reenactment troupe in Tombstone was the Wild Bunch, organized by Ben Traywick. Traywick's story is similar to other keepers of history in Tombstone. He was passing through Tombstone in 1968 when he decided to move his family there from California. Believing that the town's "true history wasn't being told," he founded the Wild Bunch in 1971 to add to the number of groups performing Tombstone's past for the entertainment and education of visitors.[66] From the onset, Traywick's group performed with an emphasis on "historically correct productions." His wife, Marie, was also involved, forming the "ladies' version" of the Wild Bunch, known as the Hell's Belles. Traywick played Wyatt Earp in reenactments of the gunfight for the next twenty years. The troupe performed the famous battle at the OK Corral "based on testimony given by Wyatt Earp at the inquest following the famous gunfight." They also performed at the annual Rendezvous of Gunfighters, a celebration of Tombstone's wild western past that featured gunfighter groups from around the country.[67] In 2014 Tombstone said good-bye to that event and the Wild Bunch, but their effect on the ways history is performed there will be felt for years to come.

Traywick was named Tombstone city historian in 1971, a post he held for thirty-nine years. His position as both performer and purveyor of history is not necessarily unique in Tombstone. Performance and "pedagogy" are impossible to disentangle in this space. While the Wild Bunch—like the Tombstone Vigilantes—contributed to a number of Tombstone charities, Traywick's objective seemed to always have been to promote the town to tourists. "The Wild Bunch gave Tombstone's tourism a tremendous boost,"

Wild Bunch with Hugh O'Brien at the OK Corral, 1982. Founding member Ben Traywick kneels center front. (Courtesy of Arizona Historical Society, http://arizonahistoricalsociety.org, AHS 78644)

he said.[68] In fact, the Wild Bunch and other reenactors and performers have given Tombstone its particular brand of westernness. While preservationists in Tombstone in the 1940s, 1950s, 1960s, and 1970s contributed to the town's appearance, the performers contributed its ambiance and made the place come alive for visitors for decades.

The various performances that take place on Tombstone's streets and in some of its establishments (Old Tombstone Western Town, for example, which is like a small Wild West theme park, and the Saloon Theater, which has a reputation for historically accurate performances) have, as we have seen, been criticized since the 1950s. The criticisms endure, as many believe these performances delegitimize Tombstone as a historical site. A historian in Lincoln, New Mexico (made famous by outlaw Billy the Kid), for example, disparaged Tombstone's performative elements as disrespectful. "In Lincoln," he said, "we respect our history."[69] Even Tombstone's own historians note the impact of popular culture on the integrity of the reenactments, including Hollis Cook, former manager of the Tombstone courthouse for Arizona State Parks, who went on to lead walking tours in town. He laughed about how the red sashes that identified the Cowboys in the 1993 film *Tombstone* found their way onto the hips of reenactment troupes in the streets of Tombstone. He conceded that the reenactors take great pride in getting their costumes right. But in the end, he said, "Hollywood creates history. Experts get it wrong."[70]

Despite the criticism, Traywick has been pleased with the successes the Wild Bunch has seen but believes there is a lot more that Tombstone could be doing to attract tourism. "We're sitting on a gold mine here, but we need to exploit it. . . . If we could all work together and do that, there's so much more we could be doing for this town."[71] Traywick retired as Tombstone city historian at "high noon" on 26 October 2011, the 130th anniversary of the Earp-Clanton gunfight. At the celebration, he encouraged the townspeople to continue to promote Tombstone's past: "If not for our history and some of the people who were here—we would be just another small town in the high desert. . . . Preserve the town's history and Tombstone will always be here. Remember the magic words; Tombstone, OK Corral, Earp and Holliday."[72] A more recent article quotes Traywick as saying, "My worry is, and always has been, that we are sitting on a goldmine [*sic*], and some of the people refuse to exploit it. . . . We need to turn this town to cater to the tourists. The only thing we have to sell is our history."[73] His words point to the ongoing struggles in the town to maintain its Old West identity. The town's residents have not always come to a consensus about what Tombstone is all about. It is not merely a tourist destination but also a living place, with all the trappings of a modern town. When the Tombstone Restoration Commission was established in 1949, the board of directors declared that the responsibility for the restoration efforts must fall in part on the entire citizenry of Tombstone. A concerted effort was both necessary and expected in order for Tombstone to survive. Yet restoration efforts in Tombstone have been under continual attack since. As early as 1955, journalist Don Dedera called the creation of Boothill Graveyard "not restoration" but "chicanery." Presaging Traywick's ideas, Dedera recommended that "what Tombstone needs most of all is unity. Is the old town to be restored, or is it to continue as a cheap burlesque of the past? . . . Tombstone also needs the support of all of Arizona, but the town hasn't proved it deserves it yet."[74]

This last comment is particularly prescient in light of the fact that Tombstone did not make *True West* magazine's list of America's top ten western cities in 2010, 2011, 2012, or 2013. "Though the town cries foul," *True West* claimed that the city did not make the list as a result of several factors, "among which is the notion that Tombstone has lost some of its authenticity."[75] Indeed, in 2004 the NPS declared Tombstone's historic designation threatened and sought to work with the community to develop an appropriate program of oversight and management. Among the alterations to the district that the NPS cited as "inappropriate" were placing "historic" dates on new buildings; failing to distinguish new construction from historic structures; building incompatible additions to existing historic structures and new incompatible buildings within the historic district; using illuminated signage, including blinking lights surrounding historic signs; and installing hitching rails and Spanish-tile-covered store porches when such architectural features never existed within Tombstone.[76]

The "threatened" status was downgraded to "watch" after town officials took steps to respond to the NPS's demands. As reported in the *Tombstone Epitaph*, "One way town officials saved themselves was by putting dirt on the streets to give visitors a more authentic experience. Last year [in 2009], Mayor Dusty Escapule ordered the dirt removed, a major setback according to *True West* magazine." The dirt controversy continues, but *True West* magazine editor Bob Boze Bell also cited Tombstone's unprofessional application as reason for passing it over. "He and his staff did not see an effort made in Tombstone's application. . . . In light of both the perceived changes to the city and their underwhelming application, Bell says that Tombstone's overall effort this year fell short of expectations and caused Tombstone to be lost among the other competitors for the Top 10 slots." Bell did have a positive outlook for Tombstone's future: "We love Tombstone; that is not the issue. . . . But sometimes you have to tell a member of your family that they need to shape up."[77] The magazine showed this adoration in 2011 and 2012 when it named Tombstone as one of the "Towns to Watch." It noted specifically the town's struggles with historic accuracy over the years but that its efforts to improve were not going unnoticed: "One hundred-thirty years after the famous gunfight, Tombstone continues to be a tusslin' town. . . . Folks, led by the city and the chamber of commerce, came together in 2010 to reopen the 1882 courthouse, which the state had closed due to budget cuts. Tombstone is, once again, the 'Town Too Tough to Die.'"[78]

Despite this recognition, the "snub" still "irked" locals, and in 2012 Bell was still citing Tombstone's issues with historical authenticity as contributing to the exclusion. In response to the omission, George Barnes, at that time city clerk and manager, was determined to hire a promotions manager to help publicize Tombstone to *True West* editors in a way that would see it included on this list in the future.[79] These efforts paid off in 2014, with Tombstone finally making the top ten. In fact, contradicting what Bell stated just two years before, the editors wrote, "To say the 'town too tough to die' is dedicated to its heritage is to absurdly understate the case. Around these parts, it's the Old West—all day, every day."[80] It is the kind of publicity that is essential to Tombstone's continued success as a monument to the Old West and a space of history and entertainment that brings in visitors.

Tombstone's Future

Much of the scholarship around tourism in the West explores the intersection of cultural memory, myth, and history—as well as contestation, economic exigencies, and environmental and cultural degradation—and casts a critical eye toward the sites to which millions of Americans and those from around the world flock each year. Chris Wilson's Santa Fe; Hal Rothman's Las Vegas, Nevada; Mike Wallace's Disneyland; Bonnie Christensen's Red Lodge, Montana—these and other sites in the West share a common legacy. Each in its growth as a lure for tourists has had a detrimental impact on local cultures and communities enticed by the hope of economic benefit only to discover that they have become commodities sold to an insatiable consumer.[81] This negotiation between economic imperative and commodification of identity and space, which tourist towns must manage, is what Rothman calls the "devil's bargain." As he sees it, although tourism promises to uplift those places that have not kept pace with the postindustrial world, it usually does not meet the expectations of communities and regions that utilize it as an economic strategy. Public identity is entrenched in ideas of particular versions of the past, and explorations into the ways these versions ebb and flow and the ways tourist towns and sites react to and reflect these shifts is imperative to a full understanding of the way the myth of the West continues to function in American culture.

Tombstone is very much a part of this overall connection between historic authenticity and economic exigency. In its constant quest to meet the expectations of tourists, it must also meet the expectations of its own citizens. This negotiation has seen continued struggle ever since the Historic Restoration Commission was established in 1949. Today Tombstone must fight against criticisms of a town whose heyday many see as long past. Perhaps epitomizing the ways the town has lost some of its luster in recent years, the park named for Edna Landin—Landin Park—has gone into disarray over the past years and has been well known for suspicious drug activity. The land was owned by Edna Landin and donated to the city in the 1950s "as a place where residents and visitors could congregate for picnics or social gatherings."[82] In 2009 the city was determined to revitalize the park, installing picnic tables and landscaping the area—mostly to make it a "safer environment" for residents and visitors. The city also intended to use part of the space for impounded vehicles, necessitating twenty-four-hour security. It is not out of step with the "wild western" history of the place to require guards with bulletproof jackets to ensure this public park would not fall further into the hands of outlaws. It does, however, seem incongruous with a tourist town bent on attracting families to spend money in a safe—albeit performatively unruly—environment.

But there is always hope for Tombstone, if we are to understand the tenacity of the town and its inhabitants, who are as interested in securing their future as they are in promoting their past. The constant controversy around Tombstone's authenticity may be exactly why the town continues to be a successful tourist destination. When something goes awry, when someone criticizes the place as inaccurately portraying its own history, citizens seem to fight even harder for what they see as Tombstone's rightful place as America's most quintessential western town. When Tombstone was designated a "Preserve America Community" by First Lady Laura Bush in late 2008, the decree was celebrated by the town's history keepers and displayed prominently on the chamber of commerce website. The press release for the designation quoted Mrs. Bush as saying, "Preserve America Communities demonstrate that they are committed to preserving America's heritage while ensuring a future filled with opportunities for learning and enjoyment. . . . I commend you for your commitment to preserving an important part of our nation's historic past for visitors, neighbors, and, most importantly, for children."[83] This designation comes with the eligibility to obtain grant monies and is invaluable to a town whose continued existence depends on its historic integrity but whose integrity as a historic site is in constant question.

Again we hear from Tombstone's Hollis Cook, who believes efforts to preserve Tombstone must continue. "Tombstone is really about the only game in town, if you're going to look for an Old West town," he says. In fact, "I really think if you brought Wyatt Earp back . . . I think he would recognize it."[84]

3

The Earp Legend in Film

The story of Wyatt Earp and the narrative of the gunfight behind the OK Corral have been told and retold, introducing each generation over the past hundred years to what in many ways has become a morality tale. Historian Paul Andrew Hutton argues that the "beauty" of the story, why it has resonated for so long for so many, lies in its simplicity: "A man who devoted his life to the law" seeks hope and opportunity in an Arizona boomtown that is overrun by lawlessness. Earp confronts the outlaws in "the classic showdown, kills them all, and rides out of town leaving law and order in his wake."[1] It is the abiding tale of the victory of law over lawlessness, of good over evil, that has come to define the winning of the West in the popular imagination. It is why Wyatt Earp and the gunfight continue to be meaningful well over a century after the event itself. It is a story that has kept readers, moviegoers, and television viewers enamored and entertained for almost a century.

But the story of Wyatt Earp and the gunfight outside the OK Corral is more than the sum of its parts. While Earp has come to symbolize the white, male fantasy of the archetypal western lawman, for many the event has come to define not just Tombstone where the gunfight took place but the whole of the Old West—the region that Robert Athearn calls "the most American part of America."[2] The public is familiar with Wyatt and the gunfight primarily because of the products of popular culture that have followed in a steady stream almost since the event happened—from novels and biographies to films and television shows. This is, in fact, how most people have come to understand the West as a whole. "For over two centuries," Richard Aquila observes, "although western images in popular culture have varied greatly, one thing has remained constant. Whether fact or fiction, story or place, the 'pop culture West' has struck a responsive chord in audiences of every generation."[3] Hollywood has been instrumental in keeping Tombstone central to public imaginings of the Wild West. Dozens of films and television shows about Wyatt Earp and Tombstone—and others that portray a showdown in the streets similar to that for which Wyatt Earp and Tombstone are known—all contribute to the sustainability of the town and can be classified as extensions of the preservation work there. In fact, the efforts of Earp himself in Hollywood in the early decades of movie making and the films produced in this time frame have had a direct and lasting impact on the town of Tombstone. Further, Tombstonians make use of Hollywood portrayals of the town and the event that made it famous by showing the two most publicly identifiable films about Tombstone and Earp on continuous loops in a number of sites, mirroring the costumes worn by the characters, and selling souvenirs bearing images of stars from the films. In other words, there is public acknowledgment in Tombstone of the role Hollywood has played in its success as a tourist destination. The relationship between popular cultural productions of Wyatt Earp and the West and the ways visitors understand the city of Tombstone is so strong that it is impossible to disentangle the two. The endurance of the Earp saga has given Tombstone its own viability, as tourists attempt to turn their two-dimensional observations into lived experiences.

This chapter explores the ways Wyatt Earp and the gunfight have been represented, interpreted, and reimagined in film and television throughout the twentieth and twenty-first centuries. Wyatt Earp and his place in the mythic West hold different meanings for different people. He has been both continually reinvented and steadfast to specific attitudes and beliefs of American culture. This chapter will demonstrate the inextricable link between popular portrayals of Earp and the gunfight and the ways audiences have imagined Tombstone and the West over time. In this framework, and similar to Tombstone itself, historicity is essential to the success of these films, while historical accuracy has not been as important as the fluidity of the main tenets of the narrative. Also as in Tombstone, the different iterations of Earp throughout the twentieth century highlight the ways "entertainment" and "authenticity" get entangled in these films, some offering bold critiques of the two-dimensionality of the Earp myth with particular prescience of Jean Baudrillard's future theories of the simulacra. The chapter will also demonstrate that precisely because he is such a contested figure, Earp has managed to maintain social significance for almost a century.

The films and television shows chosen for analysis represent the different versions of Wyatt Earp through the past seventy years and the broad appeal and power he as symbol has had in expressing and shaping perceptions of the West, law and authority, and the nation itself. The analysis begins with *My Darling Clementine*, widely hailed as the best rendering of the Earp story, and ends with *Tombstone* and *Wyatt Earp*, the two films that figure most heavily in Tombstone's current public identity and may have kept Tombstone the vital tourist destination it is today. These films and television shows—analyzed in chronological order—are quintessential Earp or lawman narratives that best illustrate the ways the story has functioned over time. The analysis relies on those films seen as classic to the genre as well as on those films resting just outside that norm, as those films that are not part of the classic western category have much to say about the ways producers envisioned Earp as western hero or antihero and the ways audiences, even those that helped develop cult followings for these productions years after their release, accepted or made use of these interpretations.

While not every film in the analysis is specifically about Earp, they all evoke the man and his position as *the* western lawman, whether idealized or vilified. They also all evoke the gunfight, a battle between two men or two factions of men as an allegory for nationalist ideals that celebrate law and order, masculinity, "civilization," and institutions of incorporation—although sometimes his story has been used to denigrate these same institutions. It is difficult to point to any western produced since the mid-twentieth century without seeing the Earp story embedded in its plot. These films also express specific ideas and attitudes about what the Earp and western myths have meant over time. That films and TV shows have relied on the Earp saga and the various events that shaped his life—most notably his time in Tombstone and the famous gun battle—speaks to the centrality of Earp to popular conceptions of the West and those ideals embodied by its myth: individualism, masculinity, and social progress—while also resisting the strict conventions and restraints brought on by that progress. Many of these popular culture productions reproduce manifest destiny, equating the development of the nation with an orthodoxy of social triumph—a success story of how "civilization" won out over "savagery." Other productions offer a sharp critique of the movement west, representing the "civilizing" process as one predicated on violence and corruption.

The epoch generally represented in popular culture (the 1880s) is also looked on with nostalgia, typically by white easterners, for the Old West as it is imagined to have been before the shuttling in of the modern age. Many of the films and television shows situated in this era reveal both a celebration of westward expansion and a sentimental yearning for what was lost in the transition. Wyatt Earp has managed to teeter easily between the Old and the New—representing both the excitement and white, masculine ideal of the Old West and the civilized nature of law and order of the New West. While "progress" has typically meant a celebration of law and authority, the Earp story has also been used to represent the greed and corruption sometimes associated with those same institutions, exposing the ambivalence or outright antagonism many have felt toward those in positions of power, particularly in films produced in the late 1960s and early 1970s—a time that also saw a reduction in the number of tourists to Tombstone. But shifting attitudes about Earp or the Old West did not seem to reduce interest in the man or the region. Whether seen as a hero or a villain, Earp, and therefore Tombstone, remains significant. The films and television shows in this chapter reveal how this simple story has a number of complex uses. From classic westerns to science fiction, Earp and the gunfight continue to resonate as the story has been shaped and reshaped to make sense to different audiences at different times.

No matter what the interpretation, the town of Tombstone relies heavily on the popularity of the most famous thirty seconds in its history. The link between popular culture and Tombstone cannot be overstated. The major tenets of the western have everything to do with how visitors interpret and experience the site. The town utilizes and benefits from the romance popular culture provides knowing that large segments of the American public continue to be captivated by the Earp myth. An analysis of films that depict Wyatt Earp specifically, as well as some that reflect on what constitutes a true western hero or what purpose the mythic West serves, is imperative to our understandings of Tombstone in the modern day.

The Myth of Historicity

The vast majority of the American public—in fact, the global public—has been exposed to the West through its representation in popular culture. The American West has been packaged and consumed as a commodity for well over a century, offering a collision of history, myth, and place and representing a variety of meanings for both producers and consumers. Scholars investigating the impact of the popular culture West on popular perceptions of the West have explored this field from a number of different perspectives. David Wrobel investigates the literature produced in the late nineteenth and early twentieth centuries by promoters trying to lure settlers and investors to the West who insisted that the "wild frontier" was a thing of the past, and "reminiscers," settlers of the West who published memoirs that focused on their encounters with the savage wilderness, exaggerating the violence of the past as much as promoters exaggerated the tranquility of the present. William H. Goetzmann and William N. Goetzmann reveal not only how artists interpreted and represented the mythic West on canvas but also how the public subscribed to the majesty and romance of the West these works presented to it. Richard White and Louis S. Warren tease out the significance of Buffalo Bill's Wild West to his audiences in the 1880s through the 1920s and of his legacy, which both White and Warren contend lives on. Henry Nash Smith illustrates the impact mass-produced fiction such as dime novels about the West and western heroes had on the popular imagination. Others have investigated western fiction writers such as Willa Cather and John Steinbeck, while still others have explored the cultural significance of rodeo. Despite the lack of depth these popular culture productions offer consumers and audiences, and the tendency of some scholars to downplay the significance of popular culture as overly simplistic nonsense, popular culture remains the most influential factor in the way the West is perceived in the popular imagination. And perhaps the single most significant way consumers learn about "the West" is through the western.

Viewing a western is not unlike taking a tour of the West—a mythic one to be sure, but one that is also grounded in actual time and space. Much like the "armchair travel" embarked on by the late nineteenth-century middle class, voracious readers of regional fiction who partly believed it presented an authentic and realistic account of specific eras and destinations while reflecting and upholding certain beliefs and values of the American bourgeoisie, westerns give audiences the opportunity to view their "creation myth" (as Patricia Limerick would say) through the lens of regional historicity.[4] Tourism scholar Edward Bruner argues that recreating the journey and giving it meaning is part of the ritual of travel, calling the experience "inchoate without an ordering narrative, for it is the story, the telling, that makes sense of it all, and the story is how people interpret their journey and their lives."[5] The meaning of the West comes in the stories that are told about it. Those stories have come to American audiences through literature, art, and, more recently, film and television shows. The western has become the "travel narrative," bringing audiences on a mythic journey through the West, which has become significant as the story of its exploration and settlement is retold. This story often functions to uphold certain ideologies already in place about the nation—ideas about individualism, democracy, masculinity, and progress—and is a reflection of changing beliefs and values throughout time.

The Hollywood western, a nostalgic eulogy to the early days of the "untamed" American frontier (most often defined in these films as the boundary between "civilization" and the "wilderness"), is the focus of much scholarship. Academics hoping to uncover the reasons the western has captivated audiences so strongly and for so long have contributed thousands of pages of research to the field. John Lenihan contends that the movie western maintained its popularity throughout times of decline in movie attendance because no other genre was "more involved with fundamental American beliefs about individualism and social progress."[6] Stanley Corkin argues that "the Western has the mythic power to define the past not simply as a body of material and ideological events that are recognizable and subject to analysis but as a triumphal moment when a compendium of quintessentially American traditions took hold."[7] These scholars and others maintain that westerns have been and remain popular because they articulate notions of a collective American past, one that offers a sense of national identity based on the perception of a shared commitment to basic American values.

Still other scholars contend that, in addition to their reflection of what are often touted as traditional American principles, another reason westerns have remained popular with audiences is the inherent "historical" quality they possess. In fact, it is the historical element of westerns that is perhaps their most exacting quality. It is not, for example, the West of the twentieth or twenty-first centuries that is the focus of most western films (although some westerns are set in more contemporary times). Because it attempts to place itself within a historical context (typically the late 1800s), the Hollywood western is viewed by audiences as being a historical record and inherently important to the construction of a meaningful past. Indeed, Jim Kitses insists that "the Western *is* American history."[8] History in the western film, then, is essential to its sustained importance to audiences who continue to seek to understand what it means to be an American.

There is an innate paradox imbedded in western films and notions of the West. Despite their historicity—or the perception that the films are historically authentic—these films do not need to be factual to be meaningful to those who view them. What is more important is that they *seem* historically authentic, the definition of which has everything to do with how the West of the 1880s has been represented to audiences over time. Aquila argues that "it doesn't matter what the actual West is like, what took place there, or what exists there. What matters is what people *believe* the West is like, took place and exists there."[9] In other words, "history" and "authenticity" are fluid concepts according to the beliefs and expectations of audiences. Raymond Durgnat and Scott Simmon assert that producers of westerns are less concerned with historical accuracy than with creating films that signify something enduring about America's true character: "Indeed, the genre is quite conscious—often pompously conscious—of representing America's essence. If it falsifies the 'little' details of history, it's only to show more clearly the crucial and underlying truths."[10]

David Pierson posits that western films and television shows are popular because their historicity lends them an air of authenticity. Again, whether they are historically precise is less important than the impression that they give to audiences who have formed ideas of what is "historically authentic" or "accurate" based on previously consumed productions of the popular culture West. Nonetheless, Pierson says, "verisimilitude to historical events adds dramatic intensity to both fictional and nonfictional programs; in this way, history serves as a prime legitimator for audiences to invest their viewing time."[11] In explaining the process through which notions of what is historically accurate were solidified, Richard Slotkin stresses that audiences develop a familiarity with the "history" of the region through their consumption of films and television shows. Through repetition, audiences become "attached" to certain devices and tropes that they then associate with the now-normalized signs of historical authenticity.[12] They then demand that all subsequent productions align with their expectations. Alexandra Keller similarly argues that it is the *resemblance* to authenticity claimed by westerns—not necessarily historical accuracy—that has given these films currency in American culture. She explains that "whether or not Westerns referred to actual events and people, they claimed an affinity with authenticity through an explicit grounding in 'History,' not in all individual texts but in the genre as a whole."[13]

We see a similar importance in the idea of history and "authenticity" to understanding Tombstone. Tourists become familiar with what they believe to be the history of the Old West and of Tombstone through the consumption of popular culture. That is to say, tourist expectations of what constitutes an "authentic old western town" are most often built on images and ideas that audiences have seen in the movies. Audiences and tourists then demand an authenticity of experience that somehow also incorporates their fantasy; in fact, now the two may be seen as inseparable. Slotkin calls this "the dilemma of authenticity," meaning that both authenticity and fantasy must exist in this paradigm.[14] Filmmakers and the history keepers in

Tombstone must meet that demand if they are to be successful. Divergence from Hollywood's version of the Old West in the town of Tombstone may be met with a less than enthusiastic response, while divergence from what is considered "historically authentic" in western films may be met with a similar reaction. This symbiosis is why films about Tombstone and those about the West in general have had and continue to have a tremendous impact on the way Wyatt Earp, Doc Holliday, the gunfight, and the town of Tombstone are conceived and celebrated in the national imaginary.

As much as westerns situate themselves in a historical context, they also reflect historical attitudes—both of the West of the popular imagination and of culture and society at the moment the film is being made. In other words, westerns can be seen both as narrativizing presumably actual events and situations from the past and as representative of the cultural attitudes and beliefs that are held at the particular time of the film's production. The malleability of the western along with its traditional archetypical images of the frontier, individualism, masculinity, racial conflict, law and order, resistance to modernity (while attempting to "tame" the "wilderness"), and the role of the gunfighter as hero allow it to be used to different purposes at different times, whether in emphasizing the value of honor and sacrifice, as did the westerns of the 1940s and 1950s, or in articulating a more pragmatic, less romantic view of the American West, as did the westerns of the 1960s and 1970s.

A number of scholars have explored this link between the history of westerns and changing attitudes, beliefs, and values of the culture at large.[15] Michael Coyne exposes the western film as a vital medium for examining the shifts and transformations in political, racial, sexual, social, and religious attitudes throughout the twentieth century. He focuses on a small sampling of westerns to show how they articulated attitudes about such issues as labor strife, miscegenation, gender and sexuality, the Cold War, McCarthyism, Vietnam, and newfound feelings of alienation in the 1970s. His work traces the trajectory of westerns from epics of national triumph to dystopic visions of life in the United States. The ideology of the western film is often taken to task by Coyne, who, like other historians of the US West, see that these films and other productions of the pop culture West articulate certain ideas of what the ideal American citizen should look like and the means by which—presumably—this ideal American citizen should maintain his (emphasis on "his") hegemonic position. Coyne states that "the Hollywood Western codified American identity as mainly white and male, largely accepted racial supremacy as given, romanticized aggressive masculinity, and, ultimately, eulogized resistance to regulated society as the truest mark of manhood."[16] Similarly, John Lenihan analyzes five hundred westerns produced during the Cold War to show "how a particular form [of movie production] is modified in accordance with the constantly changing concerns and attitudes of a society."[17] Lenihan's work reveals how the Korean and Vietnam Wars, McCarthyism, the arms race, and race issues influenced the way the genre articulated standard representations of the West (such as the image of the frontier, individualism, and the role of the gunfighter as hero).

Stanley Corkin also examines the historical significance of the western, specifically those produced between the end of World War II and the dawn of the war in Vietnam—the time when westerns reached their height in popularity. Corkin attempts to situate the western within wider cultural and political shifts that reflected and informed both national sentiment and public policy throughout the early years of the Cold War. Central to Corkin's argument is the notion that "these films metaphorically narrate the relationship between the United States and the world."[18] Concentrating on the political and social climates of the era and delving into matters of gender, family, religion, and race, Corkin effectively reads the significance of westerns at a time when Americans were attempting to define the parameters of Americanness against a backdrop of US hegemony on the global stage, the threat of communism and nuclear war, and evolving family dynamics within America's borders.

Even with the revisionist westerns of the late 1960s through the 2000s, the genre still has something to say about the nation's past and the ways that past has affected the present, perhaps even more so. These films demonstrate that with each new generation, there is something vital in the mythic West that calls for continued reference and allusion. Even with Coyne's dismissal of more recent westerns,[19] and despite the exhausted tendency to place this genre on its deathbed, westerns persist. They may be prone in recent years to representing a more pluralistic idea of the West than previous films,[20] they may be set in the twentieth-century West,[21] or they may show a more ambiguous relationship between violence and redemption/regeneration.[22] But they are still involved with the production and consumption of the meaning of the American West—a place, a history, and a myth wrought with tireless messages and significance.

Indeed, the number of western films that dots the cinematic landscape is dizzying, and every one influences the ways the West of the late nineteenth century is understood and the meaning of the region today. From *The Great Train Robbery* (1903) to *Stagecoach* (1939) to *Shane* (1951) to *Unforgiven* (1992) to *Brokeback Mountain* (2005) to the remake of *True Grit* (2010) to *Cowboys and Aliens* (2011) to the television shows *Deadwood* (2004–2006), *Justified* (2010–2015), and *Hell on Wheels* (2011–), westerns remain one of the most enduring of American genres. Within this corpus, Tombstone, Wyatt Earp, and the showdown at the OK Corral have proved persistent themes. In fact, 2012 and 2014 saw two new films featuring Tombstone and Wyatt: *Wyatt Earp's Revenge*, starring Val Kilmer, this time in the title role; and *Dead in Tombstone*, a horror western starring Danny Trejo, Mickey Rourke, and Anthony Michael Hall. Earp himself understood the power of Hollywood in shaping and shifting attitudes as he attempted to get his own story projected onto the silver screen a number of times in the 1920s. His popular characterization as the epitome of the western hero and the fact that the historic battle behind the OK Corral is imbued with the characteristics of an ancient morality play have meant that both the man and the event have served well the devices essential to the western genre. Further, and perhaps more significantly, the Earp myth has remained a powerful narrative in communicating the ideals that throughout the century have nourished and bolstered the way many Americans see themselves and their nation.

Authenticity and Invention

While a number of films about the Earps and the street fight were produced prior to 1946,[23] the commercial and critical success of *My Darling Clementine* (1946) meant it had by far the most influence on the way Wyatt Earp was conceived by the wider public up to that point. Because of its popularity, it could be argued that the film had a significant impact on Tombstone's initial efforts to become a monument to the Old West, beginning with the establishment of the Tombstone Historic Restoration Commission in 1949. *My Darling Clementine* also heavily influenced all Earp films that came after it and was instrumental in solidifying the Earp myth in the popular imagination. Even though the filmmakers claimed historic authenticity, the film was based on a book that itself was not historically accurate. Nonetheless, the film's devices helped concretize the ways the Earp story and the western hero have been imagined ever since. The film also helped set the stage for a Tombstone readying itself for public consumption. For these reasons, the plotline and setting, the intentions of the filmmaker, and the influence of previous works all deserve in-depth exploration.

Directed by John Ford, *My Darling Clementine* opens with Wyatt Earp (Henry Fonda) and his brothers Morgan, Virgil, and James (Ward Bond, Tim Holt, and Don Garner, respectively) attempting to drive a herd of cattle across the Arizona desert to California. Wyatt meets Old Man Clanton (Walter Brennan) and his son Ike (Grant Withers), who offer to buy the cattle from Wyatt at less than what they are worth. Wyatt refuses, immediately setting him up in opposition to the ranchers. Wyatt asks if there is a town close by, and Clanton tells him that Tombstone is just over the rise. Wyatt, Virgil, and Morgan head to Tombstone while younger brother James stays behind to watch over the camp and the cattle until they return.[24]

The Earps' arrival in Tombstone is marred by conflict in the town's streets. The brothers find themselves in the middle of a melee as someone starts shooting a gun outside in every direction and the town's inhabitants are under threat. No one can stop the gunman from shooting his weapon until Wyatt boldly approaches and manages to subdue the troublemaker, immediately identified as a Native American man who has had too much to drink—a familiar stereotype.[25] Wyatt's bravery is met with veneration by the townspeople and an offer to become the town marshal, which Wyatt turns down. He reconsiders after he and his brothers ride back to their campsite to find their cattle have been stolen and James murdered. Determined to find James's killer, Wyatt decides to take the job as marshal. As such, he becomes the central figure in attempts to bring law and order to Tombstone.

Wyatt meets Doc Holliday (Victor Mature), and they develop a bond that remains the focus of the film. A turning point occurs when Wyatt discovers that Holliday's girlfriend Chihuahua—a prostitute and barmaid[26]—is wearing a silver piece that belonged to James. He demands to know where she got it, and she confesses that Billy Clanton (John Ireland) gave it to her, thereby incriminating the Clantons in James's murder. Billy Clanton overhears the conversation and flees with Virgil in pursuit. Virgil is fatally shot and left in the streets of Tombstone by Old Man Clanton, who challenges the other Earp brothers to meet at sunrise for a showdown at the OK Corral. The gun battle marks the climax of the film, with history sealing the fate of the Clanton clan. The Earps' victory and the Clantons' defeat mark the moment in the film when law is indeed and finally triumphant over lawlessness, and the West changes from Old to New. In this same scene, Doc Holliday is killed, which serves an interesting purpose. Holliday is essential to the narrative: it is Doc's former fiancée, Clementine, who brings both tension and resolve to the plot, while it is his relationship with Chihuahua that leads to the defining moment in the film. With Doc being so crucial to the story, his death is imperative to the establishment of Wyatt as the hero both of the film and of the West itself. Doc's death means that Wyatt's position as the quintessential western lawman remains intact.

Henry Fonda as Wyatt Earp overlooking the vast Arizona landscape. (Courtesy of Twentieth Century Fox / Kobal Collection / Art Resource)

The final scene shows Wyatt and Morgan on their way out of town to California, their original destination. Wyatt sees Clementine, whose significance to the larger narrative of the settlement of the West is revealed in these last moments: she is staying in Tombstone to be the new schoolmarm. Like the half-constructed church tower and the gunfight, Clementine symbolizes the transition that is taking place in the West, a transition cultivated through the institutions of incorporation by the larger nation: church, school, and the law. And as the archetypal western hero, Wyatt must leave. His work is done, and he is now needed elsewhere.[27] While Wyatt seems mournful, he speeds out of town on a galloping horse, without looking back. The imperatives of the genre and of history demand that Wyatt Earp of both the film and the popular imagination move forward, farther west, leaving civilization along the way.

Given these now familiar tropes, the film was a critical and commercial success. That success may also be due in part to the fact that the film is based on the book *Wyatt Earp: Frontier Marshal* (1931) by Stuart N. Lake, which lent the film historical credibility.[28] The book, however, is far from an accurate representation of the events leading up to the famous gunfight. Lake had intended to ghostwrite Earp's memoirs as dictated by Earp himself, but his subject was less than loquacious, which led Lake to take sweeping liberties in the narrative. While written as though it were a direct transcription of Earp's dictation, Lake made up dialogue and events and wrote them as if they had actually happened. In the foreword to the work, Lake deceptively claims that "since Wyatt Earp has so long been a myth to lovers of the Old West, it is no more than fair to state definitively that this biography is in no part a mythic tale." He also writes, "Wyatt Earp was persuaded to devote the closing months of his long life to the narration of his full story, to a firsthand and a factual account of his career. It is upon this account that the succeeding pages are entirely based."[29] Neither of these statements is true, but that did not prevent the work from serving as the supposedly historical basis of *My Darling Clementine* and later idealized works about Wyatt Earp.

Of course, romanticizing the West and western heroes was nothing new in 1946. Dime novels (none of which ever featured Wyatt Earp) and Wild West shows were wildly popular precursors to the cult of Wyatt Earp that blew up in the late 1920s. Released four years before Lake's biography was Walter Noble Burns's *Tombstone: An Iliad of the Southwest* (1927). Labeling Earp the "Lion of the West," Burns crafted what Earp historian Casey Tefertiller classifies as "a triumph of blood and thunder" that captivated a wide audience "looking for heroes."[30] Lake's *Frontier Marshal* followed in that tradition, providing audiences during a tumultuous time with a comforting portrayal of a simpler era where the good guys could rid a town of the bad guys before heading on to their next adventure. Both Burns's and Lake's works cast Earp as the ideal hero who brought law and order to Tombstone and the wider Southwest, but while Burns did not collaborate with Earp on his book, Lake claimed that his work was written with Earp at his side. Of course, to the historian, historical accuracy is imperative; to the filmmaker and filmgoer, however, historical accuracy is less important than the *impression* of historical accuracy, as we have seen. Despite the licenses Lake took, or perhaps because of them, his book was wildly popular and launched Wyatt Earp as the classic western lawman and hero he became. The book also served to strengthen the claim to historical authenticity of films that used it as the basis for their narratives despite its spurious portrayal of events.

Lake is credited at the beginning of *My Darling Clementine*, with an intertitle that reads "based on a book by Stuart N. Lake." The referent for the film, in other words, is a book that could be considered as much fiction as nonfiction. But a semblance to "history" and "authenticity" are still imperative to the success of the film to both producer and audiences—although maybe not to everyone. On the one hand, screenwriter Winston Miller declared, "We made the whole thing up as we went along. . . . I wasn't interested in how the West really was, I was writing a movie." On the other hand, director John Ford was indeed interested in proclaiming authenticity when it came to the story—as already evidenced by the credit to Lake in the film as well as his remarks about the film to the press, claiming that "in *My Darling Clementine*, we did it exactly the way it had been."[31] Ford must have realized that declaring this film an accurate representation of the man and the event was crucial to the legitimacy of the narrative. If accuracy or authenticity were not important—to the writer, director, producers, and audiences— why use the historical figure of Wyatt Earp and the historical event of the street fight as the foundations for the story? Regardless of Ford's publicized intention, the storyline of the film veers from historical fact: among other inaccuracies, Wyatt's (older) brother James actually died in 1926, forty-five years after the gunfight; Newman Haynes "Old Man" Clanton died two months before the OK Corral confrontation; and Doc Holliday was a dentist, not a surgeon, and died of tuberculosis six years after the conflict. Further, as Allen Barra points out, the events in Ford's film do not even mirror those in Lake's book, which at the outset explains that the members of Earp's travel party consisted of his brothers Virgil and James and their families, not just the brothers and not Morgan, who joined them later.[32]

To complicate matters, despite asserting that the film was "exactly the way it had been," Ford also admitted to film historian Jon Tuska that the film was meant to be pure entertainment. Tuska asked Ford why he had not shot the film the way it actually happened: "'Did you like the film?' [Ford] sputtered, and when Tuska admitted it was one of his favorites, Ford shot back, 'What more do you want?'" This exchange led Tuska to conclude that "Ford didn't give a damn for the messy historical facts. What mattered in *My Darling Clementine* was the historical interpretation, the meaning that Ford gave to his story about the coming of civilization to the West."³³ Screenwriter Miller was being candid in his comments to the media, perhaps not entirely understanding the importance of historical authenticity to the success of a film set in the past. Ford, it seems, was well aware of the legitimizing power of historical authenticity to audiences who had certain expectations of what western history should "look" like. In fact, Ford's elicitation of historical accuracy and authenticity for the film is similar to that of Lake in his insistence that *Frontier Marshal* was based on words spoken by Earp himself. Ford understood that the film needed to be entertaining to win over audiences. But he (and Lake) also implied in his attempts to historically authenticate the film that the film needed to be historically authentic as well. It is this constant back and forth between what actually happened and what needed to happen in the film to make it successful—between fact and fiction—that is at the heart of the film and the genre as a whole, as well as the town of Tombstone as a sustainable and viable tourist destination.

A number of western historians criticizes these popular culture interpretations of the westward movement for perpetuating two-dimensional and often damaging representations of the West. Patricia Limerick, for example, laments the ways "conquest" has been reduced in popular culture to "stereotypes of noble savages and noble pioneers struggling quaintly in the wilderness" and how, while the "subject of slavery was the domain of serious scholars and the occasion for sober reflection[,] the subject of conquest was the domain of mass entertainment and the occasion for lighthearted national escapism."³⁴ Michael Johnson demonstrates the devastating legacy that the swirl of myths, obsession with and subsequent subjugation of the wild, and an ambivalent ideology of conquest have had on the regional and cultural landscape of the West. Johnson illuminates the ways opposing myths and binary understandings (noble savage / "red devil," wild / tame, utopia / wasteland) of the area continue to define the way the West is constructed, not only in the popular imagination but in real terms as well, as seen in degraded wilderness, decreased natural resources, and suburban sprawl.³⁵

These lamentations may speak precisely to the idea that the inherent historicity of these films means they are more readily accepted as historically accurate by audiences. In other words, the use of "history" in these films is both problematic and the reason for their resilience. Some scholars point out that these films are not necessarily meant to be historically accurate. "It is essential, of course, when viewing a film of such mythic purity and narrative power," Hutton argues, "to suspend cynicism as well as any regard for historical accuracy, remembering that Ford is presenting the absolute essence of the frontier myth and not a history lesson."[36] This may be true, but to Ford, the historical element of his western was imperative to its potency. And to audiences, westerns by their nature are always already historical, or based in history, at least in time and space if not in narrative. "In classical Westerns," Keller explains, a "seamless, totalizing presentation is achieved through a realist aesthetic that naturalizes information so that it *appears* historically accurate, even if it is not. Despite—indeed because of—this exterior appeal to apparently genuine detail and the monolithic, inviolate discourse of History itself, the Western is the bearer of its own seamless authenticity."[37] Similar to the coconstitutive relationship between preservation and historical significance, by being a western—by depicting events and focusing on heroes significant to both the region's and the nation's past—a film validates itself.

It is true that *My Darling Clementine* is riddled with historical inaccuracies, a few of which have already been mentioned, and the details surrounding the actual gunfight are complex—despite the "simplicity" of the story as relayed through popular culture. For example, it is interesting that this version of the dispute revolves around the plundering of the Earps' cattle and the murder of their young brother, James, by the Clanton clan rather than simply the possession of firearms within the town's borders or the broader issue of opposing political ideologies often cited as foundational to the historic battle. It is imperative for the trajectory of the plot that there be a definitive line drawn between the morality of the Earps and the depravity of the Clantons. Apparently, political differences are not adequate enough to prompt "the ultimate showdown," at least not to audiences in 1946. While in real life, allegiances formed on both sides, causing questions to circulate around the motivation of the Earps and Holliday to this day, Ford's reimagining leaves no ambiguity around who were the good guys and who were the bad guys.

Further, because *My Darling Clementine* is based on a book whose author fabricated much of the story and was "made up" by a screenwriter and production house that needed a powerful story to sell to filmgoers of the 1940s, the film is—in Baudrillard's term—a simulacrum, a film based on a book that itself had little basis in fact. Even Baudrillard might observe that westerns are the quintessential simulation, in which the representation of the West is more significant, more meaningful, than the West itself. Baudrillard might also observe that, similarly to westerns, the town of Tombstone has become the "hyperreal," the space in which simulating that which is simulated in western films and television shows defines the experience tourists expect when they visit. According to Baudrillard, the term *hyperreality* is used to describe a hypothetical inability of consciousness to differentiate between what is real and what is fantasy.[38] The popular media familiarize members of the public with both the history of Tombstone and what they can expect when they visit. The multiple representations of Wyatt and the gunfight in popular culture have radically shaped and reshaped the original event and person in the minds of audiences to the point of defining the experience—or notions of authenticity and "realness"—to visitors to the town where the event took place. *My Darling Clementine*'s success speaks to its power—as a shaper of the Earp myth and as a definer of the town of Tombstone. The film was pivotal in solidifying the popularity of Wyatt Earp as the ideal frontier lawman and his place in movies and television shows for the next fifty years.

The next big promotion of Wyatt Earp as western hero in Hollywood started on 6 September 1955 (the same year *Gunsmoke* premiered on CBS, Frontierland opened at Disneyland, and Edna Landin became president of the Historic Restoration Commission), when *The Life and Legend of Wyatt Earp*, starring Hugh O'Brien, premiered on ABC. This television show's unprecedented success meant it helped permanently fix "Wyatt Earp as the prototypical frontier lawman in the national, if not international, consciousness." The series traces Wyatt's adventures from Wichita to Dodge to Tombstone, ending with the direct aftermath of the gunfight. Although the series consciously relied on history as its authenticating foundation, Hutton reminds us that "the O'Brien series was steeped in Hollywood's unique version of western history."[39] Like *My Darling Clementine*, *Life and Legend* created a mystique around the narrative that helped Tombstone regenerate itself in that same time frame. The show utilized similar tropes and devices as *My Darling Clementine*, was again based on Stuart Lake's *Frontier Marshal*, and similarly attempted to historically authenticate itself while articulating the ideological underpinnings of the Earp myth. Ironically, Lake's book "subsequently became the authority for nearly all the film portraits of Earp," writes historian John Mack Faragher. "Acknowledging Lake's biography on screen lent a kind of historical authenticity to these films, but the trouble was that the book was an imaginative hoax, a fabrication mixed with just enough fact to lend it credibility."[40]

Understanding the importance of history as a legitimizer, Hugh O'Brien made the most of the bond he now had with the famed lawman. At one point he declared, "I don't think anybody is closer to Wyatt than I am. [Stuart] Lake lived with Wyatt for four years before Earp died, but I know a lot about Wyatt too. I don't mean just facts, I mean what he stood for and what he'd do under certain circumstances." Like John Ford before him, O'Brien felt it imperative to articulate a connection to the real Wyatt Earp. In this way, he could legitimize and authenticate his portrayal of the man as legitimate and authentic. The popularity of the series demonstrates, as Hutton believes, that he "obviously succeeded."[41]

The television series did make great use of the western myth as well as western history, tugging on the romantic heartstrings of its audience and their nostalgia for the Old West. The theme song for the show set the tone:

> I'll tell you a story
> A real, true-life story
> A tale of the western frontier.
> The West it was lawless
> But one man was flawless
> And his is the story you'll hear.
> Wyatt Earp, Wyatt Earp, brave courageous and bold.
> Long live his fame and long live his glory
> And long may his story be told.[42]

Similarly, the opening voice-over for the first episode laid the foundation for the promise of Wyatt Earp as the western lawman and hero audiences expected:

> This is the beginning of the story of Wyatt Earp, the greatest of the old fighting peace officers, a real western hero. So great was his character and so complete his skill at living with danger that he became a legend in his own lifetime. In the hard world of the western frontier, with all its bad men and outlaws, Wyatt Earp became the peacemaker. As a marshal, he went up against the worst of them. And the stories they tell about him are doubly fabulous because they're true.[43]

Again, we see the insistence by producers that the show is based on fact. At the same time, Hutton admonishes viewers and scholars from absorbing the series as true history: "Despite its calculated historicity, the *Life and Legend of Wyatt Earp* was always mass-marketed entertainment, meant to sell a sponsor's product, not provide a history lesson."[44] Clearly, however, the claim of historical truth was important, at least to the producers and probably to audiences as well.

One of the most interesting aspects of the Earp story, however, both historically and on screen, is its equivocal attitude toward law and authority. While reifying the dominance of law and authority on the one hand, the Earp narrative also safely reproduces suspicion and contempt toward a corrupt or ineffective government on the other, through such historical figures as Sheriff John Behan as well as countless fictional TV and film characters who help maintain this ambivalence. In episode 1 of *The Life and Legend of Wyatt Earp*, "Wyatt Earp Becomes a Marshal," for example, the "good" lawman Wyatt is clearly juxtaposed with the "bad" judge who lets the brother/accomplice of a murderer leave town with a monetary fine and a slap on the wrist. While Wyatt may come across as self-righteous in his attempt to clear the town of its criminal component (some might say he was "butting in" when there already was a capable if not fully "good" marshal in town), his position as hero—and as the representation of Wyatt Earp, widely understood as the hero—serves to excuse him from contempt by audiences. We also see in *My Darling Clementine* and repeated in subsequent films the ambivalence Earp feels himself in becoming a lawman, doing so only after extenuating circumstances force him to take on that role.

Ambivalence toward law and authority has remained a theme in films and television shows about the Earp legend as well as in the town of Tombstone itself, which banks heavily on tourists' desire to "play" outlawry and disorder while celebrating the law and authority embodied in the "Gunfight at the OK Corral" narrative. As the famous battle is continually re-enacted on the streets of modern-day Tombstone, subversive components are continually expunged. Tourists enjoy challenging the dominance of authority on the one hand, but they also are comforted with the constant reassertion of authority and control on the other. The frontier more often than not celebrated what philosophy and law professor Cheyney Ryan calls the "vigilante tradition" of people's justice. Vigilante justice subverts the law-and-order ideal, in which Earp was firmly entrenched. "As historians of American violence have shown, there has always been a 'vigilante' strain in American life that people have always found both disturbing and attractive, a strain that does not eschew violence per se but doubts whether formal law is ever adequate to achieve it."[45] Tension between the ineffectiveness of sociolegal institutions and the desire for justice on the part of the principal characters is a central motif in many westerns. This ambiguity is seen in the representations of Wyatt Earp throughout the twentieth century. Though a lawman, he is also portrayed as the "outsider," standing separate from the dominant power structure set up in conceptions of law and authority that constitute those on the "inside." This binary shows him as critical and effective while the traditional institutions of law and authority are shown as corrupt and impotent. But Earp also embodies the traits of a renegade, a man who paradoxically relies on vigilante justice to shuffle in the civilizing elements the Old West desperately needed. If he can be celebrated as a lawman or outsider of integrity, he can also be vilified as a violent and self-serving bully with vested interests in the corrupt moneymaking businesses of the West.

The continued debate over Earp's character by film and television producers (as well as journalists, biographers, and historians) may currently be indicative of a pendulum shift in attitudes toward institutions of law and authority. The conservatism of the modern-day Tea Party could find foundation in this theme—as have groups subscribing to both antigovernment/ authority and pro-"traditional" values in the past—but that does not mean Earp loses his power as a western hero. In fact, the dualism that represents him as both insider and outsider, as part of the establishment and critical of that establishment, makes him a hero from many different perspectives. By using Tombstone as the starting point for these films, a place not yet situated within the confines of society, producers and audiences are already embarking on a narrative for empire and social progress. A former mining camp, the town epitomizes the moment on the verge of civilization, with the gunfight the landmark moment when law and order are victorious over outlawry. Skepticism toward law, celebration of vigilante justice, and the welcoming of a civilized West can all be sufficiently and unironically embodied in the representation of Wyatt Earp.

Reimagining the Myth

While some films questioning the major tenets of manifest destiny as well as the ideals of masculinity and redemptive violence had been produced in the 1940s and 1950s, ambivalence about law and authority, violence, and the masculine ideal are major themes of later western films. So-called revisionist westerns of the 1960s and 1970s began to challenge the dominant romantic version of westward expansion and explore the darker side of the progression west. While some of these films were not successful, others were indeed popular in their day or have since developed "cult" followings that keep afloat those productions that point to a shift in attitudes about the "creation myth" of America. These films were very much a product of their time, when distrust in government and challenges to hegemony were gaining momentum. The "Man with No Name" series directed by Sergio Leone and starring Clint Eastwood is often cited as a prime example of revisionist westerns from the time.[46] This trend has continued through the present day.

Throughout this time Earp has remained a central, if more ambiguous, figure. In his analysis of *Hour of the Gun* (1967), Hutton quotes director John Sturges as saying "Western characters must not be glamorized," this, Hutton points out, after his very romanticized account of Earp in *Gunfight at the O.K. Corral* (1957).[47] Because *Hour of the Gun* begins with the gunfight and moves on to depict the vendetta ride on which Wyatt embarked after the street fight, it necessarily portrays a side of Earp that is more sinister than previously explored by Hollywood. But even with this in-depth look at Earp's character, in this film, Hutton argues, "Wyatt Earp nevertheless remains a powerful symbol of the law. It is from that perspective that we observe his moral suicide in *Hour of the Gun*. It remains a powerful interpretation of the Earp legend, and a film that fits perfectly with the alienation and mistrust of a deeply divided America in the late 1960s."[48]

Star Trek's "Spectre of the Gun" (1968) is yet another example of the ways the Earp myth was retooled in the late 1960s. While at first glance not a western, *Star Trek* and other science fiction productions utilize similar tropes essential to the western (not to mention the appeal science fiction and westerns both have to male audiences). This particular episode sheds more light on the ways Earp has been conceived in the popular imagination, utopian and dystopian visions of the future of the West as myth, and how notions of violence and masculinity get entangled and disentangled in a western milieu. The original *Star Trek* series offers a utopian vision of an America predicated on the (western) values of individualism and freedom, where the projects of colonialism, westward expansion, and exploration (without the messiness of mistreatment, corruption, or genocide) are successful and fruitful. The celebration of technological progress and Edenic nostalgia coexist in *Star Trek*'s vision of the future. In making great use of the western myth, the series also problematizes some of the central tenets of that myth. Because westerns typically deal with the past and science fiction typically deals with the future, the concept of history takes on different meanings in both genres, even when science fiction retools those stories that have been central to frontier narratives.

Science fiction not only has drawn from narratives of the frontier to develop conceptions of the future; it also draws on specific tropes of the genre to offer a critique of the past and the ideologies of the present. As William H. Katerberg argues, "For any redemptive project to succeed, whether as a historical narrative, a utopian vision, or a social-political movement, it must address the injustices of the past and find ways to work through, overcome, and transcend them."[49] The episode "Spectre of the Gun" uses the trappings of the western as a starting point for taking on the "burdens of western history," underscoring the flatness and simplicity of the Earp story and exposing the old triumphal frontier myth as one based on violence and conquest.[50]

"Spectre of the Gun" demonstrates shifting imaginings of the Earp narrative already tackled by Hollywood film. It attempts to expose the dark side of both the Earp myth and the mythic West, offering a critique of both the ways this western hero has been celebrated and the violence that underpins his story, historically and in popular culture. In this future, the story of Wyatt Earp becomes a death sentence for the crew of the starship *Enterprise*, and their revision of history makes a bold statement about that past, their present, and our future. Called "artistically and historically worthless" by Allen Barra, the episode nevertheless "shows how deeply the Earp story and the gunfight in back of the OK Corral had become ingrained in the imagination of the American people" and was seen by a wider public "than any Earp program ever broadcast on TV."[51] "Spectre of the Gun" manages to critique both the ideologies that were vital to westward expansion and the concepts that are fundamental to the imagined West. It also consciously takes to task the themes of the western genre, most centrally the ideas of history, authenticity, and redemptive violence.

In the episode, Captain Kirk and his crew (Spock, Dr. McCoy, Mr. Scott, and Chekov) attempt to make contact with the Melkotians, the xenophobic inhabitants of the Theta Kiokis II system. The crew is warned to leave the territory, but Kirk ignores the warning and proceeds to enter orbit and send a landing party anyway. The angered Melkotians choose to punish the crew by forcing them to reenact the legendary "Gunfight at the OK Corral," the constructed memory of which the Melkotians have crafted from Kirk's mind. The crew is immediately transported to what appears to be a stage set for a B-movie western—two-dimensional, without depth or realism. It is a frightening, barren, and bizarre landscape, canopied by a blood-red sky— here perhaps to be as unsettling as the arid landscape of the true West. The members of the crew do not yet realize that they will be playing out the gunfight; for now, they only understand that they have been placed in what the Melkotians believe to be the Wild West. "Obviously this represents the Melkotians' concept of an American frontier town circa 1880," Spock observes. Because the memory is taken from Kirk's mind, however, the set actually represents the way Kirk understands the Old West. Kirk says, "My ancestors pioneered the American frontier," to which Spock responds, "Yes, the violence of your own heritage is to be the pattern of our execution."[52]

The crew realizes that the scene is set on 26 October 1881, the day of the historic gunfight. They now begin to appreciate the Melkotians' intention.

Kirk and the crew are to play the Cowboys, the losers of the historic battle and the archetypal bad guys in the American mind. Kirk says, "We are the Clantons. And if this is a replay of history. . ." ". . . history cannot be changed," says Spock, meaning the outcome of the reenactment has been set. While it makes sense that the crew would play the part of the Cowboys in this scene—it is a punishment, after all—the fight also disrupts the traditional binary of hero and villain for the audience. As the audience of *Star Trek* is meant to identify and align with the crew, this scene sets the sympathy of the audience squarely with the Cowboys—the men typically understood as the outlaws, as the instigators of the fight, as deserving of their fate. The fact that the crew is linked in this episode with the losers of the fight serves to create an ambiguity around the purity of motivation of "the good guys" in this ultimate showdown, those men who are widely considered the heroes of the narrative, the Earps and Doc Holliday. If the heroes are made out to be the villains, then steadfast notions of good and evil begin to unravel.

Midway through the episode, Chekov as Billy Claiborne dies. This is disruptive because in the historical narrative, Claiborne does not die at the OK Corral. The notion of history as steadfast, then, has shifted. History can no longer be relied on or used to predict the outcome of the reenactment. Spock realizes that "where the laws do not operate, there is no reality. All of this is unreal." Notions of constructed history, and in many ways, constructed reality—specifically of the American West—are at the heart of this episode. The crew's only chance at survival, then, is to keep in mind that nothing in this space is real, including the bullets that would be used against them during the gunfight. Because Spock is the only character who can maintain such knowledge, he performs the "Vulcan mind meld" on the other members of the crew, hypnotizing them into maintaining the belief that this world is not real. During this scene, he repeats the most poignant statements in the episode: "The bullets are not real. They are illusions only. Shadows, without substance . . . nothing but ghosts of reality. They are lies, falsehoods . . . spectres, without body." These statements might just as well be said about Tombstone, Arizona, where the tension between fact and fiction is continually reproduced. Herein lies the critique of the ways audiences have recycled and consumed imaginings of an unreal, simplified West for generations.

The climax of the episode is the showdown. The scene is ominous, with a black background, an eerie wind, an emotionless Earp faction. The Earps and Doc Holliday are quiet, menacing, dressed all in black, attire that codes the wearer in earlier westerns as the "bad guy." Once the crew is able to maintain the belief that the bullets are not real, they are able to survive a barrage of gunfire, unharmed. In the final moments of the scene, Kirk has the opportunity to kill Wyatt Earp, but he does not—a harsh judgment on the way violence is glorified in classic westerns. Intrigued by Kirk's display of mercy, the leader of the Melkotians seeks to understand why he did not kill Earp: "Is this the way of your kind?" he asks. Kirk answers, "It is. We fight only when there is no choice." This show of clemency opens the Melkotians up to allowing further peaceful contact with the "vast alliance of fellow creatures" of which Kirk spoke when he first entered their airspace.

The lines spoken by Kirk and the crew throughout the episode are saturated with meaning about the significance of violence and redemption in the story of the Old West. Further, the episode is a rewriting of the good-versus-evil narrative that has come to define the ultimate showdown as represented through the gun battle at the OK Corral and the ways the Earps and Doc Holliday are understood in the popular imagination. Situated firmly within the revisionist westerns of the late 1960s, "Spectre of the Gun" reminds its audience of the constructedness of notions of the American West, of the ambiguity of the good-versus-evil paradigm, and of the destructive (not regenerative) qualities of violence—a violence so often celebrated in the narratives of the American West and the narrative of Earp himself. Rather than representing the West as the place of redemption and renewal and of the production and perpetuation of democratic ideals, this episode shows the Old West as a place of archaic ideas where reckless and meaningless violence and force were used to impose certain ideologies on subordinate populations. At the same time, the episode underscores the two-dimensionality of understandings of the Old West, with continual references to the unreal, to illusion, to a lack of substance in the ways the West is imagined and represented. The episode is an interesting intervention in the discussion of how violence on the American frontier is interpreted, and of the importance of history to our understandings of both the past and the present.

Unlike other films or television shows about Wyatt Earp, science fiction allows *Star Trek* to veer more pointedly away from historical accuracy, perceived or otherwise, to offer a decidedly critical analysis of conceptions of Earp, violence, the Old West, and the meanings of these issues in the present day. At the same time, the episode celebrates the underlying ideologies on which the mythic West is predicated—social progress and a better life. If, as literary critic and science fiction writer Samuel Delany argues, "SF is not about the future" but "is in dialogue with the present," and, as historian

Carl Abbott contends, "to engage the present is invariably to engage understandings of the past," then "Spectre of the Gun" offers a vision of an unfortunately violent past, a utopian future, and a present that can see this progression through.[53]

Some filmmakers of the early 1970s continued their assault on Earp as seen in the film *Doc* (1971), called "truly awful" by Hutton: "Harris Yulin's Earp is a self-righteous, totally hypocritical sadist with a delightfully Nixonian vision of the law that is totally self-serving."[54] *Doc* failed at the box office, which may indicate that while there may have been a general sense of anomie and alienation in the 1970s, audiences still wanted to revel in the traditional, romanticized story of the Old West. As Faragher contends, "Although all westerns are concerned with history, no one goes to the movies for a cynical history lesson." Faragher concludes that "the revisionist Earp films, which clearly reject the progressive interpretations of Stuart Lake and John Ford, have little to offer in their place. Mired in the disillusionment of their own times, they find nothing significant to say about the American past."[55] This may have been true, but the cynicism reflected in western films of the late 1960s into the 1970s was also reflected by tourism in Tombstone, which declined in this same time period, as Americans were less interested in celebrating the very ideals that made Earp a hero a generation before.

Perhaps most closely related to the touristic experience of "western-themed towns" such as Tombstone and reviving traditional conceptions of the gunslinger as hero, masculinity, and redemptive violence is Michael Crichton's *Westworld*, released in 1973. Unlike "Spectre of the Gun," a science fiction production that offers a distinct critique of the notion of redemptive violence in the Earp saga and the construction of the history of the West itself, *Westworld* ends up reproducing and celebrating those elements central to the western ideal. In this film, science fiction and the frontier myth are entangled in a fantasyland gone awry. The film exposes the constructed and violent nature of the mythic West but also relies heavily on those themes that made the western genre popular. While this film is not specifically about Tombstone or Wyatt Earp, it does make use of the street fight between the gunslinger and the outlaw that is central to traditional renditions of the Earp story and that serves as the climax of most other films about Earp. It also sheds light on the shifting and varying ways the West (both mythic and historical) was conceived in the early 1970s.

Westworld follows ill-fated visitors to an amusement park who desire to live out their fantasies in another time and place. Ironically called "the vacation of the future today," this amusement park for adults (run by the company Delos) offers its customers the opportunity to visit one of three historic destinations: Westernworld, which reconstructs life in the "Old West" (widely understood and seen here as the West of the 1880s); Medievalworld; and Romanworld. The desire to go back in time and space and live out certain fantasies of violence and recklessness seen as subversive to the normative confines of society reveals anxieties about the fast-paced, technologically driven world outside the confines of the park—as well as those faced by contemporary audiences and consumers of the mythic West more generally. The different "worlds" are populated by androids that visitors can kill without fear of actually causing harm. This technology also allows visitors to have what is superficially considered an authentic experience in whatever world they have chosen. In Westernworld, an outlaw android (Yul Brynner) is programmed to start duels with the guests, offering them a more "realistic" interaction with the space based on their expectations. If he is shot and "killed," he is reconditioned and out on the street the next day, thus allowing guests to live out a violent (white, male) fantasy without repercussion—but also without the redemptive quality that many scholars argue is imperative for members of the audience to align themselves with the western hero. In some ways, the violence in *Westworld* is meaningless, not regenerative, although the end of the film offers a chance at regeneration for the lead character, Pete.

In Westernworld, Pete (Richard Benjamin) and John (James Brolin) continually negotiate between authenticity and reality, between what is expected in the real world and what is expected in this construction of the Old West. Throughout the film, Pete, who, unlike John, has not visited Westernworld before, must be instructed in the ways of both the Old West and proper masculine behavior. As in so many representations of the West of the 1880s, in Westernworld, the Old West and masculinity are coconstitutive. Pete's normative masculinity seems to be in constant question, remedied only by the experiences unfolding in the masculinist milieu of the 1880s West. For example, when Pete orders a martini at the saloon (a drink made famous by the antithetically British, elegant, groomed, and urbane James Bond), he is glared at by the bartender and told they only have whiskey. When Pete complains about the rugged unpleasantness of the accommodations, asking, "We're paying $1,000 a day for this?" John answers, "It's authentic, the West of the 1880s." "Well, at least they could have made it a little bit more comfortable," Pete says. "That's the point," John responds. "This is really the way it was!"[56] This exchange reveals both Pete's effete nature—some would argue a result of living in a modern, disinfected, disconnected world—and the ways that authenticity gets skewed in the film.

The ideas of reality and authenticity are brought up a number of times. The movie opens with a reporter outside the Delos park interviewing visitors on their experience. One guest exclaims:

TED MANN: "Oh, you're not going to believe this but I've just been the sheriff of Westernworld for the last two weeks!"
ANNOUNCER: "Did it seem real to you sir?"
MANN: "It's the realest thing I've ever done."

The notions of realism and authenticity are imperative to the experiences of the guests, much as they are in spaces such as Tombstone. But authenticity is disrupted in the film whenever a scene cuts to the central control room, in which electrical engineers manage and direct what happens out on the streets. This disruption reminds the audience that these worlds are completely manufactured. Reminders of the constructedness of the experience are juxtaposed with the constant encouragement to believe in the authenticity of the place. Of course, the "authenticity" is at a safe distance from any dangers a real western gunslinger might have encountered in the Old West. This distance also works to sustain Pete's feminized character.

Performative danger becomes true danger when the androids inevitably rebel and start killing the guests. When the danger becomes real, Pete is transformed, finally exhibiting the masculine traits he'd been lacking all along. Many of the workers and guests are killed while others frantically run for their lives. Rather than flee the conflict going on in the streets, Pete stays on, vowing to kill Brynner's renegade android before heading to safety, which he does. In this way, the film offers some redemption to Pete, but not in the same way so many other westerns do. The hero of the classic western is typically redeemed through actions that come to the aid of broader society and unambiguously place him in the realm of "good" in the battle between good and evil so often depicted in these films. In *Westworld*, however, Pete is really redeemed in terms of normative gender codes—regaining the masculinity lost in the antiseptic modern age, through violence, both real and unreal.

In many respects, Pete is similar to William Munny, Clint Eastwood's character in *Unforgiven* (1992), a pig farmer and aging outlaw who has seemingly relinquished some of the masculine trappings of a gunfighter (drinking, straight-shooting, and the ability to control a horse) only to have this masculinity restored at the movie's end by going on a murderous rampage in the town of Big Whiskey in retaliation for the torture and murder of his partner, Ned Logan (Morgan Freeman). While revealing the underbelly of the western myth, both films reproduce those elements of the story that fit in with the larger cosmology of the Old West: the imperatives of masculinity and regeneration of the hero through violence. As science fiction, *Westworld* manages to expose anxieties around technology and the crisis of masculinity in the modern world. As a western, the film also delivers a commentary on notions of authenticity both in the construction of the mythic West and—interestingly—in the construction of touristic experiences as lived yet distanced, as "authentic" yet unreal, as "wild" yet tidy. In this way, *Westworld* is firmly entrenched in the context of "revisionist" westerns that many argue began with the production of *High Noon* (1952).

But the film also adheres to the tropes of traditional westerns and provides a filmic experience (and commentary on that experience) similar to the kind many visitors to Tombstone bring to the site. Like the tourists of the Delos amusement park in *Westworld*, visitors to Tombstone arrive with the desire to reenact the 1880s as they understand them to have been based on their interaction with popular films and television shows. Like many believe of Tombstone, the worlds of *Westworld* are simulacra—recreations of, in the case of Westernworld, not the West as it actually was but a replica of the West as seen in westerns throughout the twentieth century. John and Pete base the authenticity of their experience in Westernworld on their understanding of the period and the place as developed through their engagement with popular culture. And like Tombstone, Westernworld must continually create a world that visitors expect. If being sheriff in Westernworld is not the "realest thing" Ted Mann has ever done, if the room John and Pete stay in were not "really the way it was," then people would stop visiting. The fact that there is an opportunity for Pete to triumph over the evil android outlaw and reclaim his masculinity—the purpose of the trip to Delos in the first place—is just the resolution of the typical western narrative, the icing on the cake, so to speak. It is the dream of every visitor to Tombstone as well: the promise of playing out the Earp narrative, being at once renegade and lawman, ridding the space of its savage element, all from the safe distance of a simulated, "hyperreal" experience.

Revisionism in western films and television shows reflects a shift in the ways the romanticized West and American values were being seen more generally, in popular culture and in popular history, in the 1960s and 1970s. It was an unprecedented moment of political and cultural change in the United States that included the civil rights and feminist movements, the Vietnam War, Watergate, and the fragmentation of any consensus around the ideologies undergirding American society. This ambiguity had been reflected in westerns produced earlier in the Cold War era, most notably *High Noon* (1952), but the 1960s and 1970s saw the production of films and television shows that portrayed a depth of character not common in films that came before. These films had stronger roles for women, offered richer and more sympathetic depictions of Natives and Mexicans, and portrayed a different kind of vision of westward expansion that was far more critical of manifest destiny and cynical about American exceptionalism. These movements also coincided with a decline in the number of visitors to sites such as Tombstone, which represented to many the paradox of the American experience, one that celebrated a history that was exclusive and violent. As mentioned, tourism in Tombstone hit a wall in the early 1970s, leading to the report by Garrett and Garrison that was instrumental in stimulated restoration efforts there. These ruptures in the national story also led to a reimagining of the history of the West and the narrative Americans tell themselves about it. Scholars of public history, cultural memory, and the US West led the charge in academia to reveal the ideological underpinnings of the narrative of the West and include voices that had been silenced for centuries.

Upheaval in America, revisionist westerns, and new western historians all reflected changes in attitudes about the past. The new western history in particular gained traction in the late 1980s and early 1990s and was featured in many a news article. Perhaps unintentionally, the publicity surrounding new western history seemed to touch off a renewed interest in the American West, even if the narrative had somewhat changed. The unprecedented success of *Dances with Wolves* (1990), followed by the critically acclaimed *Unforgiven* (1992), started a new trend of westerns that also renewed the focus on the region that had for twenty years been relegated to the periphery of the American experience.[57] But it was two other westerns in this time frame that had a direct and powerful impact on the small town of Tombstone, Arizona.

Tombstone (1993) and *Wyatt Earp* (1994)

The release of *Tombstone* in 1993 and *Wyatt Earp* in 1994 reinvigorated the significance of history and the popular culture West and renewed interest in Tombstone, Arizona. These two films did little to "revise" the genre or reflect consciously on notions of masculinity and violence that previously defined the western film but were imperative to resuscitating Wyatt Earp and revitalizing the town of Tombstone for modern audiences. In fact, these films may be the two biggest reasons the town has survived into the twenty-first century.

Like many of its predecessors, historic authenticity (both in its adherence to the tropes of the genre and in its devotion to accurately depicting the events) is fundamental to the presentation of the Earps, the town, and the Tombstone gunfight in the 1993 film *Tombstone*, directed by George B. Cosmatos and starring Kurt Russell and Val Kilmer. The film opens with a sepia-toned, fast-paced introduction choreographed to saloon-style piano music. The sequence provides a summary of recent events in Tombstone and the Arizona Territory that led up to the narrative starting point of the film: the arrival of the Earp brothers in Arizona. Voiced by western film legend Robert Mitchum, the introductory recitation explains that the end of the Civil War and resulting economic explosion brought a great migration west. This introduction is also meant to explain why Wyatt Earp as lawman is essential to the taming of the town of Tombstone and the West as a whole: with a great migration west, "cattle drovers turn cow towns into armed camps, with murder rates higher than those of modern-day New York or Los Angeles. . . . Attracted to this atmosphere of greed, over one hundred exiled Texas outlaws band together to form the ruthless gang recognized by the red sashes they wear. They emerge as the earliest example of organized crime in America. They call themselves, 'the Cowboys.'"[58]

At this point, a Cowboy faces the camera and shoots his pistol directly at the audience—a shot many may recognize from the 1903 film *The Great Train Robbery*. In fact, many of the shots in this opening sequence are lifted from that earlier film. Intertextuality—the complex interrelationship between texts, and the shaping of meaning of one text by others—is important to *Tombstone*; it is, in fact, essential to all westerns in maintaining certain codes and significations of meaning for audiences. The borrowing of shots from what is widely considered the first western film ever produced, and the use of Mitchum to narrate this opening sequence, lends *Tombstone* an air of authenticity, a component central, as we have seen, to the production of western films as well as to the town of Tombstone. Intertextuality in *Tombstone* goes beyond the genre as well: this opening sequence also connects the violence of the frontier to modern-day concerns of urban criminality. As Hutton argues, the audience is expected—whether consciously or not—to link the red sashes that identify the outlaw set in the film to the colors worn by gang members in inner-city Los Angeles in the early 1990s.[59] Wyatt Earp's vigilante justice, then, as represented in this film (like so many films before it), may be an answer to what seems to be an ineffective and impotent institutional legal apparatus.

If this introduction does not fully convince the audience that the "Cowboys" are cold-blooded, murderous desperados, the next scene further solidifies this characterization. The audience is brought to a Mexican wedding at a nameless border town. Johnny Ringo (Michael Biehn) and Curly Bill Brocius (Powers Boothe) ride into the plaza with their outlaw posse—red sashes visible—and shoot up the party after accusing the groom of killing two Cowboys. They are impervious to the screams of crying women and children; Ringo even shoots the priest as he quotes the Book of Revelation and prays for all of their souls. The scene then cuts to the train station in Tucson. Wyatt (Kurt Russell), his brothers Virgil (Sam Elliott) and Morgan (Bill Paxton), and their wives have arrived by rail to continue on to the boomtown of Tombstone to start a new life. Wyatt's reputation as a lawman precedes him, and he is immediately approached by the US marshal to join up with the law. While the real Wyatt does indeed become a lawman in Tombstone (briefly), just as in *My Darling Clementine*, Russell's Wyatt refuses; he is starting anew in Tombstone. It is worth noting that despite his refusal to become a lawman in Tombstone throughout the first half of the film, Wyatt continuously interferes when outlawry is afoot, pistol-whipping those men in town he feels are deserving. A certain amount of sanctimonious hypocrisy is very much a part of Wyatt's personality in this movie, a trait common among his representations in film and television throughout the twentieth century. Before moving through the depot, Wyatt makes his family stop to look at their reflection in a store window, the picture of the perfect and peaceful life he is expecting. This shot thus begins a relatively syrupy rendering of the traditional story of Wyatt Earp and the gunfight, with the exception of the final third of the film, which presents the vengeful aftermath of the fight. In fact, according to this film, it is through this rampage that Wyatt's mythic status as the ultimate hero of the West is solidified.

While it is clear that *Tombstone* was meant to provide a more accurate representation of Wyatt's time in Tombstone, the film relies heavily on mythic styling, resulting in an almost cloying interpretation of the events. There is constant juxtaposition between the "good guys" and the "bad guys" through actions and behaviors coded as either polished and civilized or vulgar and unrefined. For example, after the drunk and rowdy Cowboys shoot their pistols at the actors during a performance at the Birdcage Theatre, the Earp brothers have an existential discussion about God, spirituality, and death provoked by the performance of a scene from Faust that same night. The Earps and Doc Holliday (Val Kilmer) are presented as firmly entrenched in bourgeois aesthetics while the Cowboys are completely uncouth—with the exception of Johnny Ringo, who is clearly cultured and well educated. Doc and Ringo go head to head in an intellectual battle at a local saloon, speaking Latin to each other. "Obviously Mr. Ringo is an educated man," says Holliday. "Now I really hate him." The enmity between them is unambiguously articulated here, a hostility that follows the two throughout the remainder of the film.

In another cue taken from *My Darling Clementine*, Curly Bill starts shooting haphazardly in the town streets, not because he is drunk but because he has been smoking opium with Chinese Tombstonians (the only time the Chinese—who were a large part of the population of Tombstone in the 1880s—are presented in this film or any of the productions discussed in this study).[60] No one is bold enough to challenge and stop Brocius, not even Sheriff Behan. The town marshal, Fred White, finally and reluctantly confronts Brocius, but White is shot and killed. Non-lawman Wyatt is then forced to take care of things and take Brocius into custody. Doc, Virgil, and Morgan come to Wyatt's aid to ensure no further trouble ensues. (This particular historic event is reenacted on the streets of modern-day Tombstone to entertain tourists.) Despite his willingness to get involved, Wyatt is still set against becoming a lawman. His brother Virgil is the first of the brothers to feel obligated to impart some order on the town. Virgil replaces White as the town marshal, declares weapons illegal within the town's borders, and begins to bring some sense of order to Tombstone. Morgan agrees with Virgil's intentions and decides to help him. Wyatt, however, continues to resist pinning on the badge—right up to the moment of the famous showdown. In fact, Wyatt argues with his brothers and Doc as they walk toward the OK Corral that fighting the Cowboys "over a misdemeanor" (carrying firearms) is not worth the risk. In this film, Wyatt's assessment of the situation may be right. Beyond carrying firearms within town limits and Brocius killing Marshal White (a crime for which he is not charged), the only crimes the Cowboys as a unified gang seem to have committed within the borders of Tombstone have been a denunciation of the confines of civilized society, exhibited by their being constantly drunk, causing trouble, smoking opium, and perhaps getting emotional over card games. In fact, it is a dispute over a faro game with Doc Holliday that causes Ike Clanton to vow vengeance against him and the Earps. As they walk toward the OK Corral, Virgil counters Wyatt, "You're damn right I'll risk it. They're breaking the law." So Wyatt, the quintessential law enforcer of legend and archetypal western hero, is hesitant till moments before the gunfight. In this film, Virgil is the ultimate lawman; the promise of an ordered and civilized society rests with him. It is quite a shift from the Wyatt of *My Darling Clementine*;

while Fonda's Wyatt was initially uncertain about becoming a lawman, he does so within the first fifteen minutes of the film. In spite of his reluctance, Russell's Wyatt is still the star of *Tombstone* and still revered as the hero of the Old West.

The Earp myth is crystalized in *Tombstone* not through the gunfight but in its wake, when Wyatt goes on a mission to avenge the maiming of Virgil, who had been shot in the arm, and the death of his brother Morgan, who is killed in retaliation for the gunfight at the OK Corral. Wyatt now becomes a deputy US marshal—not to bring civilization to the Old West, as has been the overarching theme of this tale, but to bring wrath and punishment to those who wronged his family. Wyatt vows to kill anyone he sees wearing a red sash, telling Ike Clanton to let all the Cowboys know, "The law is coming! You tell them I'm coming! And Hell's coming with me!" He and Doc and some reformed Cowboys join forces to administer "frontier justice" in an attempt to clear the territory of lawlessness and brutality. Earp's vendetta ride, as shown in John Sturges's *Hour of the Gun* (1967) and now in *Tombstone* (and only hinted at in *Wyatt Earp*), depends heavily on Earp's ambiguity as an officer of the law, on his duel persona as both insider lawman and outsider gunslinger—but as one (*Hour of the Gun*) offers a critique of such violence, the other (*Tombstone*) celebrates that violence as the moment when the West is won and Earp becomes the western hero.

In this film, Wyatt Earp defends the dominant power structure constituted by institutions of law and order, domesticity, and capitalism—affirming the basic values of American society. Interestingly, he does so (to borrow a phrase from Richard Slotkin) *in the style of* an outlaw.[61] If Earp's legendary status is solidified through his vendetta ride, as *Tombstone* suggests, then this status is set by both upholding the law and stepping outside of its confines. He uses vigilante justice as a means to sustain the bourgeois ideal. Legitimizing violence and condemning it, at once lawman and outlaw: herein lies Earp's resilience. This is also a moment at which we glimpse both a nod to the tropes of the classic western and a reliance on revisionists—filmmakers and historians alike.

In the final moments of the film, we hear another voice-over by Mitchum wrapping up the Earp tale. He tells the audience that Wyatt and Josephine Marcus (Dana Delany)—the mistress of John Behan when she first arrived in Tombstone—"embarked on a series of adventures" (presumably after Wyatt abandoned Mattie Blaylock, his common-law wife who suffered from addiction and who, Mitchum neatly reveals, died of a drug overdose). According to this sentimental denouement, Wyatt and Josephine "never left each other's side" over the forty-seven years until Wyatt's death in 1929. The audience is told that movie legend Tom Mix was a pallbearer at Wyatt's funeral—an interesting moment when the friendship of a western film star serves to legitimize Wyatt's life as a western lawman rather than the other way around. The final words, "And Tom Mix wept," further solidify the relationship between movie star and western legend, between Hollywood and history. They also serve to establish the film's historicity, and Wyatt's status, in the popular imagination.

People tend to reference *Tombstone* more than *Wyatt Earp*, which failed at the box office but is the more historically accurate of the two films. "Lawrence Kasdan's *Wyatt Earp* is as self-important as *Tombstone* is unpretentious," Faragher argues. "Crawling along for more than three hours, it tells viewers far more than they ever wanted to know about Earp. The filmmakers clearly did their research well, taking their commitment to history seriously. Too seriously." Faragher makes clear that the significance of the Earp story lies far more in the meanings it articulates than in the "messy historical facts." He calls *Wyatt Earp* "lifeless," claiming that while it loads "us down with facts, it presents very little of what Earp's life might have *meant* and finally has nothing important to say."[62]

Tombstone was a box-office success, not despite but most probably because of the grittier personification of the famous lawman. Both films set out to demystify the standard portrayal of Earp and, in the process, create a character that resonated with audiences of the 1990s. Hutton writes that the writers and directors working on *Tombstone* and *Wyatt Earp* "were determined to expose the darker truth about Earp's career. Their revisionism came too late for the more truthful Earp they presented was not shocking to 1990s audiences. . . . Earp's murderous vendetta against the Tombstone cowboys actually proved a satisfying tonic to modern audiences fearful of rising crime rates and frustrated by legal red tape."[63] Philip Deloria, however, argues that *Tombstone* "reasserts the primacy of white male violence and the uninverted western, suggesting that traditional masculinity is the underpinning for the 'family values' on which society is founded."[64] As *Tombstone* presented a Wyatt Earp that made sense to modern audiences, it also remained true to the limitations of the western genre. Earp has most often served to assuage the fears surrounding a criminal faction that eschewed the rules of civilized society. While exposing the bloodier side of westward expansion and frontier justice, the Earp myth has also managed to reify order and authority as necessary to the progress of the nation.

Despite the fact that this film and its contemporary *Wyatt Earp* were produced more than twenty years ago, the influence of these films on the ways the place and the event are popularly understood cannot be overstated. For those experiencing Tombstone today, these two films stand as the most dominant representations of the town. Tourism in Tombstone experienced a massive resurgence after the release of these two films, and it has been riding that wave ever since. When asked what they think of when they hear the word "Tombstone," many people make reference to the movies.[65] "I'm your huckleberry" (possibly the most famous line from the 1993 film, spoken by Kilmer's Holliday) is often invoked along with mentions of Val Kilmer and "the movie" (meaning the movie *Tombstone*). Some people even watch the films before visiting Tombstone to learn the "history" of the town and to get an idea of what to expect when they arrive.[66] Beyond setting expectations for those planning to visit the town, both films are central to the ways Tombstone represents itself to visitors. References to the films throughout Tombstone and in the minds of the public underscore the importance of popular culture in crafting and perpetuating perceptions and understandings of the town and its history. These pop cultural productions, and the many other western films and television series that have been released since the early 1990s, all have a hand in maintaining interest in this old western town and set the expectations of visitors and potential visitors that Tombstone must then negotiate.[67] It is imperative that Tombstone measures up to those expectations: it must "do" the Old West better than other western towns, or at least as well as Hollywood, all while maintaining its historical integrity.

As we have seen, the simplicity of the Earp narrative has allowed for its continued recitation. But the cultural and social underpinnings of the story are far from simple. In fact, the depth of the story has allowed Wyatt to be reformulated as representing both insider and outsider; both lawman and vigilante; and, in some cases, both savior and murderer. Despite these varying interpretations, Wyatt remains the quintessential western hero—a hero whose shortcomings can be forgiven if he continually rids the West of its savage elements. Every hero of western film can in some way reflect back to him. The same is true for the town of Tombstone. Wyatt put Tombstone on the map; popular culture has kept it there. It now is considered by many to be the quintessential western town, the reflection of which can be seen in every western film and television show produced in the past seventy years.

4

The Global Mythic West

Tombstone, the OK Corral, and Wyatt Earp have figured largely in global conceptions of the Wild West almost since the year Ed Schieffelin christened his first mine there. While mythologized stories of the frontier had been popular in Europe prior to Tombstone's founding, the publicity surrounding the street fight behind the OK Corral contributed to a sense that the West was a place of wildness and danger, of outlaws and lawmen, of opportunity and adventure. What better ways to express this mythic landscape than with the names "Tombstone," "OK Corral," and "Wyatt Earp" (not to mention "Johnny Ringo" and "Doc Holliday")—names that seem ready-made for folklore? In fact, while any reference to the Old West can affect the power and sustainability of the town of Tombstone, these names have in many ways become synecdoche for the Wild West worldwide and have found various uses throughout Europe and Japan for those looking to experience the West of legend and others looking to profit from that experience.

Just as in the town of Tombstone, central to discussions around global productions of the Tombstone or western myth is the concept of authenticity. Are western films produced in Europe true westerns or mere imitations? Can western towns in Europe offer an authentic experience to visitors? The question about authenticity that has plagued Tombstone for decades finds similar expression in a global context. As we discuss notions of authenticity and the meanings articulated and inferred in an academic sense, it is clear that on the quotidian level, Tombstone and its history have provided international filmmakers, theme park owners, and western-style heritage site and museum proprietors fodder for their businesses, and audiences signifiers of the Old West. At the same time, those places and people relying on the "Tombstone" brand around the world have contributed to keeping Tombstone relevant and afloat as well.

One of the first mentions of Tombstone in a British newspaper was on 22 May 1880, when the *Leeds Mercury* printed an article on page 1 titled "The New El Dorado: Tombstone in Arizona." While the author admits that such a moniker might typically connote a town in the "process of decay, that its hills are deserted and its houses in ruins, and that the dead in its cemeteries outnumber the living in its streets," nothing, he says, could be further from the truth: "despite its lugubrious title," the "picture is not in shadow but in sunshine. Tombstone is in its infancy of its growth. It has only just sprung into being. It is a germ of prosperity, and from its development great results are expected."[1] The piece has a number of the elements that Londoners had already come to know of the American West: the extreme temperatures found in the desert (while noting that Tombstone's elevation of about five thousand feet keeps it cooler than Tucson—"pronounced Took-sohn"), the aridity of the area, and of course a discussion of the gambling houses and saloons that had popped up within a year of the town's founding.

In September 1883 another article with ties to Tombstone, titled "American Cow-Boys," appeared in a West Yorkshire newspaper, the *Hadderfield Daily Chronicle*, clarifying for its readers what the term "cow-boy" means in the United States. It quotes first mayor of Tombstone and former editor of the *Tombstone Epitaph* John P. Clum, who describes cowboys (as well as editors and "a few other renegades") as "the classes who principally amuse themselves with revolvers, bowie knives, and shot-guns in that quarter of the States." In an attempt to explain the cowboys' reputation, the author writes, "The fact that they are employed only half the year in the regular occupation of cattle-driving may help to account for this other fact, that they are given on occasion to train-wrecking and similar desperate diversions. Such indeed is the reputation they have acquired, that cow-boy, as used in America, is synonymous with desperado." The author then recounts a story about "Curley [*sic*] Bill" Brocius, the Cowboy who shot Fred White, first town marshal of Tombstone and known ally of the Earp brothers, on the town's streets in 1880; had participated in the assassination of Wyatt Earp's brother Morgan in March 1882; and was said to be killed by Wyatt Earp that same month—according to Wyatt himself.[2] The story about Brocius in the article recounts an event that does not seem plausible, as it states that Brocius was killed in Shakespeare, New Mexico, in October 1882 by a man named "Wallace" (perhaps Jim Wallace, a friend of Brocius and fellow desperado) in retaliation for Brocius killing Wallace's friend "Barter" (perhaps Richard "Rattlesnake Dick" Barter, a horse rustler in California who was killed in 1859 by a sheriff named J. Boggs). The validity of the story notwithstanding, the article is interesting in that it perpetuates specific ideas about the American West to Britons, and two of the names mentioned have direct connections to Wyatt Earp and the Tombstone, Arizona, of the early 1880s, though Tombstone is not the focus of the piece.[3]

British newspapers also reported on the fires that wreaked havoc on Tombstone in the 1880s. *The Bristol Mercury and Daily Post*, for example, contained an item in its "News of the Day" section reporting that "destructive fires have occurred at Leadville, Colorado, and at Tombstone, Arizona. Losses nearly one million dollars."[4] And the March 1884 hanging at the Cochise County Courthouse in Tombstone of the five "bandits" responsible for the Bisbee Massacre was reported in the *Derby Daily Telegraph, Yorkshire Post and Leeds Intelligencer, Edinburgh Evening News, Stamford (Lincolnshire) Mercury*, and Scottish *Aberdeen People's Journal*.[5]

Tombstone's fame also benefited from the tremendous popularity Buffalo Bill Cody enjoyed during his tours throughout Europe. In 1886 Cody was invited to perform with his Wild West show at London's American Exhibition in the Earls Court complex. A number of London's elite visited Cody's encampment prior to the show's opening, including the Prince of Wales, and many more attended the show itself, including Queen Victoria, who, according to Cody's publicist John Burke, stood and bowed during the opening ceremony when a rider entered the arena with the American flag. While it seems that Burke may have been stretching the facts with the story of the queen bowing in reverence to the flag during "The Star Spangled Banner," these stories, as Louis S. Warren points out, were entertaining and powerful in that they validated the American nation in the eyes of its former colonizer, the monarch of which at the very least was charmed by the narrative of America's frontier history, American entertainment, and American culture.[6] When Buffalo Bill's Wild West performed for the Queen's Jubilee Day celebrations, the event was attended by an assortment of heads of state, various princes and princesses, and of course England's royal family. Over the next number of years, the Wild West show traveled through France, Spain, Italy, and Germany, playing to crowds as large as ten thousand for up to eight days in major cities. "By the time Cody returned to England for another command performance for Queen Victoria," Robert Rydell and Rob Kroes explain, "his show had earned a reputation on both sides of the Atlantic for its 'authentic' representation of the American West and for inspiring dreams of freedom in European societies that seemed locked into class-based social hierarchies."[7]

As we have seen, while Buffalo Bill's Wild West was not the first time Europeans came into contact with the mythic West, his show was by far the most popular articulation of the stories and ideologies connected with the ever-shifting American frontier. But something in Cody's productions changed in the later years of the nineteenth century: audiences were coming into contact with a hybrid "West," one not solely representative of America and her ideals but one that now articulated values that coincided with those found in other nations. Productions became amalgams of the stories of empire and conquest found globally. Buffalo Bill began incorporating signifiers of different exotic "others" into his pageants in the 1890s, including "twelve Cossacks and six Argentine gauchos, as well as two detachments of regular European cavalry—twenty Germans, and twenty English."[8] This internationalization may have contributed to the success of German author Karl May, whose two-thousand-page "Winnetou" series released in 1893 featured "a German immigrant to the American West, Old Shatterhand, [who] out-lassos, out-hunts, out-shoots and finally out-wits Yankees and Indians alike." In Lone Ranger style, May included a faithful Native partner for Old Shatterhand named Winnetou, "the stoical 'red gentleman.'" By doing so, "May had created both a patriotic [German] epic and a popular monument to the Native American race."[9] With 80 million copies of his work in circulation, translated into more than thirty languages, and a number of film adaptations of his novels, Karl May is arguably the most popular German novelist of all time. As such, German studies scholar Susanne Zantop argues, "May's works, since their inception, have generated a whole culture industry that almost obsessively reiterates and thereby reproduces the idea of a special affinity between Germans and Native Americans based on shared experience."[10]

The "West" then came to represent not solely the American frontier but that space west of the imagination that could encompass the imperialist and colonial ideologies of nations around the globe looking to make sense of a modernizing world and define their place in a global context. Exported and reproduced outside of the borders of the American nation for more than a century now, the western myth has carried with it notions of, as Richard Slotkin puts it, "wide-open land of unlimited opportunity for the strong, ambitious, self-reliant individual to thrust his way to the top."[11] From rodeos staged throughout the world, to western films produced in Russia, France, Germany, Italy, Spain, India, and Australia, to hobbyist groups throughout Europe, to the Wild West show at Disneyland in Paris and Westernland at Tokyo Disney, to the (originally) German-owned Apache Spirit Ranch (now Tombstone Monument Ranch) in Arizona, the West of the imagination has been adopted on a global scale. That the West has become a global space speaks to its adaptability and salience to people who do not necessarily have a physical connection or cultural attachment to the United States.[12] Despite the contention that the American West is the story of the American nation or articulates purely American experience, the narrative and its ideological elements have resonated worldwide. As Michael Steiner reminds us, "Endlessly malleable for every need, the frontier has far more power as an ongoing story than it did as an actual experience."[13] And by Patricia Limerick's account, "The idea of the frontier and the pioneer have clearly become a kind of multicultural common property, a joint-stock company of the imagination."[14]

Not only are international audiences and travelers intrigued with images of the frontier, but they are also employing the central precepts of the mythic West in these new cultural contexts, making use of the dialectic and polemic possibilities the mythic West offers. International producers and consumers are making use of those parts of the narrative that appeal the most to them, retooling and reinterpreting them in ways that make sense. Kroes believes there are "crucial questions of mediation and reception, questions to do with the manifold ways in which people at the receiving end recontextualize American culture as it reaches them" that must be addressed.[15] In other words, American culture is both crucial to and secondary in the ways people around the world reinterpret the messages it transmits. Kroes and others strongly assert that European appropriation of American culture has everything to do with their notions of their own cultures and identities and less to do with their perceptions of the United States. Mary Yoko Brannen has a similar perspective: "I posit that what is missing in our knowledge base is an understanding of the process of recontextualization. . . . In order to understand recontextualization, we need to not only examine the process of transnational transmission but also develop a deeper understanding of the dynamics of host country reception."[16]

Indeed, a tour throughout Europe and Japan reveals a devotion to the ideals of the mythic West as well as Wyatt Earp and demonstrates the broad appeal of Tombstone and the West to audiences well beyond US borders. Western-style films have been produced internationally since the early twentieth century, and a number of western-themed towns and amusement parks around the world claim a connection to the frontier fantasy that some argue is most or only relevant to Americans. The continuing fascination with the West as a mythic space on a global scale is evident in the myriad ways the myth circulates, including these films and western-themed towns and destinations, built environments that offer a third dimension to visitors' preconceived notions and whimsy about the mythic West partially constructed through the films produced in the United States for generations. These movies and places stand as testaments to not only the resonance of Tombstone and Wyatt Earp but also the ongoing fascination with and celebration of the ideals, principles, and values that undergird the West of the imagination.

The Frontier and International Cinema

As in the United States, a principal way people around the world consume images of the mythic West has been and continues to be through film. Since the very early years of cinema, film and television series have had a tremendous impact on Tombstone's success as a tourist destination and have helped sustain western-themed towns globally as well. One of the earliest westerns ever produced was the French western *Le Cowboy*, directed by Joë (Jean) Hamman and released in 1906.[17] The transnationalization of the West—or the flow of the western myth between and among the different nations of the world—continued throughout the twentieth century. Westerns were produced in Germany in the 1920s and 1930s fueled by a "long-standing German occupation with the iconography of the Far West," which allowed audiences to come to terms with "Germany's abrupt step into the age of machines, urban traffic, democratic will formation, and mechanical reproduction."[18] Japanese filmmaker Akira Kurosawa, American filmmaker John Sturges, and Italian filmmaker Sergio Leone traded plot lines in the 1950s and 1960s. American actor Clint Eastwood starred in Leone's "Man with No Name" series, all shot in Spain; French actor Pierre Brice played the Mescalero Apache chief Winnetou in the German films of the 1960s adapted from the books of Karl May; American singer and actor Dean Reed starred in a number of East German westerns in the 1970s; and Yugoslav actor Gojko Mitic portrayed Native Americans fighting white villains in East German *Indianerfilme*.

Western film scholar Christopher Frayling argues that the context within which each non-US film was made (cinematic tradition, social and cultural ideologies, cultural belief language) informed the production of the films as well as made them meaningful to audiences in specific nations. For example, specifically European themes played a key role in the revival of German westerns of the 1960s and 1970s: the noble savage or the theme of gold or the mighty dollar as a neglected symbol of the implications of the western myth. In his quest to show how the cultural context within which these films were made informs the films as much or more than the American cultural component, Frayling goes into detail about why Germans connected so readily with the myth of the West and with the Indian, especially the influence of our old friend Karl May. He also discusses in depth the romance Italians had for westerns in the 1960s. Frayling reveals the "Italianization" of the western, and the ways that Italian history, Italian culture, and Italian cinema not only greatly influenced the production of Italian westerns but also made them meaningful to Italian audiences. "Perhaps it is politically significant," he writes, "that Italy, like Japan and Germany, should produce 'westerns' in which the hero lives on his wits, prefers survival to honour, revenge to social morality, and has little faith in the 'progressive' aspects of the era in which he lives—this is an atmosphere of extreme brutality: for all three were defeated nations in the Second World War. 'Axis westerns' so to speak."[19]

European filmmakers were developing and exploring their own genre, one of critical cinema—using the western as the formula while deconstructing and commenting on the ideologies and conventions of the original. In many ways, though, non-US westerns aided the progression and evolution of the genre by heightening the violence aesthetic and producing heroes that did not fit easily within the good-evil binary, something US audiences were also after—and something representations of Wyatt Earp also experienced. Indeed, British film scholar Edward Buscombe credits the revival of the western genre in the United States in the 1960s to directors, writers, and audiences outside the United States. Frayling similarly argues that the "significant resurgence in popularity of the (American) western film" revealed in the 1967 Hollywood production total (thirty-seven) "was largely due to the impact of the international western."[20] Of the films that had the most influence in that time frame were those by Japanese filmmaker Akira Kurosawa, specifically *Seven Samurai* (1954), which was remade into the US production of the *Magnificent Seven* (1960), and *Yojimbo* (1961), which was the basis for Leone's *Fistful of Dollars* (1964); westerns by Sergio Leone; and the German Winnetou films based on May's novels.[21] Buscombe highlights the aesthetic of violence of, specifically, Italian westerns, saying "Italian directors displayed a fascination with the violence which was inherent in the dramatic tensions the Western had traditionally explored. . . . This was developed by the Italians into a fully-fledged obsession, taken to extremes of parodic excess."[22] Violence, whether regenerative or purely poetic, is a large component of non-US western films of this time period—taking their cue from the ways violence had been glorified in traditional narratives and representations of the westward movement in the United States. The violence on the frontier translated into stylistically excessive and artistic violence on the screen. Sergio Leone made this approach to western filmmaking famous, an approach that has been used ever since.

Tombstone and Wyatt Earp have figured into these international westerns for decades, most notably during the 1960s, when Leone and his signature style were gaining popularity in Italy. *Cavalca e uccidi (Ride and Kill)*, a Spanish western directed by José Louis Borau and released in 1964, portrays a group of corrupt Tombstone officials extorting money from the town's citizens in exchange for protection. When the sheriff tries to intervene, he is killed by the officials' gunman and replaced by someone the gangsters think they can control: the town drunk. *Gunmen of the Rio Grande*, an Italian western directed by Tulio Demicheli and released in 1965, tells the story of US marshal Wyatt Earp, who is sent to a lawless mining town on the US-Mexico border to rid the place of its outlaw element and protect the beautiful saloonkeeper from bandits. Italian western *La Grande Notte di Ringo*, also released in 1965, begins with the robbery of a stagecoach on its way to a bank in Tombstone. Another Italian western, *Black Killer* (1971), portrays the citizens of Tombstone, assailed by the five outlaw O'Hara brothers, seeking justice through the newly established institutions of law and authority. Clearly these films are using names of people and places that are familiar to their audiences, even if the narratives are not at all based on history. Again, the terms "Tombstone" and "Wyatt Earp" (and in other cases, "Johnny Ringo," "Doc Holliday," and "Curly Bill") evoke notions of the Old West even in these distant regions of Europe almost a century after the event that put Tombstone on the map and propelled Earp into American national consciousness.

More recently, in 2011, French film students at Ecole supérieure des métiers artistiques (ESMA) in Toulouse garnered international attention for their animated tribute to (Italian) westerns with their short film *Little Tombstone*, a film that uses Tombstone as the archetypal setting for violence and corruption in the Old West. The film won critical acclaim in France, Italy, Spain, Switzerland, England, Tokyo, China, Korea, Ukraine, and the United States.[23] *Little Tombstone* marks a return to the aesthetic violence so often utilized in westerns of the 1960s and 1970s, particularly spaghetti westerns produced in Italy but also referenced in Mexican American filmmaker Robert Rodriguez's *El Mariachi* trilogy, released in the 1990s and 2000s.[24] That Tombstone is not only referenced but is the central way in which these French film students chose to signify their short film as a "western" speaks to the centrality of Tombstone to popular conceptions of the Wild West internationally.

The aesthetic of violence shown in *Little Tombstone* and captured by Leone and Rodriguez is nothing new to Japanese filmmakers, whose samurai films have brought blood spatter and mutilation, first in black and white and then in Technicolor, to Japanese audiences for decades. In 2007 a western-style film utilizing that same tradition was produced in Japan and has been playing at theaters there ever since. *Sukiyaki Western Django*, directed by Japanese horror moviemaker Takashi Miike, relies on the poetic violence of Leone's "Man with No Name" series as well as on the aesthetics of Japanese cinema.[25] But it also bases its narrative on Japanese history and symbols that draw from Akira Kurosawa's *Yojimbo* films. Its name is even a combination of Japanese cuisine (sukiyaki) and the film *Django*, a spaghetti western directed by Italian director Sergio Corbucci, released in 1966. This cultural mingling is important as we attempt to understand how these tropes resonate with Japanese audiences, but it is also seamless.

Borrowing from samurai tradition (and Kurosawa's samurai films), the film is inspired by the historical rivalry between the imperial family (Genji) and the samurai clans (Heike) beginning in the eighth century. *Sukiyaki Western Django* is set "a few hundred years after the Genpei War," a conflict in the late twelfth century that saw the defeat of the samurai and the rise of the shogunate (military dictators). In a similar plotline to Kurosawa's *Yojimbo* and Leone's *Fistful of Dollars*, a lone gunman comes upon a remote mountain town named "Yuta" in "Nevata" where two gangs—the Whites and the Reds—remain faithful to political factions that seem irrelevant in this isolated space. Another key component to the rivalry is the treasure said to be hidden somewhere in town. Each gang attempts to win the loyalty of the quick-drawing gunman, who ends up playing both sides in an attempt to rescue a female gunslinger, now a prostitute, and her son, mute from the trauma of witnessing his father's murder. Even though *Sukiyaki Western Django* does not reference Tombstone or Wyatt Earp directly, its relevance lies in its reconfiguration of the western myth and the way it has resonated with Japanese audiences, which have been enticed by the West for generations and who continue to explore the ways Japanese history and culture meld with the elements of the Old West.

While many of the western-style films produced outside of the United States mimic the themes of American westerns, such as individuality, freedom, and fortitude, other western-style films—particularly those produced in the former Soviet Union—inverted the messages and meanings of the typical American western to critique more pointedly American ideologies that US westerns tended to espouse. We have already discussed the relevance of Karl May to Tombstone, but it is worth noting that, despite Karl

May's popularity in Germany prior to World War II, in 1940, German novelist and social critic Klaus Mann proclaimed May "the cowboy mentor of the Führer."[26] At the conclusion of World War II, in 1946, the Soviet military government founded DEFA (Deutsche Film AG) in the newly formed East Germany. It remained the only film-producing entity in East Germany for more than forty years. DEFA was entirely subsidized and controlled by the state, and while there were no censorship rules in place per se, all films had to be approved by the Ministry for Culture.[27] In 1952 party leaders introduced a new doctrine in filmmaking: "to intensify the 'methods of socialist realism,' using 'positive heroes' and dealing more with 'problems of the German working-class movement.'"[28]

Construction of the Berlin Wall began in 1961 with one particular story producing some of the most vivid photographs of an event that illustrated the system that was in place there: on October 22 (almost exactly eighty years since the gunfight outside the OK Corral), a quarrel between an East German border guard and an American official on his way to the opera in East Berlin led to American and Soviet tanks facing off at Checkpoint Charlie for sixteen hours. It nearly turned into what one observer at the time called "a nuclear-age equivalent of the Wild West Showdown at the OK Corral," broadly understood as a confrontation of epic proportions.[29] After that altercation and well-known Tombstone reference, East German party officials hoped to strengthen the expression both of socialist realism and anti-Americanism, banning films that did not comply. Karl May had been labeled a fascist in East Germany, and his works were rejected and replaced with those that conformed more with the socialist realism party leaders demanded. As a result, DEFA began making *Indianerfilme*, which did not challenge Soviet directives and, in fact, whose ideological goal, according to Gerd Gemünden, "was to articulate an unspoken critique of the colonialism and racism that fueled the westward expansion in the United States."[30] Further, he argues, "Not surprisingly, in the DEFA films, the various responses of the Indian tribes to the ever-advancing Western frontier of the United States look like a blueprint for a better socialist Germany."[31]

Perhaps the East German film that is most closely tied to 1880s Arizona is Gottfried Kolditz's *Apaches* (1973), one of East Germany's *Indianerfilme* based loosely on the legend of Apache warrior Ulzana and possibly posited as a response to the Indian chief portrayed in Robert Aldrich's film *Ulzana's Raid* (1972). In Aldrich's film, though considered a revisionist western, Ulzana and his men go on a vicious rampage against white settlers. In the East German film the Apaches are portrayed as victims of American imperialists who are motivated by greed and violence. As tensions mount between the

United States and Mexico in what would eventually erupt into the Mexican-American War, Ulzana sets out to avenge his tribe's massacre at the hands of an American mining engineer. Ulzana is played by Gojko Mitic, whose characters, according to Gerd Gemünden, offer "a fantasy designed to resonate with the commitment to antifascism, the founding principle, or foundational fiction, of the GDR."[32]

Other *Indianerfilme* include *Sons of the Great Bear* (1966), *White Wolves* (1968), *The Falcon's Trail* (1968), *Fatal Error* (1969), *Osceola* (1971), *Tecumseh* (1972), *Ulzana* (1973), *Blood Brothers* (1975), *Severino* (1978), *The Scout* (1982), and *Atkins* (1985). Two more westerns were produced in East Germany during the Cold War, but they were not *Indianerfilme*: *Kit & Co.* (1974) and *Sing Cowboy Sing* (1981), both starring American musician/actor Dean Reed, whose socialist political views were well known and who resettled in East Germany in 1973. The celebration of the struggle for survival and the critique of US policy (ironically accomplished by turning the myth of the American West on its head) resonated with East German audiences through their affinity for an imagined connection to Native Americans. These westerns also echoed the popular ethos of progress in the face of tremendous odds and demonstrated the contempt for the racist policies enacted by the United States during westward expansion and during the civil rights struggle of the 1960s—thereby having the added benefit of distancing East Germany from its Nazi past and its capitalist cousins to the west. Soviet westerns were also produced in Russia, Czechoslovakia, Lithuania, Romania, Uzbekistan, and Kyrgyzstan beginning in the silent era (*The Extraordinary Adventures of Mr. West in the Land of the Bolsheviks* [1924]) and continuing into the early 1980s. These films elicited tropes familiar to the genre while still promoting ideologies that many interpret as being in direct opposition to those advocated by filmmakers in the United States. Soviet westerns work similarly to the ways Wyatt Earp has operated in western films and television shows throughout the twentieth century. As both lawman and outlaw, insider and outsider, he has served to signify all the greatness and inadequacies of America at different cultural and historical moments—remaining relevant no matter the portrayal and giving expression to both the celebration and criticism of the ideals of America.

Theme Parks and Western Towns in Europe and Japan

While western films might be one of the most widely consumed representations of the West—both those from Hollywood and those produced in the nations in which their audiences reside—the Old West is also consumed in other ways. Western-themed towns and amusement parks have been built from England to Japan, offering a third dimension to the two-dimensional imaginings of the American West. These towns and parks allow travelers to live out their Wild West fantasies in much the same way Tombstone does for its own visitors. Similarly to Tombstone, in addition to family fun and entertainment, much of their marketing is geared toward emphasizing authenticity in experience as well as an educational component that has been very much a part of the strategy of US heritage and open-air museums for decades.

Disney theme parks do not specifically reference Wyatt Earp or Tombstone, but they have approached the construction of their western-themed areas with an understanding of the power of the frontier myth and the built environment, and they contribute to the continued circulation of and romantic fascination with the American West. Disney theme parks have become some of the top tourist destinations globally. According to *Travel+ Leisure* magazine, as of October 2011, of the world's fifty most-visited tourist destinations, Disney World's Magic Kingdom in Orlando, Florida; Disneyland Park in Anaheim, California; and Tokyo Disneyland rank eighth, ninth, and eleventh, respectively, while Disneyland Paris ranks seventeenth. Tokyo Disneyland attracts 14.5 million visitors per year; Disneyland Paris, 10.5 million per year. By far the most popular attractions at Disney parks in Paris and Tokyo are the western-themed Frontierland and Westernland. Frontierland at Disneyland Paris and Westernland at Tokyo Disney are based on Frontierland at the original Disneyland in Anaheim, California, which built-environment scholar Michael Steiner calls "the prototype for the architectural merchandising of the frontier myth."[33] It can also be called the model for the ways three-dimensional experience informs understandings of the frontier myth itself. The idea of the built environment affecting experience is central to understanding how western-themed sections of the Disney theme parks and western towns throughout Europe and the United States, including Tombstone, continue to draw visitors.

Visitors to Disneyland Paris can attend "Buffalo Bill's Wild West Show with Mickey and Friends," which opened in 1992 and is the most popular attraction at the park. Buffalo Bill, Sitting Bull, Annie Oakley, and the Rough Riders are joined by Mickey and friends, who "invite spectators to share in their adventures across the American Wild West" and "see how the West was won."[34] Despite, or possibly because of, stretching the historical truth by inserting Mickey Mouse and friends into the story of the settlement of the West, this show has welcomed more than 9 million spectators since its opening. The seamless marriage of Buffalo Bill and Mickey Mouse—two of America's most popular imports—speaks volumes about the ways the mythic West is inextricably linked to a consumer- and commodity-driven culture.

Buffalo Bill's Wild West has been part of Disneyland Paris since the park opened in 1992, thirty-seven years after the original Disneyland theme park opened in Anaheim, California, with Frontierland as one of its main attractions. Steiner asserts that "the transnational lure of the mythic West is embodied in the multitudes who forsake French cuisine to chow down on barbecue ribs, chili, and grits at the antler-festooned Chuckwagon Cafe or who eagerly stay at Antoine Predock's pseudo sunbaked Santa Fe Hotel, where French staff members outfitted as cowpunchers say 'howdy' at the drop of a hat." While it is "a long way from Crockett's rustic stockade in Anaheim to Predock's enigmatic pueblo in Marne-la-Vallée," Steiner argues, "both places indicate that the frontier is America's most potent myth and Disney its most effective merchandiser."[35]

The western myth as articulated by the Disney Corporation has been equally salient in Tokyo. Those present on opening day in April 1983, "many wearing ten gallon hats and cowboy boots," waited for "the Western River Railroad, the Mark Twain riverboat ride, or the southern fried chicken served at the Lucky Nugget Cafe in Westernland." The conflation of signifiers of the American West with those of the American South seems inconsequential, as the overall articulation and sensation of "westernness" are what matter most. Already well versed in American western lore as well as in the consumer world of Disney, the Japanese flock to Westernland, which, Steiner argues, "was designed to provide crowded island-bound people—especially Japanese men—with the illusion of open space and plenty of swagger-room where good always defeats evil."[36] It is clear that the symbols that many associate with the American West have tremendous power in Japan. It is important to resist assuming that this sway is purely in celebration of the American nation. Indeed, cultural studies scholar Masako Notoji argues that Tokyo Disney is a celebration of *Japanese* nationalism, a space in which to extol the virtues of Japan and appreciate how far they have come from the privation of war.[37] Westernland makes great use of the signifiers of freedom and masculinity, ideals that have cultural significance far beyond the borders of the United States.

Tapping into Japan's desire to explore the themes bound to the Old West was Kenichi Ominami, owner of Western Village, a Wild West theme park in rural Japan in a town called Imaichi. Before the park closed in 2007, "750,000 visitors annually [took] stagecoach rides and [ate] chuckwagon barbecue."[38] Ominami opened the park in the 1970s on four acres of family land. The space opened as a campground, where people could fish in the pond, go horseback riding, and take lasso lessons. In 1975 he expanded the ranch to what would become Western Village, with "all wooden façades, horses, and dusty thoroughfares, as though you'd stepped onto the set of a John Ford Western."[39] Takeui Yoshida, head of Western Village's overseas marketing when the park was still operational, remarked that "the Japanese are fascinated with the idea of the US West, the ingenuity of the pioneers, and the freedom and wide open spaces they sought. It's a contrast to the controlled Japanese regimen of living, where space is so carefully planned."[40] The dialectic of personal, lived experience in a controlled Japan with limited space and that of the freedom and wide-open spaces articulated through symbols of the American West is imperative to comprehending the impact of these symbols on Japanese visitors to Western Village, but also on Ominami himself. He explains, "When I was a child I would go to the movies and see American westerns. . . . I watched *Rawhide* on television." Of course the Earp-Clanton fight is referenced as part of the experience of Western Village as well. During the park's heyday, "Japanese cowboys stage[d] mock gunfights, performing a sort of Far East equivalent of the Shootout At The OK Corral." Hollywood is also mentioned as part of the experience, as "a Stagecoach-era John Wayne with cyborg heart exposed stands by the park entrance," and "hidden away in the Sheriff's office, Clint Eastwood drawls in lazy Japanese about how he ran the bad guys out of town."[41] After visiting South Dakota to buy props for Western Village after seeing *Dances with Wolves* (1990), Ominami spent $27 million on the construction of a replica of Mount Rushmore. In another example of the ways the mythic West flows outside the United States, then back again, on hearing of the reproduction, South Dakota officials named Ominami honorary governor of South Dakota, and Rapid City and Imaichi became sister cities. After almost forty years, Western Village closed in 2007, after being foreclosed in 2006 and finding it too expensive to reopen, perhaps due to its remote location and years of competition with Tokyo Disney. Ruins of its former self remain, lending it an air of even more authenticity as a true ghost town.[42]

Western-themed towns are also found in other countries throughout Europe. One such place is Laredo Western Town in Kent, England. As in Tombstone, and unlike Western Village in Japan or Disneyland in Tokyo or Paris, Laredo Western Town presents itself as faithfully representing the American past. The town asserts that it portrays the "American Wild West, as it would have been in 1860 to 1890" with a saloon, marshal's office, courthouse, gunsmith, Wells Fargo bank, photography studio, undertaker, mining company, and dentist.[43] Laredo Western Town claims to be "the most authentic in ENGLAND & EUROPE." Billing itself as "the one and only true western town in the UK," Laredo Western Town markets itself specifically for events or to studios that can film there "inside and out," which "makes things easier" because it saves "valuable studio time." Its website proudly declares that it "has been used for filming with look-alikes Clint Eastwood, John Wayne, Lee Van Cleef, Steve McQueen and Yul Brynner" and can be visited by appointment only. It is ironic that Laredo Western Town's "authenticity" rests in the hands of "look-alikes" of Hollywood actors and not real frontiersmen. Further, that this town is not really open to the public but only accessed via reservation seems to confound the basic tenets of the openness of the frontier and the freedom espoused by the frontier myth.

Another western-themed town in Britain is Deadwood Western Town, located on Wattlehurst Farm in Surrey and, of course, named for Deadwood, South Dakota, itself a western town on the National Register of Historic Places and open for business. Unlike the original Deadwood, however, Deadwood Western Town in Surrey is a complete replica, though it still claims authenticity of experience for visitors. Its logo—an American bald eagle—declares "Go Western: Line Dancing, Authentic Camping, Theme Weekends."[44] The town was built by a "group of western re-enactors" who had hoped to recreate "a typical old west town of the 1870's–1880's." Visitors are welcome "on open weekends between 10 am and 5 pm, [to] look around inside the buildings and meet the towns folk, who love to chat about the history and creation of the town." In addition to regular weekends, the town holds what its creators call "authentic weekends . . . when westerners camp in authentic tents on a field just outside the town." Authenticity is important to the "re-enactors" at Wattlehurst Farm: "All visitors are . . . invited to camp over night with their authentic tents on the authentic field." As in Laredo Western Town in Kent, Deadwood Western Town includes a saloon, blacksmith shop, schoolhouse, bank, gunsmith, Western Union office, trading post, general store, marshal's office, and a small "Boot Hill" graveyard, perhaps a nod to Tombstone, Arizona. Inside the buildings, visitors "will find wood burning stoves, oil burning lamps, and general decor of how the buildings would have been back in the 1880's." The town also presents an interesting exhibit of a "poor Irish immigrant's encampment who migrated from his home land escaping the Great Irish Famine, 1845/1850 'An Gorta Mor' [which means the Great Irish Famine in Irish] seeking fame and fortune in them thar black hill's [sic] of Dakota!"[45] This is a moment at which the creators of Deadwood Western Town are claiming some legitimate personal experience, connecting with the droves of people who migrated to the American West in the mid-nineteenth century. They are also recovering the West somehow, bringing it back to England in a tangible way for their visitors.

In the south of France, located in the Bouches-du-Rhône region between Marseille and Toulon, a western-themed amusement park called the OK Corral (where overnight guests can stay at Le Monde des Tipis [Tipi World]) opened in 1966. The French version of the OK Corral more specifically references Tombstone and the 1881 gun battle between the Earps and the Clantons that made the town famous; there is even a Tombstone Saloon. Unlike Laredo and Deadwood Western Towns in the United Kingdom, the OK Corral in France does not declare itself an "authentic" representation of the Old West, although it is a place "where the family can enjoy a return to America's heyday." The park in fact models itself more after Disneyland, with roller coasters, boat rides, and "Splash Mountain."[46] Other rides are named the Hopi Snake, the Black Eagle, Mountains of the Grand Canyon, Sitting Bull's Teepee, the Rodeo, Crazy Horse, the Colorado Rapids, and Mexican Twist. In addition to rides, the OK Corral also "specialize[s] in re-enactments of some famous western stories, including the gunfight at the OK Corral, which will have the youngsters enthralled."[47] Further, "visitors can also watch the most famous scenes of the Conquest of the West at the Silver Dollar City show area which opened in 2010."[48] Families are invited to stay on the park's grounds, "in one of the teepees provided by the park [which] accommodate up to 2 adults and 4 children." Of course, these "tee-pees" are equipped with modern amenities "that a Native American would be envious of (kitchen area, electric lighting, separate toilet for each teepee and a site swimming pool)."[49] The OK Corral theme park is approximately 484 miles from Disneyland Paris, and it seems to be satisfying a desire of residents and visitors in the south of France—who flock to the theme park in the hundreds of thousands every year—to experience something they might consider akin to the Old West.[50]

Similar frontier-style towns are found in Austria (No Name City), Czech Republic (Wild West City, Šiklův mlýn), Spain (Oasys Theme Park, Almería, Rio Bravo), and Germany. Fort Fun in the Sauerland of Germany has theme park rides as well as an Old West town with street perfor-mances that include "The Secret of the Silver Mine," which culminates in a shootout between the sheriff and the outlaw Doc Smith, clearly making use of the signifiers of Tombstone and other articulations of the West in popular culture. Pullman City in Bavaria is also a western town with a sa-loon, sheriff's office, silver mines, and a Boot Hill Cemetery. Visitors come to Pullman City to see Indian dances, western shows that include rope and gun demonstrations and shoot-outs, and country western bands to which they can line dance and two-step. Pullman City also offers a forty-minute "American History Show" that starts with the American Revolution and ends with the conclusion of the Indian Wars. This show includes a lecture on Native American culture by "the half blood Cheyenne Native American Hunting Wolf," who has visited Native American communities in order to educate Pullman City visitors about Native history as well as some of the issues Native Americans deal with today, including crime and unemployment.[51] When asked why people visit Pullman City, Detlef Jeschke, a Nuremberg-born former champion European rodeo cowboy and Pullman City's program manager, said, "People dream of a free, beautiful country, of romantic campfires and heroes in the saddle."[52] Ruth Ellen Gruber observes that while western-themed towns in Germany and the Czech Republic each have their own character, they all "feature full daily programs and special entertainment with an emphasis on activities for families and children, and are all anchored by a Main Street that doubles as an outdoor stage."[53] The performative component to these towns in Germany and elsewhere mirrors that experienced in Tombstone, where history, celebration, and entertainment are inextricable.

Clearly we see the influence of Karl May in Germany, where hobbyists and western lovers continue to flock to the Karl May Museum in his home town of Radebeul (also referred to as "Little Tombstone"), opened in 1928, and to the German town of Bad Segeberg for an annual Karl May Festival, which started in the 1950s and is visited every summer by three hundred thousand people.[54] Radebeul is a sister city to Sierra Vista, Arizona, which is about twenty miles southwest of Tombstone. The towns participate in an exchange program in which students from Germany and Arizona can experience each other's culture. Interestingly, both towns survive on the tropes of the American West, so students from Radebeul bring their expectations of the West to Sierra Vista and their lived experiences back with them, while students from Sierra Vista bring their lived experiences of the West to a town that perpetuates these notions to its other German visitors. Further exemplifying the global flow of the mythic West, a Karl May museum was opened in Tombstone, Arizona, in 2012 to mark the one hundredth anniversary of the author's death. Cosponsored by the Karl May Foundation and Tombstone Monument Ranch, located just a few miles outside of Tombstone, the museum displays numerous artifacts of Native American life and various images of the mythic West.[55]

These western-themed towns rely on built environments that are based more on romance than on reality. In his book *The Myth of Santa Fe*, Chris Wilson defines this phenomenon as romantic regionalism, which can be disrupted through critical regionalism: "If romantic regionalism earlier in the twentieth century was intertwined with the rise of the urban bourgeois and consumerism, critical regionalism reacts against the tendency to turn culture and the environment into exploitable commodities." He credits architecture critic Kenneth Frampton for extending "the debate over critical regionalism when he charged that most of what passes for regionalism today is 'cardboard scenographic populism' and 'a consumerist iconography masquerading as culture.'"[56] The American West as both a place and a concept has found itself caught within this paradox of romance and critique, reworking its own past and contributing to both a collective memory and a historical amnesia that has allowed it to remain resonant for decades.

Steiner does similar work looking at the ways the built environment makes meaning for people. He argues that "Disney realized that the lure of refabricated frontiers rested in their ability to transform abstract concepts and flat images into lived experience. He sensed that architecture, more than any other medium, sharpens vague feelings into concrete form. Cartoons and movies project two-dimensional abstractions, while people *participate* in architecture."[57] He goes on to pinpoint one of the most enduring components to all of these built western-themed towns and destinations: "Remodeling what was often a dirty, brutal, chaotic experience into the cleanest, happiest, most predictable place on earth became a mission."[58] By creating these experiences for their visitors, Disneyland Paris, Tokyo Disney, Laredo Western Town, Deadwood Western Town, Radebeul, and OK Corral, much like the actual town of Tombstone, are offering the realization of the nostalgia that makes visiting these towns so important to people in the first place. They offer comforting versions of a West that never really was—or at least one that is far less frightening, dirty, and dangerous.

Back at the Ranch

Back in the actual American West is a transnational space glorifying the Old West and celebrating its surroundings and proximity to Tombstone. Originally called Apache Spirit Ranch, Tombstone Monument Ranch lies about two miles from Tombstone's central business and historic district, and it was opened in 2011 to cater specifically to German visitors. As a place where European fantasies about the Old West are played out on a daily basis, Tombstone Monument Ranch is unique in our discussion of the global West. As outsider, it plays on romantic notions of the region; as insider, it offers entrée into a world only imagined by its visitors. Although the ranch changed owners in 2014 and has expanded its services to welcome American visitors as well, the initial focus of the ranch was to allow German guests the opportunity to live out romanticized encounters with the American Southwest written about by Karl May and continually perpetuated through both American and German popular culture.

Apache Spirit Ranch's original German owner, Peter Stenger, declared that the inspiration for building and opening the ranch "was definitely [May's Native American character] Winnetou. Winnetou was my childhood hero, back when I used to read Karl May books. I absolutely ate them up." Stenger did not evoke actual images of the American frontier or even Hollywood westerns in his constructed images of the Old West; instead, he was inspired by May, who had never visited the American West but only imagined it based on his own consumption of the stories of his time. Stenger's experience reading about Native American culture as imagined by Karl May was reinvigorated when, as an adult, he "had the wonderful experience of meeting a real Apache on a ranch holiday in New Mexico. We rode out together just the two of us, rounded up horses. It was like all of my Christmases coming up at once. It was at that time that I realized I wanted to experience that kind of thing more often." This is when the idea for Apache Spirit Ranch was born, "with the idea of creating our own thing and making the ranch experience available to other people, taking them back in time to the year 1881."[59]

The ranch is just minutes from the town of Tombstone and may be interpreted as essentially a small-scale replica of Tombstone—with a saloon, town marshal's office, post office, blacksmith shop, bank (these "offices" are actually the guesthouses on the ranch), "authentic cowboy coffee by the fire" at dawn, horseback rides, and barn dances. "Our goal," said Stenger, "was that if we were going to do this, we have to do it as well as we possibly could. Sticking as closely to the original as possible, like a real western town, and therefore creating a journey back to the year 1881 for our guests."[60] The "original" in this case is Tombstone itself—although it could as easily refer to the settings of May's stories that Stenger read as a child, as these are the foundation on which the ranch was initially conceived and constructed.

The ranch publicizes its proximity to Tombstone as one reason to visit, even naming rooms after Wyatt Earp and Doc Holliday and one guesthouse "the Cochise County Courthouse." They also have had two three-course meals named for Holliday and Earp available to guests who eat at Schieffelin's Restaurant. When the ranch first opened, it specifically promoted its links to Native culture and history, as well as the idea that the ranch was built on "sacred land": "The history of the Apache village comes alive when the Apaches tell tales of their forefathers, taking you into their world, the world of their ancestors Cochise and Geronimo. A traditional Pow Wow with *real* Native Americans ignites the spirit of the Wild West in you."[61]

Authenticity of experience and legitimacy of historical context were imperative to both the owner and the visitors to this ranch. Stenger also relied on notions of history and authenticity to market the destination as one of historic and "spiritual" significance: "The ranch is situated among spiritual and historic surroundings reflected in the site's architecture and design."[62] Apache Spirit Ranch's quest for authenticity was further articulated when it sponsored the Karl May Museum, which opened in Tombstone in May 2012. Of course, the continual reference to *stories* about the West—as imagined by May, who never visited the American West; by Hollywood screenwriters and producers; by filmmakers in European and other nations throughout the world; by businessmen in Japan, reenactors in Great Britain, and Walt Disney—rather than the West itself points to the ways producers and consumers of the mythic West worldwide define "authenticity" and "history" and what purpose these terms serve in their quest to capture some of what the West signifies.

The ranch had some trouble in its first couple of years—not because Germans do not want to experience the mythic West, and not because Apache Spirit Ranch did not live up to its own marketing. It was mostly because Stenger was hard and fast about maintaining the *Germanness* of his endeavor, essentially closing off the ranch to local, regional, and American tourists. The ranch changed ownership in 2014 but continues to be a transnational space, purchased by two Tombstonian businesspeople, a Briton, and a seasoned dude-ranch owner. Two Germans manage the property. British businessman and coowner Dave Cole invested in the ranch in August 2014. Like Stenger, Cole turned his love for the West and for Native history and culture into an everyday lifestyle. He calls it "the personal fulfillment of my own American dream." Germans Marcel and Regina have been managing the ranch since it changed ownership. Marcel has had a long fascination with the West and was an investor in Apache Spirit Ranch and a repeat visitor. His and Regina's love of horses and the western way of life prompted the new owners to hire them as managers, resulting in their permanent move to the ranch in 2014. When asked what the biggest

Tombstone Monument Ranch, 2015. (Courtesy of Tombstone Monument Ranch)

difference is between her life as a lawyer before coming to the ranch and her life now, Regina says, "Everyone I encounter now is happy."[63]

Changing the name to Tombstone Monument Ranch, the new owners moved away from representing the ranch as one of spiritual significance that promotes a romantic ideal of Native life to one that more explicitly celebrates cowboy culture, demonstrating the differences in the ways the "West" is understood by Germans and Americans and the expectations each might bring to the ranch as guests. Germans and many other Europeans have claimed "Indianness" as a means of defining their own cultural experience—perceived through the lens of indigeneity, masculinity, spirituality, and romance. Their imagined connection to Native Americans, their history, and their plight during westward expansion has generated an entire industry that allows for the articulation of this relationship and the kindred spirituality they believe to be at the core of the Native worldview. Americans, on the other hand, have historically seemed more enamored with the clothing, activities, and attitude of the romanticized cowboy: cowboy boots and hats, chaps, horseback riding, roping, cowboy coffee at twilight, and guns. As the name change suggests, Tombstone Monument Ranch is far more linked to the idea of Tombstone than the idea of the spiritual ancestral lands of the Apaches. Although the ranch remains popular among American and European tourists and was recently featured on the online show *Best of America by Horseback*, not everyone is pleased with the transition. One seventy-year-old guest who has been visiting the ranch from Quebec, Canada, twice a year since 2009 was first drawn to Apache Spirit Ranch because of his interest in the area and the history of Native life there, as well as in Native crafts and the relationship between Native and white people. Growing up in France, he loved to play the Indian in games of "cowboys and Indians." He was captivated by the American West as portrayed in western films and television shows and found himself feeling sad at the end of western movies because the Indians always lost. He describes himself as having a "strong relationship with Natives, rather than with my white fellow men." He explains that "the tradition of Natives and their relationship to their cosmic environment exerts a deep fascination" in him. The feeling that Apache Spirit Ranch was more about a spiritual journey and connecting with Native culture compelled him to travel there regularly. Now he feels that it is much more a celebration of cowboys and whiteness, of violence and conquest, and he is unsure how many times he will return.[64]

Tombstone Monument Ranch is similar to Tombstone in its commodification of the hyperreal West for which Tombstone is now famous. In many ways, though, Tombstone Monument Ranch offers a more "authentic Tombstone experience" (what could be called a "hyperauthentic" experience) than the town itself, the authenticity of which arguably has been compromised or at least called into question for so many decades by its performative character, souvenir shops, and conspicuous reliance on popular culture for its own identity. Further, as an actual living town, with a mayor, city council, schools, and all the trappings of a modern community, Tombstone must constantly answer to the needs of its own citizenry. Most important, however, is that, as a nationally recognized historic district, Tombstone must strive to legitimate its historicity or risk losing the designation. Tombstone is confined by the guidelines set up by the Department of the Interior and must be so in order to remain "historically significant." Tombstone Monument Ranch has no such rules to which it must adhere beyond those guiding the expectations of its visitors; it resides outside of Tombstone and outside the limitations Tombstone must itself observe. Tombstone Monument Ranch also resides inside the imagination of the people who visit there. One visitor commented that their stay at what is now Tombstone Monument Ranch was the "highlight of our trip to Tombstone," while another stated that the ranch is the "best place in town." Similarly, one guest remarked that the ranch is "the best way to enjoy the Tombstone experience"; another claimed that the ranch offered the opportunity to experience an "authentic looking" western town; and still another stated that the ranch is like "the old west plus." All of these reviews reveal how successful the ranch is at meeting its visitors' expectations, some believing the ranch to be the best part of their visit to Tombstone and others pointing to the authenticity of its construction. Yet another visitor remarked, "All the dreams of living in the time of cowboys and Indians come true at [Tombstone Monument Ranch]. . . . The ranch looks like a western movie town, the cowboys are the real thing and the Indians are friendly." This final reference to a "western movie town" reveals the "experience" from which this reviewer—and so many others—bases his judgment.[65]

★ ★ ★

The ideas and practices performed around the symbols of the Old West in spaces such as Tombstone, Arizona, are clearly meaningful to people outside of the United States. Masako Notoji argues that "American culture is deconstructed and recontextualized into the everyday experience of the people. American popular culture is not the monopoly of Americans; it is a medium through which people around the world constantly reorganize their individual and collective identities."[66] However, it is not just American popular culture but all the cultural productions of other nations that reference the mythic West that work globally. All of the examples in this chapter bear out this concept. The significance of the OK Corral, Tombstone, and the mythic West are maintained globally through the connection consumers imagine they have with these spaces, which still offer some wish fulfillment to the fantasies of a global community. Tombstone and the mythic West allow for both a sense of belonging and a sense of rebelliousness, a way to feel both connected to and distanced from something. People of other nations who subscribe to the ideologies embodied by the imagined West are not necessarily imagining a connection with the United States—though that may be part of it. They seem more interested in imagining how the tropes of the Old West help them construct a relationship with their own pasts and with the promises of their own futures.

5

Historians' Gunfight

The gunfight behind the OK Corral lasted only thirty seconds, but the debate about the details of that fateful afternoon and about the one man to emerge from the battle without a single bullet wound has raged on for 135 years. For a man who has represented both law and vigilantism and for a town that has been teetering between "wild" and "tame" since its founding, it makes sense that contention and controversy have plagued and continue to plague that story. Professional and grassroots historians as well as journalists and fiction writers in the ever-expanding field of Earp scholarship that has come to be known as Earpiana have debated the Earp legend in ways worthy of Tombstone's wild western past, debunking or rebuilding the traditional saga, battling over sources, crafting elaborate hoaxes or exposing those who have done so, and taking sides in the now famous gunfight. Ever since the Earps and the Clanton clan battled it out on the streets of Tombstone, ever newer versions of the story continually grace bookshelves, history journals, blogs, magazines, and newspapers with the promise of revising the old story and perhaps settling the matter once and for all. Renewed interest in debating the heroic or exaggerated reputation of Wyatt brings rekindled interest in the town itself, as history buffs and Wild West enthusiasts seek their own answers and experiences in the town at the center of it all. With the different ways Wyatt has been constructed and deconstructed and the different meanings his story makes for so many different people, the debate over Earp—as well as the contest around who gets to tell his story—keeps both his legacy and Tombstone alive.

Earp historians and experts have so debated and challenged the facts surrounding the story of Wyatt Earp and the famed street fight over the years that an accurate history has often been muddied by personal and professional motivation. "No other figure in the Western past," contends Earp historian Gary L. Roberts, "has been so obscured by the deliberate distortion of the record, or so trivialized by mean-spirited dialogue [than Wyatt Earp]."[1] This makes understanding the events leading up to the fight and what happened on and after the afternoon of 26 October 1881 difficult and dependent on the whims of the people telling the tale. Perhaps it is this confusion that engenders recurrent interest in this historical narrative. But the most important component of this discussion is that it keeps coming back to Tombstone. Indeed, it is the very idea of Tombstone and its raucous history that offer a figurative and literal space that both provokes these disputes and benefits from them. These fights help maintain intrigue in Tombstone and bring more people to its historic district. Through these debates, it is clear that there is power not only in the narrative but also in the telling of that narrative. Earp historians all want a hand in creating and perpetuating the legend, even as they attempt to demythologize the man.

There was never consensus over what happened all those years ago on the streets of Tombstone. Debates about the dispute and who was to blame began almost immediately after the battle occurred. Tombstone's two newspapers, the *Epitaph* and the *Nugget*, were the first to offer biased and contradictory accounts of the gunfight and the motivations of each side. *Epitaph* founder and editor John P. Clum was unapologetic about his Republican leanings, his Christian beliefs, his confidence in the advancement of incorporation and capitalism as civilizing powers in the Old West, and his support of the Earps and Doc Holliday. Writing the day after the street fight that "nothing ever occurred equal to the event of yesterday," Clum declared the Earps and Holliday to be "entirely justified in [their] efforts to disarm these men, and that being fired upon they had to defend themselves, which they did most bravely."[2] *Nugget* editor and Sheriff Behan's undersheriff Harry Wood agreed with Clum that this event was unrivaled in the town's history, writing that this was "a day always to be remembered as witnessing the bloodiest and deadliest street fight that has ever occurred in this place." But that's where the agreement ends. Wood, an equally unapologetic proponent of Sheriff Behan and the Democratic ideal, called the outcome of the fight "tragic" and insisted that the McLaurys and Billy Clanton were upstanding citizens and that the Earps and Holliday were ruthless ruffians whom Wood implicated in criminal acts even before the shootout. In his account of the fight, he called Billy's ability to survive his wounds for a full hour afterward a demonstration of his "wonderful vitality," and he reported that the McLaurys "did not bear the reputation of being of a quarrelsome disposition" and that they generally "conducted themselves in a quiet and orderly manner in Tombstone."[3] The linguistic battle over whether the Earps and Holliday acted with or against the law was carried within the pages of the *Epitaph* and the *Nugget* as well as other area newspapers throughout the Spicer hearing to decide whether the case should be brought to trial. It continued during Wyatt's infamous vendetta ride, which he and Doc embarked on ostensibly to rid the territory of its criminal element once and for all. Called a "pestiferous posse" made up of "desperate men" by the *Nugget* and more kindly referred to as "the Earp Party" by the *Epitaph*, which offered a "journal of their adventures and wanderings" to *Epitaph* readers, lines were clearly and forever drawn within the pages of Tombstone's most influential and notable tabloids.

Other newspapers and magazines were still reporting on Earp's years in Tombstone as well as his life in California years later, including the *San Francisco Examiner*, which in August 1896 published a series of favorable articles, presumably penned by Earp himself, titled "How Wyatt Earp Routed a Gang of Arizona Cowboys."[4] This series appeared only a few months before Earp was highly criticized for calling a boxing match he was judging in San Francisco for the man all others thought lost, Tom Sharkey—most likely because Sharkey was knocked out by the defending champion, Robert Fitzsimmons, and had to be carried out of the ring after the fight. Newspapers lobbed accusations of a conspiracy and reawakened debates around Earp's contentious past in Tombstone and the Arizona Territory. The *San Francisco Call* reported that Fitzsimmons's manager had called Earp "the bad man from Arizona" and wanted him removed as referee of the match. While National Athletic Club manager John D. Gibbs is quoted as calling Earp "a cool, clearheaded person of an unimpeachable character," the article's focus is on Earp's being charged for carrying a concealed weapon into the arena without a permit and features a sketch of the "formidable," "one-foot long" .45-caliber Colt that was taken from him.[5] A few days later, the *Call* published "The Swindle Is Revealed," reporting that Earp was implicated in court proceedings in fixing the match, although the judge ended up throwing out the case.[6]

Controversy over this match swirled for months afterward as Earp's character was raked over the coals. In January 1897 an article titled "Look at His Phiz: Wyatt Earp, a Bad Man and He Looks It," printed on page 1 of newspapers in a number of states, including the *Columbus (NE) Journal* and the *Independence (KS) Daily Reporter*, claims that Earp "led the life of a coward" and even perfidiously asserts that Earp shot and killed Ike Clanton, who the author states was married to Earp's nonexistent sister, Jessie. (The author also claims Curly Bill was the Earps' cousin.) In this article Earp is said to be part of the "Stage Robbers" faction in Tombstone along with his brother Virgil: "The Stage Robbers were in politics republican and stood up stages and plundered express companies for a livelihood." The author accuses Virgil and Wyatt of working with the Wells Fargo agent to be tipped off whenever a large amount of cash was being transported. They would hold up the stage, driven by their brother Warren, who would easily surrender the money. The Earps would then "pretend to chase the robbers," all the while duping the system and living off the profits. "He is exactly the sort of man to referee a prize fight," the author concludes, "if a steal is meditated, and a job put up to make the wrong man win. Wyatt Earp has all the nerve and dishonesty needed to turn the trick."[7]

Criticism continued through the early years of the new century. The *Richmond (VA) Times* ran a first-page piece in July 1900, "Murders Were Their Pastime," following erroneous reports that Wyatt had been shot in a saloon he managed in Nome, Alaska, supposedly "by a customer he had tried to bully."[8] The *Richmond Times* story labels the Earps "bandits" who "amused themselves with plunder and slaughter." It also uses the occasion of Wyatt's alleged shooting to rehash the old Fitzsimmons-Sharkey controversy and perpetuate falsehoods that had been printed in "Look at His Phiz" in 1897, including that his "sister" Jessie married Ike Clanton, whom Wyatt supposedly killed in cold blood, and that Curly Bill was the Earps' cousin.[9]

The 1920s—a moment of renewed interest in the signifiers of the Old West—saw a number of conflicting accounts of Earp and his time in Tombstone. In 1922 the *Los Angeles Times* ran a short, highly critical article by one J. M. Scanland titled "Lurid Trails Are Left by Olden Day Bandits," in which Earp and his brothers are described as a villainous gang who, after being "driven out of Dodge City" by Bat Masterson, settled on Tombstone as the home base of their presumably illicit operations. Scanland blames the shootout on the fact that "four cowboys refused to recognize the right of the Earp gang to rule the town."[10] That same year, Frederick R. Bechdolt's compilation of articles written for the *Saturday Evening Post* on the Old West was published under the title *When the West Was Young*. Unlike the newspapermen who came before him, Bechdolt researched his subject and conducted interviews in the 1910s with Tombstone old-timers, including Billy Breakenridge and former Cochise County sheriff John Slaughter, who had relatively negative opinions about the Earps. Bechdolt's work reflects their belief that the Earps were involved in criminal activity in Tombstone, although Bechdolt does describe the Earps as "bold" and writes that out-lawry in Tombstone "took on a new lease on life" with their departure.[11]

Renewed interest in the Old West and Wyatt Earp in particular brought Tombstone back into the spotlight. Indeed, while Wyatt had been a topic of debate for decades, author Mark Dworkin points out that Bechdolt's articles in the *Saturday Evening Post* and his book "focused national attention on the town [of Tombstone] for the first time in almost forty years."[12]

Tombstone's next opportunity to benefit from that attention came in 1928, with the publishing of Billy Breakenridge's memoir of his time in Tombstone, *Helldorado: Bringing the Law to the Mesquite*. To say that Breakenridge, another of John Behan's deputies, wrote an unflattering account of Earp would be an understatement. In addition to painting him as a thief and a murderer, Breakenridge accuses Earp of shooting the Cowboys behind the OK Corral after they had already surrendered their weapons and threw up their arms.[13] "It is my belief," he writes, "that the cowboys were not expecting a fight. . . . If they had expected that the Earps were coming to kill them, they could have shot down the whole Earp party with their rifles before they got within pistol shooting distance."[14] It seems that in the thirty years since the Fitzsimmons-Sharkey match, Wyatt was demythologized to the point of vilification. This is particularly interesting given the upsurge in enthusiasm and attention that the West as a region was experiencing in the 1920s. Breakenridge's memoir was so popular that it, like Bechdolt's work, recentered Tombstone in the narrative of the West. Tombstone wanted to take advantage of this renewed interest in the region but, at the same time, perhaps wanted to maintain some distance from Wyatt Earp and his soiled reputation. The town named its first festival Helldorado Days in celebration of its wild western past. The fact that Tombstone chose to name its annual festival after a book that depicted Earp so unfavorably indicates that Earp's reputation was ambiguous, even in Tombstone, and that original attempts by Tombstonians to capitalize on their history were based on a broader perspective of a raucous past of which Earp was only a part. While both Breakenridge's and Bechdolt's books deride Earp, his brothers, and Doc Holliday, they also both signal a departure from the unresearched sensationalism that graced the front pages of newspapers for years prior. In the coming decades, a work's legitimacy sprang from the author's assurances of authenticity of sources and vigilance to research. These assurances, however, did not always carry with them the promise of an authentic—or even honest—telling of the story, as we shall see.

In this same time frame, Walter Noble Burns's epic *Tombstone: An Il-iad of the Southwest* was released in 1927 after he had conducted extensive research in Tombstone about the men that had made the town famous. In this quixotic account, Burns describes Wyatt as the "Lion of Tombstone," a moniker that romanticizes Earp and casts him as civilizing the Arizona Territory. Burns was meticulous in his inquiry, relying on issues of the *Epitaph* as well as interviews with Tombstonians to get at the heart of the Earp tale. One of his main sources was southwestern historian Lorenzo Walters, who expressed frustration, especially with the testimony given at the Spicer hearing, that "men who were considered absolutely reliable gave evidence directly opposite to that given by other men who were considered equally reliable." Indeed, this is a frustration, as Dworkin and others point out, "shared by subsequent historians attempting to sort through the facts surrounding the various versions of the street fight" for decades to come. Perhaps because of the ambiguity, Burns crafted a work that "treads a fine line between history and fiction," embellishing the story and using "colorful dialog" to elevate the narrative to Homeric proportions.[15] Other early twentieth-century writings about Earp and the fight took their cue from Burns and tended to glorify Wyatt and excuse his use of force at the OK Corral and throughout the Arizona Territory. Indeed, these works celebrated his use of what some termed vigilante justice as heroic and necessary for the ushering in of progress and modernity. After Burns's account of what happened in Tombstone came Stuart Lake's biography in 1929, one that is more hagiographic than historic. Lake's work was so popular that it was pivotal in the shifting of attitudes about Wyatt Earp and would become the basis of a number of Hollywood productions of Earp's time in Dodge City and Tombstone. Later historians would attempt to revise and rewrite the romantic story of Earp and the factors leading up to and following the gunfight as portrayed by Lake and film producers in the early twentieth century, but Lake's version would prove the most steadfast of imaginings of Wyatt Earp for decades.

Years of examination and consideration over Earp's character continued unabated, with a general impression, despite the record that shows otherwise, that Earp had been continuously glorified and celebrated since his time in Tombstone. Hollywood got in on the mythologizing endeavor starting in 1932 with *Law and Order*, followed by *Frontier Marshal* (1939), *Tombstone, the Town Too Tough to Die* (1942), and *My Darling Clementine* (1946)—all of which portray Earp as the quintessential western hero. As a response, historians and biographers looking to reshape Earp in a more realistic light joined the many that came before in contributing to the Earp narrative while disrupting the Earp myth. Frank L. Waters's *Earp Brothers of Tombstone: The Story of Mrs. Virgil Earp*, released in 1960, and Ed Bartholomew's *Wyatt Earp: The*

Untold Story and *Wyatt Earp: The Man and the Myth*, released in 1963 and 1964, respectively, paint Earp in ways that hark back to newspaper articles of the late nineteenth century and to Breakenridge in the 1920s. Historian Paul Hutton takes exception with those writers who have criticized previous, romantic representations of Wyatt Earp, those who "viciously assailed the historical reputation of America's favorite television and movie lawman," specifically Waters and Bartholomew. Hutton believes they and others "went far beyond the mild corrective that was in order. Their Earp—a con artist, thief, and killer who hid behind the badge to commit his crimes—was in turn mindlessly copied by a generation of popular writers anxious for a sensational story or too quick to believe the worst about a popular myth."[16] In *The Earp Brothers of Tombstone: The Story of Mrs. Virgil Earp*, for example, Waters begins by telling his readers that his book "is an exposé of the Tombstone travesty, laying bare under the scalpel of her merciless truths the anatomy of one of the legends contributing to the creation of a unique and wholly indigenous myth of the American West."[17] Calling the Earp story "a fictitious legend of preposterous proportions," Waters believed—as Hutton points out—that if you debunk the Earp myth, you unravel the entire story of progress embodied by the frontier myth. By making this analogy, however, Waters was acknowledging that the Earp yarn is as meaningful to and profound as the mythic West itself. With equal fervor and similar objective, Bartholomew set out purposefully to "unmask" the legendary Earp. Making it clear that his work was crafted from careful research, he states in the introduction to *Wyatt Earp: The Untold Story*, "The author has spared not time and travel in his search for documented facts; his travels to the West have been unrelenting. . . . He has leveled his six-shooter at the Earp myth and has blasted it to shreds."[18] The fact that these works were published in the 1960s, when the nation was beginning to cast a more critical eye on the narratives that make up the American story of progress and exceptionalism, seems reasonable and timely, but it also appears that these writers allowed their personal inclinations about the man to cloud their ability to objectively tell his story.

In fact, perhaps far more sinister than a personal agenda to revise the Earp myth—and further complicating the Earp narrative—has been the revelation of apocryphal or even spurious accounts by both professional and grassroots historians of events in Tombstone in 1881. The authors who celebrated Earp as well as those who vilified him fell victim to their own personal motivations for writing their tomes and included erroneous information—or outright lies—in order to paint the picture of Earp they felt was justified. The first of these, as discussed in chapter 3, was Stuart Lake's

Wyatt Earp, Frontier Marshal. On its release in 1931, it was publicized and accepted as historically accurate, even once Lake admitted after the fact that it was not. "Lake clearly used many sources for his information, then credited Earp, while adding quotes Earp never said," explains Earp expert Casey Tefertiller. Lake later wrote why he chose to use such a device: "There had been so much erroneous matter printed about the Earp exploits, none ever put down in the order of cause and effect, that I was hunting for a method which would stamp mine as authentic. Possibly it was a form of 'cheating.' But, when it came to the task, I decided to [employ] the direct quotation form sufficiently often to achieve my purpose."[19] In other words, Lake had a specific story in mind and by crediting Earp directly with the narrative, he legitimized his work. Despite the licenses Lake took, or perhaps because of them, his book was wildly popular and launched Wyatt Earp as the classic western lawman and hero he became.[20]

Just as Lake's work had been debunked in the years following its publication, other notable works in Earp historiography have faced similar charges. In July 1955 *Argosy* magazine published "The Truth about Wyatt Earp" by western writer and magazine contributor Edwin V. Burkholder. Burkholder called Earp a coward and a murderer and, like others not satisfied with what research and facts revealed, manufactured evidence to prove it. As Gary Roberts says, "Here was fakery in its most blatant form, designed to be as outrageous as possible." A few years later, after being lauded for supposedly shedding new light on the old story in his own work, Waters's claim that the entire narrative for *The Earp Brothers of Tombstone* came straight from the mouth of Virgil's wife, Allie Earp, was widely discredited. Apparently, dissatisfied with what his own research exposed, and to satisfy his own motives—similar to Stuart Lake—Waters "could not resist the temptation of altering Allie's story" to create what he believed the narrative should be.[21] This is particularly interesting given his propensity for describing Lake's work as "fictitious" throughout his book.[22] Despite his claims to careful research, Bartholomew's argument, according to Roberts, was based on "rumors, gossip, and innuendo piled on top of one another until the effect was somewhat overwhelming."[23] Earp author Richard Erwin laments how Bartholomew was obviously biased in his approach, and "apparently so determined to destroy what he considered to be the Earp myth that he put an adverse spin on almost every fact that turned up in his research." In fact, says Erwin, Bartholomew "invariably sought to use the tactics of guilt by association in order to degrade Wyatt Earp."[24] Again, Waters and Bartholomew were writing at the onset of the turmoil of the 1960s, a decade that witnessed the revision of the western myth as a whole.

As Waters's belief in Earp's centrality to the story of progress embedded in the frontier myth attests, it makes sense that there would be some attempt to disrupt the stories of those on whose shoulders the mythic West rested. In these circumstances, Earp was ready-made for criticism, but much of it was created and had only a fleeting relationship with truth.

Over the course of the next thirty years, a number of works came out either in favor of Earp or intent on destroying his reputation. Film representations of Earp brought *Hour of the Gun* in 1967 and *Doc* in 1971, both portraying Earp as a flawed and questionable hero. But it was the 1990s that saw a full-fledged revival of both Wyatt Earp and Tombstone for a new generation of western enthusiasts, movie audiences, and tourists. Hollywood returned to the Earp story in 1993 and 1994 with the release of the overwhelmingly popular *Tombstone* and, to a lesser degree, *Wyatt Earp.* The 1993 *Tombstone,* as discussed in chapter 3, offers a depiction of Wyatt made heroic despite his shortcomings and because of the vendetta ride. *Wyatt Earp* offers a more balanced portrayal of a complex Earp and the events leading up to the showdown. Both films had a tremendous impact on the popularity of Tombstone and refocused scholarly attention on Earp's character as well as on the works that defined him in these last decades of the twentieth century. Indeed, the late 1980s and early 1990s saw renewed attention not only on Wyatt Earp and Tombstone but also on the narrative of progress that had been central to imaginings of the Old West. After filmmakers had been revising the western myth for decades, new western historians began to demythologize the West and explore the complexities of the history of the region. These attempts were highly publicized in the press and highly controversial in the field. Similar to the battles being fought over Earp's character in the pages of newspapers and biographies, battles among respected western historians such as Gerald Nash and William Goetzmann and those looking to revise the story were fought in academic journals and at conferences in ways that are in keeping with the Wild West aesthetic. Gerald Nash accused new western historians of being both Nazis and Communists, and Goetzmann said they should go to Russia, while William Savage Jr. simply called them stupid. Patricia Limerick and John Mack Farragher accused the older generation of idiocy and of being irrational, and their insults deplorable.[25] The exchange of vitriol led one journalist to label the situation "Showdown in the New West."[26] While shots were exchanged on both sides, the reality was that the "American attitude about America" had changed. Larry McMurtry, in an article decrying the revisionists as having no imagination, attributes the shift in attitude to the fact that "old, brutal, masculine American confidence has been replaced (at least among historians) by a new, open, feminine American self-doubt—a moral doubt, the sort that can produce a malaise of the spirit."[27] The conclusion that new western historians of the 1980s and 1990s were gripped by the feminization of American culture would be put to similar use by Glenn G. Boyer, an Earp biographer whose work came under fire amid this shakeup in western historiography.

Like the works of Lake, Waters, and Bartholomew, Boyer's *I Married Wyatt Earp: The Recollections of Josephine Sarah Marcus* (1976) and *Wyatt Earp's Tombstone Vendetta* (1993), two prominent, highly regarded, and presumed historical works, were discovered to be largely works of fiction in the early 1990s. These books have become the focus of discussions around historical authenticity and the questionable ability to fully grasp and understand the story of Wyatt Earp and his place in the story of the West. These two books were both supposedly based on different manuscripts and primary sources Boyer claimed he had in his possession, including a memoir that he credited to Earp's wife, Josephine Marcus. *I Married Wyatt Earp* had been published as a nonfiction memoir by the University of Arizona Press since its first printing in 1976, but when Boyer's well-known and heavily influential *Wyatt Earp's Tombstone Vendetta* was published in 1993, other Earp historians were faced with inconsistencies and inaccuracies that just did not make sense. Questions began to circulate about the validity of his sources, and after a few years of inquiry, both works were exposed as entirely false. This revelation led to a years' long battle between Boyer and the many Earp historians who felt not only misled but swindled by Boyer's assertions of historical authenticity.[28]

Although squarely situated in the Earp camp, *I Married Wyatt Earp* was considered by many to offer a balanced version of the Earp story. The seemingly unbiased work was seen as a must-use, standard source by other scholars and formed the basis for films about the Earps following its initial publication (including a made-for-television movie of the same name starring Marie Osmond as Josephine). Indeed, according to Earp expert Allen Barra, Boyer's book had been "the text quoted in virtually everything written on Wyatt Earp in the . . . two decades [since its publication]—Paula Mitchell Marks's *And Die in the West* relies heavily on it."[29] And in his introduction to *The Truth about Wyatt Earp*, Erwin classifies Boyer as "an important researcher and writer," saying that "he mostly told the story to the best of his ability"[30]—this despite the fact that Boyer had been less than forthcoming about his sources, at least since 1998, telling a reporter at the *Tucson Star* at the time that the original manuscripts were lost "years ago" in "a messy divorce settlement." In light of questions about authenticity but without any real proof whether the sources were authentic or even existed, Barra concluded, "In lieu of further evidence, what we have in *I Married Wyatt Earp* is a novel with footnotes and with vocabulary and syntax altered to fit Boyer's conception, however informed, of what Josephine, Wyatt, and others might have said."[31]

This is a far more generous assessment than that given by Earp authority Jeffrey J. Morey, who publicly questioned Boyer's integrity in a 1994 article titled "The Curious Vendetta of Glenn G. Boyer." Morey first takes to task Boyer's 1993 work *Wyatt Earp's Tombstone Vendetta*, a book Morey calls "so bizarre it stands as emblematic of all that is troublesome in Earp litera-ture."[32] Boyer claimed *Tombstone Vendetta* was the memoir of a journalist working for the *New York Herald* named Theodore Ten Eyck (a pseudonym, according to Boyer), who apparently was in Tombstone in 1881. Morey de-bunks point for point Ten Eyck's supposed firsthand accounts, pointing to inconsistencies and out-and-out falsehoods contained in the narrative. Ca-sey Tefertiller, who had admired Boyer's previous work, knew immediately that Ten Eyck was fictitious and seemed personally offended by Boyer's use of him in his work. Tefertiller was preparing to review the book for the *San Francisco Examiner*, but he realized that "it was such a transparent fraud that I was absolutely stunned. Mr. Boyer had told me that it was written by a top-level journalist, but this Ten Eyck character knew nothing about fron-tier journalism. At that point I knew I had been lied to."[33]

Boyer's responses to his critics were combative, confusing, and evasive. While sometimes claiming Ten Eyck was a real person whose name had been changed, as he did to Tefertiller, Boyer also reveals in his foreword to *Tombstone Vendetta* that, "'in a few instances,' he blended other voices to form Ten Eyck's singular perspective."[34] In an interview with *Wild West* magazine in 1998, Boyer calls the use of Ten Eyck a "literary device":

WILD WEST: So there was no newspaperman?
BOYER: There was a newspaperman. There were a lot of people. But there was no newspaperman by the name of Ted Ten Eyck. Nor did he work for Tombstone's *Nugget*.
WW: But in the book you actually said that it was a *Nugget* newspaperman.
BOYER: In the book I actually said so broadly, or hinted so broadly, that it is a literary device that anybody with an iota of sense recognized instantly . . . that this man was a composite. That's what I intended.

In the *Wild West* piece, Boyer criticizes those who did not see his work as "creative," referring to them as "morons." In the same piece, however, he references his own importance in the field and claims that "writing about Earp and failing to mention me and my work is something like writing about Catholicism and neglecting to mention the Pope."[35] In other words, referencing his work was imperative, but referencing his work also opened one up to Boyer's harsh condemnation. More confusing was Boyer's own classification of the book as a "non-fiction novel."[36] In an apparent effort to revise his own career, he even refers to himself at times as a novelist, not a historian.[37]

Despite these caveats, it is difficult not to be critical of a man who had been considered one of the foremost authorities on Earp history. As Morey puts it, "It is tempting to be flip and dismissive of a book whose Library of Congress classification incessantly proclaims it as 'Juvenile Literature,' but Glenn G. Boyer has assumed a position of preeminence on the subject of Wyatt Earp."[38] Morey's suspicion about Boyer's Ten Eyck and *Tombstone Vendetta* prompted him and others to look more deeply into his previous works, especially the extremely influential *I Married Wyatt Earp*, supposedly based on the recollections of Josephine Marcus as well as on a manuscript Boyer called the Clum manuscript, now understood to have never even existed. Ironically, Boyer had—like Waters had of Lake—exposed Lake and then Waters himself as "manufacturing quoted material out of whole cloth," a "formidable performance," as Roberts calls it, given Boyer's seemingly complete fabrication of his own source material.[39] As Tefertiller contends, the questions around sources demanded a clear, if not mature, response from Boyer. Instead, Boyer offered only hostile and puzzling responses. Perhaps in an attempt to deflect the controversy, Boyer "accused [his critics] of theft and dishonesty, belittled their skill, envisioned deep-seated conspiracies to 'get' him, alluded to their weight and appearance, called them thieves, idiots, perverts, and drunks, and questioned their sexual orientation."[40]

Indeed, an interview in 1998 with Tony Ortega for the *Phoenix New Times* reveals the vitriol with which Boyer and his wife, Jane Candia Coleman, a western novelist, viewed their detractors. After telling Ortega, "This is an artistic effort. . . . I'm not a historian, I am a storyteller," he further claimed he did not "give a shit about young historians. . . . I do not have to give a shit about young historians, middle-aged historians, old historians, dead historians, or historians who are not yet born. This is my fucking prerogative. I happen to be a literary artist performing." Then, in response to questions about the people Boyer believed responsible for his trouble, Boyer's wife asked Ortega, "Do you think Casey Tefertiller is a homosexual?" Ortega concludes that "Boyer, who has come to believe that the various cowboys aligned against the Earps in Tombstone were likely homosexuals, thinks it's an interesting parallel that he, as living link to the Earps, should be fending off attacks from a bunch of people he imagines to be switch-hitters, homos, and pedophiles."[41] Answering the allegations with character and personal attacks rather than with evidence of his legitimacy kept the controversy in the spotlight for years.

Of course, the revelation that these two esteemed books were fiction opened the door for inquiry into his other works. In usual form, Boyer's defense seemed at best muddied and illogical. Indeed, he called his own pamphlet about Doc Holliday written in 1966 a hoax. In the interview with *Wild West* magazine in 1998, Boyer was asked how making this claim might have affected the credibility of his future, more serious work. He answered, "I don't give a damn about the credibility about the more serious work, let's put it that way." He then went on to again insult those who he believed could not tell the difference between the hoax that was his pamphlet on Doc Holliday and the legitimate history that was his most recent work. "Anybody that can't tell, if they have read much of my serious work, that it's bona fide is a candidate for mental examination. I've told the truth as I've seen it." Not only did he claim he wrote his work on Doc Holliday without knowing that he would be taken seriously later in his career, but he also claimed that his misleading works were serious in that they were meant to expose what he apparently considered the sinister practice of historians utilizing secondary source material without investigating the accuracy of the research previous historians had done: "The serious purpose was to prove that the people writing at that time copied liberally from each other without checking facts for accuracy." He then claimed credit for setting "afoot a historical experiment, not knowing I ever intended to be anything that somebody could characterize as a historian."[42] If this were true, he would have had to realize how his works would be received and know that he would be considered a serious historian in order to reveal the supposedly widespread practice of "liberally" copying others' work. His own statements contradict whatever argument he put forth.

The feud between Boyer supporters (who included Tombstone city historian Ben Traywick) and Boyer detractors continued for a few years in the press and in letters among the various players, most notably between Boyer and either Tefertiller or Allen Barra, both of whom referred to *I Married Wyatt Earp* as a hoax. The climax of this drama was witnessed at what has come to be known as the Showdown at Schieffelin Hall in Tombstone the first weekend of November 2000. This event was covered in *True West* magazine in February 2001 by editor Bob Boze Bell, but his account was perceived by a few who were there to trivialize what they considered to be a serious situation. Essentially, a number of Earp authorities who regularly contributed to the blog BJ's [Billy Johnson's] Tombstone History Discussion Forum, which Mark Dworkin calls "easily the most popular Tombstone and Wyatt Earp Internet site," were gathering in Tombstone that weekend, including Gary Roberts, Casey Tefertiller, Allen Barra, Mark Dworkin, and Jeff Morey. Glenn Boyer was scheduled for a book signing at Schieffelin Hall on Saturday, 4 November 2000, at one o'clock, sponsored by Tombstone city historian Ben Traywick. According to witnesses, Boyer's event got heated when two of his most outspoken critics—Tefertiller and Barra—arrived at Schieffelin Hall around three o'clock, two hours after the Boyer event began, after attending a hike and tour of Charleston, a nearby ghost town. An agitated Boyer accused the men of being cowards from the stage, threw verbal assaults at them, and finally, after being asked a question by Barra, physically intimidated Barra, his wife, and their daughter. According to Billy Johnson, Barra had asked Boyer to clarify a recent blog post by Boyer saying Barra and his wife were getting a divorce. At this point, "Glenn Boyer, [Tombstone writer and resident] Ron Fischer, Ben Traywick and [Boyer and Jane Coleman's son] Danny Coleman stormed toward the now seated Barra family and surrounded them in an intimidating fashion. Glenn, Danny and possibly several other Boyer supporters were wearing guns and holsters."[43] The setting of Tombstone and Schieffelin Hall for this heated encounter seems fitting for a moment when bravado and audacity trumped mature discourse as weapons of choice in the debate. Perhaps Boyer and his friends felt justified in their aggression as defenders of the ways of the true Old West. It seems they also felt that Earp and Tombstone scholarship had been hijacked by effete "cowards" and "homosexuals" unable or unwilling to physically fight for what they believed in—a sentiment they apparently shared with the old western historians debating the feminization of the field by new western historians. Indeed, Morey remembers the intense atmosphere in the hall when he arrived on hearing what was happening there. "What really alarmed me now, though," he wrote on Johnson's blog, "was Boyer's holstered pistol on his hip. . . . Glenn would occasionally brush his jacket back to appear ever more menacing."[44] The display of guns in holsters and the overall feeling of danger in the hall gave Boyer's group the opportunity to experience the violence of masculinity that so defined Tombstone in the 1880s and that they may have thought was sadly missing from the Earpiana of the 1990s and 2000.

The attacks continued. According to witnesses, who reported what they said and saw that day on a blog set up by Jeff Morey, Tefertiller had been attempting to smooth things over, asking that they all call a truce, but Boyer was persistent. Within this short time, accusations about Boyer's works were interspersed with verbal assaults on character and personal lives. Circling back to Boyer's legitimacy as a historian and attempting to expose Boyer's often contradictory and always convoluted responses to these questions, Tefertiller indignantly announced: "You say, *I Married Wyatt Earp* is a story. We say IMWE is a story. You say *Wyatt Earp's Tombstone Vendetta* is a novel. We say WETV is a novel. Where do we disagree?" Morey reports that Boyer was nonplussed by Tefertiller's approach and did not respond. Then Morey himself was emboldened to ask about a letter Boyer had written to Earp researcher Robert Mullin in 1977 in which Boyer, contrary to what he told *Wild West* magazine in 1998, claimed Ten Eyck was authentic—in other words, a real person. According to Morey, Boyer now replied, "Ten Eycke [*sic*] was representative of a typical authentic frontier type." Morey pressed on: "If that's the case, why, after my critique appeared, did you ask, in one of your responses, 'Why didn't Morey cite the many letters where Robert Mullin and I were trying to determine just who Ten Eycke [*sic*] was?'" This too baffled Boyer, who responded, "Yes, we were trying to learn who Ten Eycke [*sic*] was IN TOMBSTONE." Morey and the others in the audience who stood in opposition to Boyer were "astonished" by "the absurdity of his answer," and Morey said, "But, you're Ted Ten Eyke [*sic*]!" Boyer responded with "Morey you are a hopeless case!" but gave no satisfactory answer to Morey's questions.[45]

By these accounts, it had been an incredibly tense and at times threatening afternoon, one in which Barra and his family felt physically vulnerable and in which Boyer refused to back down—in true showdown fashion—and take responsibility for his actions. Bob Boze Bell did write about the event in the winter 2001 issue of *True West*, but many of those in attendance felt that he did not treat the situation with the seriousness it deserved. On Johnson's Tombstone History Discussion Forum, Dworkin wrote that the magazine "lost [an] opportunity to support western historical scholarship through its failure to place the events of the now legendary Scheiffelin Hall showdown in proper historiographical context." Johnson also criticized Bell's report of the accounts: "Contrary to the *True West* article written by Bob Boze Bell in the winter edition portraying the Schieffelin Hall event in a facetious and light-hearted mode, this was a very dangerous situation. Arrests could have, and probably should have, been made at this armed attempt at intimidation of the Allen Barra family."[46]

Tefertiller helps put Boyer's actions in the context of the field of Earp history, Tombstone history, and history as a discipline, claiming that many see the situation as a showdown between good versus evil, perhaps (ironically) with Boyer (who had adamantly declared his personal connection to the Earps and was an Earp devotee his entire career) and his supporters as the Cowboys, and Barra, Morey, and their supporters as the Earps and Doc Holliday, with Tefertiller, as peacemaker, in the role of Wyatt Earp: "What Boyer has done is wrong in all regards. It is wrong to fabricate history; it is wrong to fabricate outrageous attacks against others. I really see no middle ground. Trying to serve as a peacemaker between good and evil is a difficult situation, particularly when evil flat-out refuses."[47]

Despite being unable to defend himself against his critics, Boyer nonetheless said he would take the fight to his grave. Indeed, he did, as he died on 14 February 2013, never admitting any wrongdoing. Even with all the controversy, *True West* gave him an honored send-off, calling him the "Icon" who was "charming and disarming" in the face of criticism.[48] The Showdown at Schieffelin Hall demonstrates the passion with which those enmeshed in Earpiana approach their subject, as well as the power assumed by the one who tells the story. But it also demonstrates the often ambiguous line between authentic or true history and historical fiction, between historian and, in Boyer's term, literary artist. The idea that the historiography of Earp and the nature of the showdown in the streets of Tombstone in 1881 can be so riddled with inaccuracies and falsehoods calls into question the role of those who choose to tell this tale. What responsibility to "true" history do those who call themselves historians have? Do "history buffs" and "western enthusiasts"—or even Hollywood—have a place in the scholarship of Wyatt Earp? Indeed, perhaps to the chagrin of new western historians, if not for them, the hype around the story and Tombstone may have dissipated long ago.

Perhaps physical showdowns over Earp history died with Boyer as hopefully did the penchant for manipulating the historical record for personal gain, but the debate over Earp's character has raged on as more recent journalists and historians become engaged in the passionate Earpiana that has come before them. A number of books attempting to debunk the Hollywood version of Wyatt Earp as most recently seen in *Tombstone* and *Wyatt Earp* hit bookshelves in the last few years. *The Last Gunfight: The Real Story of the Shootout at the O.K. Corral—and How It Changed the American West* by former journalist Jeff Guinn and *The McLaury Brothers of Arizona: An O.K. Corral Obituary* by Paul L. Johnson (both 2011) have contributed to the efforts of those interested in telling a less sanguine story of the Earps and the famous gunfight. Their works received a fair amount of attention from the press, which seems to have a limited acquaintance with the scholarship on Wyatt Earp (excluding Allen Barra, himself an expert on Earp).[49] Of course, as we have seen, writers have been interested in "telling the whole story" or "setting the record straight" for almost a century. These recent works managed, however, to once again recenter Wyatt Earp in the popular press. This is a man who has received public attention for 135 years. These books and the press about them show that his story continues to resonate with the general public, whether he is lauded as the gallant lawman or criticized as the self-serving, ruthless businessman and cold-blooded killer.

In 2013 yet another work about Wyatt Earp was released, this time by professional historian Andrew Isenberg: *Wyatt Earp: A Vigilante Life*. This book is the most recent example of the endless debate over Earp's character, a debate that has been brewing ever since the gunfight took place. Isenberg's book is in keeping with other efforts to revise the frequent but not entirely recent glorified representations of Wyatt and the famous showdown, an endeavor many before Isenberg have undertaken. Like many of the previous works in this chapter, Isenberg's study generally paints Earp as a self-motivated narcissist whose unchecked ambition led to the showdown in Tombstone on 26 October 1881. His work has provoked both academic historians and Earp experts to respond to his claims. Paul Hutton says the book is "useless as a work of scholarship but quite interesting as yet another entry in the popular culture/cultural debate over Earp. It falls in the Frank Waters class of Earp book."[50] Allen Barra calls Isenberg's study an "indictment, coming down hard on his subject for not living up to his TV and movie white knight image."[51] One reviewer highlighted Isenberg's seeming obsession with knocking Earp and his most successful biographer down, writing, "Like a child who won't let things go after a schoolyard brawl, Isenberg can't let more than a few pages pass without reminding us of Lake's flaws and, by implication, the author's scholarly virtue."[52] Indeed, Isenberg's apparent desire to demythologize the man central to the debate seems unnecessary. "It's been more than half a century," writes Barra, "since anyone accepted the hagiographic version of Earp's life offered by Stuart Lake in the 1931 book *Frontier Marshal*, but Isenberg insists on judging Earp" for not living up to Lake's ideal.[53] Further enmeshing himself into the traditional Earpiana milieu, Isenberg responds to Barra's review with the biting "If you want the Earp myth, dust off your DVD of *Gunfight at the O.K. Corral* or *Tombstone*. If you prefer to get your history from historians rather than Hollywood, you'll appreciate *Wyatt Earp: A Vigilante Life*."[54] Isenberg's response situates him as very much a part of the heated discussion with other impassioned Earp historians, as well as in debates around the legitimacy of both grassroots historians and Hollywood in contributing to the field of Earpiana. The claim that Hollywood only purveys the Earp myth (which has not been true for decades) or that other researchers or biographers of Wyatt over the past century have only written positive accounts (which has never been true) and that Isenberg, as a historian, is more suited to interpreting the historical record than others most definitely earns him a place within the disputes discussed in this chapter.

It may be little wonder that, just as in Wyatt's time, feuds like this one continue to take place in and about Tombstone, Arizona. Wyatt's life was beleaguered by such distortion during his own day; Tombstone's current performance of the events in October 1881 is still criticized as inauthentic. Earp historians lament the fact, however, that the field of history—especially that of outlaw-lawman history, which continually must legitimize itself—has been plagued by such seemingly purposeful distortions of the facts. It is also intriguing that these men become so impassioned, so involved, with Wyatt Earp, as we have seen with Lake and Waters, Boyer and Barra, and many others, and with each other's work, to the point of heckling, grandstanding, and almost coming to blows. The contestations within Earp historiography follow in a long history of disputes in the space that we call Tombstone, Arizona. An incredibly violent thirty-second event in October 1881 has come to define Tombstone and Wyatt Earp more than a century later. It is perhaps all of these contestations that help the man and the place remain vibrant spaces of interest and intrigue. The passion that Earp historians reveal in their verve to tell the story reflects the continued infatuation with the mythic West both in the United States and around the world. Their shouts of authenticity and historical accuracy echo those that critics have been lobbing at the city of Tombstone as a tourist destination for decades. These writers seem to also metaphorically be performing the mythic battle fought between the Earps and the Clantons a century earlier. They are replaying and reinforcing ideas about white masculinity, violence, and individualism that underpin the western myth itself and that get played out daily by reenactors and tourists on the dusty streets of Tombstone.

Epilogue

Vigilantism and the Border

In 2011 Tombstone's water line, which carries water from springs in the Huachuca Mountains—in the Miller Peak Wilderness area protected by the US Forest Service—was damaged during a massive fire known as the Monument Fire and monsoons that brought mud and boulders down the side of the mountain, crushing water lines and destroying reservoirs. The town and the federal government have been locked in a battle to access and repair the water line ever since. The city claimed the feds blocked emergency repairs. The feds claimed there is no emergency and "Tombstone is using the fire's aftermath as an excuse to 'upgrade and improve' its water system." In a feud dubbed by CNN the "Showdown at the H$_2$O Corral," the federal government allowed Tombstone to repair the line as long as the work complies with the 1964 Wilderness Act, which states that Tombstone "can dig with shovels, not bulldozers" and that "the new pipe can come up the mountain on horses, not in trucks."[1] In response, Tombstone organized a protest/work party called "The Tombstone Shovel Brigade" for June 2012. The litigation and the shovel brigade event underscore the continued tension between the powers of incorporation and federalization of the region and those that wish to remain on the periphery—as mythic as that position has always been.

The water battle rages on. In 2015 a federal judge rejected arguments that Tombstone had a perpetual right to the water or that it had the right to access the site of the damage.[2] But the water issue had another effect on Tombstone: in 2012 Tombstone's mayor at the time, Jack Henderson, was the first mayor to be recalled in Tombstone's history. Supporters of the recall accused Henderson of failing to protect the infrastructure of Tombstone, citing neglect of the city's water system, fire department, and graveyard as evidence. In addition, Henderson was accused of spending the city's money on things that have "no immediate benefit to the residents of Tombstone." His recall came in the wake of the resignation of three public officials a little more than a year earlier when recall efforts began: Patrick Greene, chamber of commerce executive director and Historic District Commission chair; Don Taylor, chamber of commerce president and city historian; and James Neubauer, Historic District Commission commissioner. Letters from Greene, Taylor, and Neubauer cited malfeasance on the part of the Henderson adminis-tration, including slander, unprofessional behavior, and ethically compro-mising business tactics. These resignations came on the heels of Greene and Taylor being investigated by the Arizona attorney general's office for misappropriation of state funds. Both Taylor and Greene were cleared of any criminal charges, but all of these local battles demonstrate the strug-gles and contestations that continue to brew in Tombstone about how best to manage this municipality, its tourist industry, and the monies generated from this industry, and about the fundamental disagreement over who should have control, both at the federal and state levels, as well as within Tombstone itself. Despite a long history of federal involvement in the West, many saw the debate over water in Tombstone as yet another example of Washington overextending its reach. One Tombstonian understood it as business as usual, claiming, "People in Washington just don't understand the West. They don't understand the wide open spaces and how we live and how we manage the land."[3]

"Wide open spaces" take on a different meaning in the disputes taking place at the US-Mexico border just south of Tombstone. Here there are claims that the federal government is not doing enough and that the space is in fact too open. Calls for reinforced barriers to keep Mexican and Cen-tral American immigrants from illegally crossing the border have reached a fevered pitch in the past ten years, and Tombstone is central to this ongo-ing dispute. The border between the United States and Mexico just thirty miles south of Tombstone is hotly contested; it is no surprise that issues surrounding immigration and illegal activity have found a home in this almost-border town. As the epitome of the Wild West of the late nine-teenth century, Tombstone also has come to symbolize the New West, a place characterized as inhabited by former urbanites whose connection to the region is through recreation and entertainment—although they are unlikely to position themselves in those terms. While the mythic West has been utilized by film producers, reenactors, hobbyists, businessmen, advertisers, marketers, sports fans, and everything in between to play on the fantasy of freedom and individual fortitude, Tombstone and its home state of Arizona have become central to notions of a closed and militaristic space unwelcoming to those seeking to make the dreams of the imagined West—of the imagined America—a reality.

The state of Arizona received international attention on 23 April 2010 when its legislature passed and its governor signed into law Arizona Senate Bill 1070, the nation's strictest anti-immigration measure in recent US history. Probably the most condemned portion of the bill is that it theoretically allows law enforcement to stop people believed to be undocumented and demand proof of status without due cause. While Arizona SB 2162, which passed a week later, made it clear that police officers could check immigrant status only during a lawful stop, detention, or arrest, the law received intense criticism, and Arizona dealt with an almost immediate backlash principally through boycotts of the state by would-be visitors and conventioneers.

Tombstone is in many ways at the crossroads of the immigration controversy. The border patrol militia group the Minuteman Civil Defense Corps (MCDC) was founded by Chris Simcox and Carmen Mercer in Tombstone, Arizona, in 2002. Simcox's initial organization was called Civil Homeland Defense, a Tombstone-based vigilante militia group that "he brags has captured more than 5,000 Mexicans and Central Americans who entered the country without visas."[4] In December 2004 Simcox teamed up with Jim Gilchrist, who already headed up an organization called California Coalition for Immigration Reform, to form the Minuteman Project. While the national Minuteman Project disbanded in 2007, local chapters continue to work in their efforts to secure the border.

Chris Simcox is now a local celebrity. After a failed marriage in Los Angeles, he arrived in Tombstone in 2002—no doubt drawn to the town by its popular cultural identity as a place where vigilante justice prevails—and since has become one of the best-known spokesmen for the American anti-immigrant movement. After working for a while as a gunfight show performer, he bought and became editor of the (now defunct) *Tombstone Tumbleweed* as a forum for his anti-immigration sentiments. "ENOUGH IS ENOUGH!" declared the *Tumbleweed*'s front page in October of that year. "A PUBLIC CALL TO ARMS! CITIZENS BORDER PATROL MILITIA NOW FORMING!" His "call to arms" attracted the attention of Tombstone residents and people around the country, who carried pistols and donned baseball caps "emblazoned with the American flag." The group would patrol the area between Tombstone and Mexico, "searching for people who look like illegal immigrants."

Simcox claimed that immigrants, when caught, "are 'humanely' placed under citizen's arrest and turned over to the U.S. Border Patrol."[5] But Simcox was never himself off the radar of local law enforcement: "In January 2003, while on patrol with Civil Homeland Defense, Simcox was arrested by federal park rangers for illegally carrying a .45-caliber semi-automatic handgun in a national park. Also in Simcox's possession at the time of that arrest, according to police records, were a document entitled 'Mission Plan,' a police scanner, two walkie-talkies, and a toy figure of Wyatt Earp on horseback."[6] Simcox gained national attention in 2010 when he ran against John McCain for US Senate but then went on the lam that same year to avoid being served an order of protection from his ex-wife.[7] Despite loud criticism from civil rights groups and all of the negative press, the group survived under the control of cofounder Carmen Mercer.

Carmen Mercer is a German immigrant who settled in Tombstone, Arizona, in 1992 shortly after divorcing her soldier husband.[8] She became a US citizen only after being asked to leave a local planning committee in Arizona when it was discovered that she was not. She was naturalized in 1999, almost twenty-five years after coming to the United States. She started working at the OK Café in 1993 and bought the restaurant in 1998, solidifying her place in the historic district and in the lore of Tombstone. She started working with Chris Simcox in 2002 after seeing his "Enough Is Enough" editorial. She says she became aware of the problems of illegal immigration only after Simcox enlightened her: "I would come home from Sierra Vista after doing my shopping at night and I would see hundreds of people walking along the San Pedro River, thinking they were tourists. . . . I met Chris Simcox and told him what I had seen, and he said, 'You can't really think those are tourists. Those were illegal aliens that just broke into our country.'"[9]

Simcox's and Mercer's connection was instant, and they founded the Minuteman Project together that same year. She has stood by Simcox over the years (there are rumors that they were a couple for a while) and contributed one thousand dollars to Simcox's Senate campaign in 2009.[10] Also in 2009 she self-published a book, *America: De-Fence-Less*, in which she credits Simcox for motivating her to work against illegal immigration: "[Simcox's] words about our border insecurity and what needed to be done truly inspired me. From a two-person operation, we grew eventually into 12,000 volunteers in several states. Truly amazing, and proof that when Americans set their mind to do something, we can do it!"[11] Like Simcox, Mercer's efforts have not been without controversy. In 2009 she was named by the Arizona attorney general as part of a property-tax scam that bilked victims out of $189 apiece for a property-tax reduction. After receiving hundreds of complaints about the scam, the attorney general filed a suit against the parties he says were involved, including Mercer, who purportedly owned the post office box used in the solicitation. Mercer claimed that she opened the PO box "for a friend" and has turned over more than one thousand responses to the scam.[12]

In March 2010 Mercer was widely criticized for an email message she sent out to MCDC members across the country, an "urgent alert" that encouraged them to come to the border "locked and loaded" prepared to "forcefully engage" with the "criminals" who make it across the border. Like so many before her, Mercer accused the federal government of being impotent in efforts to curtail the number of people attempting to cross the border: "President Obama and John McCain have left us no choice—this March we return to the border locked, loaded and ready to stop each and every individual we encounter along the frontier." Stating that the operation was not "for the faint of heart," she reminded her followers that the MCDC "will forcefully engage, detain, and defend our lives and country from the criminals who trample over our culture and laws. Long arms will be allowed and frankly, encouraged."[13] Merely a week later, on 26 March, Mercer disbanded the national MCDC, claiming she had received many responses to her call to arms email that seemed overly enthusiastic about the prospect of shooting people who attempted to cross into the United States from Mexico. She felt this exuberance was indicative of both the frustration many Americans felt at the lack of action on the part of the state and federal governments and the possibility that people would use any means necessary. Mercer denies that she meant for members to come to the border really locked and loaded, saying that that is not what the group was all about. Nonetheless, the enthusiasm on the part of some members and the criticism on the part of civil rights groups prompted the disbandment of the MCDC. Some critics also believe she disbanded the group among allegations of fiscal mismanagement.[14] Mercer encouraged members to continue in their efforts and to remain committed to more localized MCDC chapters. "She said these local chapters are to follow the same guidelines as national members of MCDC, which solely consist of reporting suspicious border activity to law enforcement and never physically confronting illegal immigrants."[15]

Mercer and Simcox's efforts reveal an underbelly of Tombstone that is one of the most idealized components of its public identity: vigilante justice. Despite the 1881 gunfight being revered as a moment when law and order finally came to the American West, it has been the area's "wildness" that continues to draw the attention of tourists for decades. As Katherine Benton-Cohen reminds us: "Clear away the smoke from the OK Corral and a different Tombstone comes into view. The Saturday-matinee version has shaped popular understandings of the American West for nearly a hundred years. Yet Tombstone's real history resides firmly in a borderland world far more complex than a simple division between good guys and bad guys."[16] Mercer and Simcox, and Arizona as a whole, exemplify this complexity and the impossibility of disentangling vigilantism from the popular understanding of Tombstone and the broader West.

Indeed, the battles at the border follow in a long history of disputes in and about Tombstone and the man that made it famous. Violence and wildness are central to Tombstone's existence and viability as a tourist destination. Richard Slotkin argues that "in American mythogenesis the founding fathers were not those eighteenth-century gentlemen who composed a nation at Philadelphia. Rather, they were those who . . . tore violently a nation from implacable and opulent wilderness." As a result, "Regeneration ultimately became the means of violence, and the myth of regeneration through violence became the structuring metaphor of the American experience."[17] Violence and wildness are crucial to Tombstone's public identity. It makes sense that these battles take place in Tombstone, Arizona, a town whose vitality is inextricably linked to constructed notions of its wild past.

Introduction. The Tombstone Mystique

1. In 1850 Frederick Brunckow joined the Sonora Exploring and Mining Company, a Cincinnati-based company that brought Brunckow west. Eight years later, Brunckow struck out on his own to develop his own mine, the San Pedro Silver Mine, located approximately eight miles from where Tombstone would be founded a little more than twenty years later. Brunckow was discovered murdered in his cabin—now known as the Brunckow Cabin, a site infamous for connections to a number of murdered men and a current site for ghost tours. See William B. Shillingberg, *Tombstone, A.T.: A History of Early Mining, Milling, and Mayhem* (Spokane, Wash.: Arthur H. Clark, 1999).

2. The showdown actually took place in an empty lot and alleyway behind the OK Corral and adjacent to C. S. Fly's boardinghouse. The street fight became known as the Gunfight at the OK Corral only after the 1957 John Sturges film of that name solidified the event's legendary place in the public consciousness.

3. Frank L. Waters, *The Earp Brothers of Tombstone: The Story of Mrs. Virgil Earp* (New York: C. N. Potter, 1960), 87, 88. Frank Waters is well known for his animosity toward Wyatt Earp and the myth Earp himself had a hand in constructing. Waters's work notoriously rakes Earp over the coals for pumping up his own status as a legendary lawman. While Waters's perspective was clouded by a desire to debunk the myth and much of his work should be looked on with skepticism, his description of Tombstone in this time period is uncontested.

4. Shillingberg, *Tombstone*, 81.

5. Waters, *Earp Brothers of Tombstone*, 82, 89.

6. Allen Barra, *Inventing Wyatt Earp: His Life and Many Legends* (New York: Carroll & Graf, 1998), 95.

7. Casey Tefertiller, *Wyatt Earp: The Life behind the Legend* (New York: Wiley, 1997), 39.

8. In an attempt to maintain the blind eye toward cattle rustling they had enjoyed for years, the cowboys of Pima County rigged the reelection of Democrat Shibell for sheriff, who ended up getting 103 votes to the one vote his challenger, Bob Paul, received in the San Simon Cienega precinct, which had only 15 voters. Paul challenged the results of the election, which then went in Paul's favor, and he was declaired the winner. By that time, however, Cochise County had been formed from the eastern portion of Pima County, so the election now was moot. See Andrew C. Isenberg, *Wyatt Earp: A Vigilante Life* (New York: Hill & Wang, 2013), 141–142.

9. Barra, *Inventing Wyatt Earp*, 103. Famous Cowboys in the area at this time include Curly Bill Brocius and Johnny Ringo.

10. Ibid. Historian Andrew Isenberg disputes Barra's and many others' assessment of the antagonism between the Earps and the Cowboys that has been

portrayed by Hollywood as well as biographers for generations as being exaggerated and having nothing to do with politics. He asserts that while Wyatt was not apolitical—he ran for public office a couple of times—he was not necessarily interested in Republican ideology. Indeed, Isenberg says, "Earp wanted to hold public office because it gave him opportunities to make money—he wasn't ideological." Email correspondence with author, 29 September 2015.

11. Wyatt Earp, "How Wyatt Earp Routed a Gang of Arizona Outlaws," *San Francisco Examiner*, 2 August 1896.

12. Barra, *Inventing Wyatt Earp*, 108.

13. See Isenberg, *Wyatt Earp*, 147–148. In fact, Wyatt attributes the events of the afternoon of 26 October 1881 to this secret bargain. Earp, "How Wyatt Earp Routed a Gang of Arizona Outlaws."

14. Barra, *Inventing Wyatt Earp*, 173.

15. Earp claims to have killed Curly Bill Brocius, but no body was recovered, and this assertion has never been confirmed. And though Earp at one time claimed he had killed Ringo, Ringo's death in July 1882 was declared a suicide after Earp and his posse had left Arizona. "It is simply impossible for Earp to have killed Ringo," says Andrew Isenberg, "even though in his unpublished memoirs he claimed to have done so." Email correspondence with author, 29 September 2015.

16. Eric L. Clements, *After the Boom in Tombstone and Jerome: Decline in Western Resource Towns* (Reno: University of Nevada Press, 2003), 15.

17. Richard Slotkin, *Gunfighter Nation: The Myth of the Frontier in Twentieth-Century America* (1992; reprint, Norman: University of Oklahoma Press, 1998), 384.

18. A short chapter on tourism in Tombstone and the ways the town has been represented in five Hollywood productions appears in Warwick Frost and Jennifer Laing, *Imagining the American West through Film and Tourism* (New York: Routledge, 2015), 61–76.

19. Odie B. Faulk, *Tombstone, Arizona: Myth and Reality* (New York: Oxford University Press, 1972), 207.

20. David M. Wrobel, *The End of American Exceptionalism: Frontier Anxiety from the Old West to the New Deal* (Lawrence: University Press of Kansas, 1993). See also Michael L. Johnson, *Hunger for the Wild: America's Obsession with the Untamed West* (Lawrence: University Press of Kansas, 2007).

21. Arizona Office of Tourism, "Arizona 2012 Tourism Facts: Year-End Summary," 3, http://www.azot.co/system/files/1146/original/2012%20AOT%20Tourism%20Facts%2003.05.pdf?1395843739 (accessed 23 November 2015).

22. This figure—as seen in tourism literature, Tombstone websites, and articles about Tombstone—varies from source to source. According to "Bronco Bill" Pakinkis, a Tombstone historian and member of the historic district commission who is heavily involved in planning and promoting special events, the number has been as high as 650,000 (email correspondence with author, 5 March 2015). Finding an exact number has been difficult because each site in Tombstone keeps its own visitation numbers, which means there are no totals for those visiting the town as a whole. See Ann O'Neill, "Showdown at the H_2O Corral," CNN, 10 May 2012, http://www.cnn.com/2012/05/10/us/tombstone-water-fight/index.html (accessed 3

September 2015); and Ken Belson, "Cleaning Up the Old West the Modern Way," *New York Times*, 21 January 2012, A14, http://www.nytimes.com/2012/01/22/us /cleaning-up-tombstone-the-modern-way.html?_r=0 (accessed 23 November 2015).

23. Dydia DeLyser, "Authenticity on the Ground: Engaging the Past in a California Ghost Town," *Annals of the Association of American Geographers* 89, no. 4 (December 1999): 602–632.

24. Ibid., 606.

25. Julian Smith, "Living Arizona's Wild West," Arizona Office of Tourism, http://www.visitarizona.com/experience-and-share/featured-article/living-arizonas -wild-west (accessed 23 November 2015).

26. DeLyser, "Authenticity on the Ground," 604. See also Erik Cohen, "Authenticity and Commoditization in Tourism," *Annals of Tourism Research* 15 (1988): 371–386; Eric Hobsbawm and Terrance Ranger, *The Invention of Tradition* (New York: Cambridge University Press, 1983); Dean MacCannell, *The Tourist: A New Theory of the Leisure Class* (Berkeley: University of California Press, 1976); and Umberto Eco, *Travels in Hyperreality* (New York: Harcourt Brace, 1986).

27. Eco, *Travels in Hyperreality*, 7.

28. Eco quoted in Edward M. Bruner, "Abraham Lincoln as Authentic Reproduction: A Critique of Postmodernism," *American Anthropologist* 96, no. 2 (June 1994): 397.

29. DeLyser, "Authenticity on the Ground," 604, 613. See also Edward M. Bruner, *Culture on Tour: Ethnographies of Travel* (Chicago: University of Chicago Press, 2004).

30. Bruner, "Abraham Lincoln as Authentic Reproduction," 398, 399, 400.

31. See www.tombstoneweb.com (accessed 24 November 2015); tombstonebird cage.com (accessed 24 November 2015); http://tombstonecourthouse.com/ (accessed 24 November 2015). See also Alyssa Thompson and Kyle Sandell, "Fight on to Save Tombstone Courthouse," *Tucson Sentinel*, February 5, 2010, http://www.tucson sentinel.com/local/report/020510_courthouse/fight-save-tombstone-courthouse/ (accessed 25 November 2015).

32. Larian Motel, https://www.tombstonemotels.com/attract.html (accessed 25 November 2015); Gunfight Palace, www.gunfightpalace.com (accessed 24 November 2015).

33. See, for example, quotations from then-mayor Dusty Escapule: "We're not a movie set or something fabricated; we work hard to preserve it," in Julie Alfin, "Magazine's Omission Irks Locals," *Tombstone Epitaph*, 29 January 2010, 2; "[Tombstone is] not a movie set or a theme park, but a real old town," in "Landmark Status No Longer Threatened: Tombstone Still Listed as Historic," *Tombstone Epitaph*, 3 April 2009.

34. For more on the West of the imagination and the West as myth, see Liza Nicholas, Elaine M. Bapis, and Thomas J. Harvey, eds., *Imagining the Big Open: Nature, Identity, and Play in the New West* (Salt Lake City: University of Utah Press, 2003); Richard Slotkin, *Fatal Environment: The Myth of the Frontier in the Age of Industrialization, 1800–1890* (1985; reprint Norman: University of Oklahoma Press, 1998); Robert G. Athearn, *The Mythic West in Twentieth-Century America* (Lawrence: University Press of Kansas, 1986); and, of course, Henry Nash Smith, *Virgin Land:*

The American West as Symbol and Myth (1950; reprint, Cambridge, MA: Harvard University Press, 1978).

Chapter 1. Making History

1. National Park Service, http://www.nps.gov/nhl/index.htm (accessed 24 November 2015).

2. Author visit to Tombstone, April 2010.

3. John Urry, *The Tourist Gaze* (London: Sage, 2002).

4. Ibid., 3.

5. Adrian Franklin, *Tourism: An Introduction* (London: Sage, 2003), 8.

6. There are about forty cemeteries throughout the United States that are named or referred to as "Boothill" or "Boot Hill," including those found in Virginia City, Nevada; Virginia City, Montana; El Paso, Texas; and Deadwood, South Dakota. Ted Robbins, "A Wild Resting Place for Gunslingers and Cowboys," National Public Radio, *Morning Edition*, 14 August 2012, http://www.npr.org/2012/08/14/158585753/a-wild-resting-place-for-gunslingers-and-cowboys (accessed 3 September 2015).

7. Doug Kreutz, "Boothill Gets a Face-lift: Wood 'Headstones' Replace Inauthentic Metal Markers," *Arizona Daily Star*, 17 February 2012, http://tucson.com/news/local/wood-headstones-replace-inauthentic-metal-markers/article_1b75c512-773e-5cb9-b4ba-ce964f1e2988.html (accessed 3 September 2015).

8. According to former Tombstone city historian Ben Traywick, Lester Moore was employed as a Wells Fargo station agent in the border town of Naco. Hank Dunstan came to claim a package one afternoon, but it was damaged. "An argument ensued, and both Moore and Dunstan reached for their six shooters. When the smoke cleared, Les Moore lay dead behind his window with four .44 slugs in his chest. Dunstan, too, lay dying, a hole blasted through his ribs by the one shot Moore had been able to get off before he collapsed." Moore was given a space in Boothill and one of the most famous epitaphs of the Old West. Dunstan's burial place is unknown. Ben Traywick, "Tombstone's Cemetery: Boothill," *Wild West*, 12 June 2006, http://www.historynet.com/tombstones-cemetery-boothill.htm (accessed 25 November 2015).

9. J. Stuart Rosebrook, "The Best of Heritage Travel 2014," *True West*, 9 December 2013, http://www.truewestmagazine.com/the-best-of-heritage-travel-2014-2/ (accessed 24 November 2015). The editor's choice went to Concordia in El Paso, Texas.

10. Review of Boothill Graveyard, TripAdvisor, http://www.tripadvisor.com/ShowUserReviews-g31381-d3834325-r15067899-Boothilll_Graveyard-Tombstone_Arizona.html#UR15067899, accessed 5 February 2015.

11. "Wyatt Earp's Return to Tombstone," 29 October 2008, http://www.prweb.com/releases/bronze/sculpture/prweb1508184.htm (accessed 26 October 2012).

12. Meredith Littlejohn, "Wyatt Earp Returns to Tombstone in Bronze," *Tombstone News*, 21 November 2008.

13. There are Doc Holliday's Saloons in towns around the United States, including Nashville, Tennesee; Cottage Hills, Illinois; and Glenwood Springs, Colorado. There is no indication that this is a chain.

14. Conversation with author, February 2015.

15. Conversation with author, March 2007.

16. Hal Rothman, *Devil's Bargains: Tourism in the Twentieth-Century American West* (Lawrence: University Press of Kansas, 1998), 11.

17. Franklin, *Tourism*, 2, 4, 5.

18. Victor Turner, "Liminality and Communitas," in *The Ritual Process: Structure and Anti-Structure* (Chicago: Aldine, 1969), 94–113, 125–130.

19. Conversation with author, Crystal Palace Saloon, Tombstone, Arizona, March 2007.

20. Conversations with author, Crystal Palace Saloon, Tombstone, Arizona, 14 February 2015.

21. Shillingberg, *Tombstone, A.T.*, 105.

22. Arizona Office of Tourism, http://visitarizona.com/experience-and-share/featured-article/kid-friendly-arizona (accessed 25 November 2015). A number of visitors point to the idea that Tombstone is a good place to bring children as a major reason they like it here and keep coming back. Conversations with author in and around Tombstone's Historic Landmark District, esp. February 2015.

23. Conversation with author, Historama, Tombstone, Arizona, April 2010.

24. Urry, *Tourist Gaze*, 13.

25. Tombstone Merchants Brochure, Fall 2014, in author's possession.

26. Scott Simmon, *The Invention of the Western: A Cultural History of the Genre's First Half-Century* (Cambridge: Cambridge University Press, 2003), 277.

27. Al Larson, "Mountain Justice: An Examination of Three Mountainous West County Courthouses," *Material Culture* 31, no. 1 (Spring 1999): 22.

28. Alyssa Thompson and Kyle Sandell, "Fight on to Save Tombstone Courthouse," *Tucson Sentinel*, 5 February 2010, http://www.tucsonsentinel.com/local/report/020510_courthouse/fight-save-tombstone-courthouse/ (accessed 3 September 2015).

29. Arizona Parks Commission, http://azstateparks.com/Parks/TOCO/index.html (accessed 21 September 2010).

30. Katherine Benton-Cohen, *Borderline Americans: Racial Division and Labor War in the Arizona Borderlands* (Cambridge, MA: Harvard University Press, 2009), 69, 71.

31. The Cochise County census of 1882 put Tombstone's population at 5,300; the *Tucson and Tombstone General and Business Directory* set the population at around 6,300; and an Arizona business directory estimated the population to be 6,000. Clements, *After the Boom*, 135. See also Benton-Cohen, *Borderline Americans*, 71.

32. Clements, *After the Boom*, 135.

33. Benton-Cohen, *Borderline Americans*, 74, 77.

34. Hartmut Lutz, "German Indianthusiasm: A Socially Constructed German National(ist) Myth," in *Germans and Indians: Fantasies, Encounters, Projections*, ed. Colin G. Calloway, Gerd Gemünden, and Susanne Zantop (Lincoln: University of Nebraska Press, 2002), 167.

35. Julie Vanderdasson, Tombstone Courthouse State Historic Park Manager, email correspondence with author, 9 March 2015.

36. The Bisbee Massacre occurred in Bisbee, Arizona, on 8 December 1883,

when a gang robbed a general store and killed four people. Five of the six men responsible were later convicted and sentenced to hang in Tombstone (the first criminals to be legally hanged in Tombstone). John Heith escaped that sentence but did not escape the "vigilante justice" carried out by a mob of men from Bisbee dissastisfied with the ruling.

37. Linda Weiland, "Tombstone Courthouse State Historic Park," *Tombstone Times* 8, no. 3 (March 2010), http://www.tombstonetimes.com/stories/courthouse 10.html (accessed 20 January 2013). These two hangings resulted in the death of seven men. The first of these hangings, which occurred on 28 March 1884, was of five men convicted of murdering three men and a woman during the Bisbee Massacre of 1883. The five men were Daniel "Big Dan" Dowd, Comer W. "Red" Sample, James "Tex" Howard, William "Bill" Delaney, and Daniel "York" Kelly. "Old West Legends," http://www.legendsofamerica.com/we-johnheath.html (accessed 25 November 2015). The second hanging, on 16 November 1900, was of brothers William and Thomas Lee Halderman, who had been convicted of killing Constable Chester L. Ainsworth and wounding his deputy, Teddy Moore, in a brief gunfight in the Chiricahua Mountains in 1899. R. Michael Wilson, *Legal Executions in the Western Territories, 1847–1911* (Jefferson, NC: McFarland, 2010), 42.

38. Weiland, "Tombstone Courthouse State Historic Park."

39. Seven of the parks that were slated for closing are historical state parks, including the Yuma Territorial Prison. Before reaching agreements with a number of individual communities, the Arizona State Parks Board chose only one of the eight historic parks in Arizona to remain open: the Yuma Quartermaster Depot State Historic Park.

40. Conversation with author, Tombstone Courthouse State Historic Park, April 2010.

41. Conversations with author, Tombstone, Arizona, February 2015.

42. David Wrobel, Introduction, "Tourists, Tourism, and the Toured Upon," in *Seeing and Being Seen: Tourism and the American West*, ed. David Wrobel and Patrick Long (Lawrence: University Press of Kansas, 2001), 5.

43. Conversation with author, April 2010. Major Wolcott's "Regulators," who worked out of the Powder River area of Wyoming from 1887 to 1892, were known as the Red Sash Gang and did in fact wear red sashes. They had no connection to the Cowboys in Tombstone. "Outlaw Gangs of the American West," http://www.legendsofamerica.com/we-outlawgangslist5.html (accessed 3 September 2015).

44. Franklin, *Tourism*, 9.

45. Conversation with author, Tombstone Chamber of Commerce, April 2010.

46. Meredith Littlejohn, "Neon Signs in the Historic District Major Concern for HDC," *Tombstone News*, 28 May 2010.

47. Southeastern Arizona Economic Development District, "Cochise County Tourist Attractions, Analysis and Overview," http://seagoedd.org/ceds-home/sea go-region/current-situation-and-trends/tourism-regional-analysis/cochise-county -tourist-attractions-analysis-and-overview/ (accessed 24 November 2015).

48. In addition to heritage tourism, other types of tourism have flourished here, including paranormal and supernatural tourism, biker tourism, and gun tourism.

49. National Historic Landmarks Program, http://tps.cr.nps.gov/nhl/detail .cfm?ResourceId=88&ResourceType=District (accessed 2 November 2010). The citizens of Tombstone did not vote on this measure, which was taken up and approved by the city council.

50. "Dust in the Wind Causes Major Problems for Allen Street Shops," *Tombstone Epitaph*, 24 April 2006.

51. Betty Krug, "In Regard to the Dirt on the Streets of Tombstone," letter to the editor, *Tombstone News*, 8 September 2006. See also Chelsea Kerzner, "Tombstone Left in the Dust," *Tombstone Epitaph*, 3 April 2009, 1.

52. Overheard by author, July 2012.

53. See Adam Daley, "Mayor Embroiled Again in Brouhaha," *Tombstone Epitaph*, 3 April 2009, 1.

54. Meredith Littlejohn, "Council Approves Closure of 4th and 5th Streets," *Tombstone News*, 27 February 2009, http://thetombstonenews.com/council-approves -closure-of-th-and-th-streets-p1997-1.htm (accessed 25 November 2015).

55. Conversation with author, Tombstone Chamber of Commerce, April 2010.

56. Maria Polletta, "Despite Budget Cuts, Tombstone Refuses to Let Its State Park Close," *Cronkite News*, 30 September 2010, http://cronkitenewsonline.com /2010/09/despite-budget-cuts-tombstone-volunteers-refuse-to-let-state-park-die/ (accessed 3 September 2015); Julie Vanderdasson, email correspondence with author, 9 March 2015.

57. Conversation with author, Tombstone Courthouse State Historic Park, April 2010.

58. Thompson and Sandell, "Fight on to Save Tombstone Courthouse."

59. Ibid.

60. "Tombstone Celebrates Grand Reopening of Courthouse," *Tombstone News*, 1 November 2010, http://thetombstonenews.com/tombstone-celebrates-grand-re opening-of-courthouse-p2667-1.htm (accessed 3 September 2015).

61. Yoohyun Jung, "In Tombstone, a Dispute over the Historical Record," *Arizona Sonora News*, 11 December 2013; Alex P. Wainwright, "Cuts May Threaten Tombstone Records," *Tombstone Epitaph*, 19 February 2014; Meredith Littlejohn, "Foundation for the Tombstone Archives Fails to Pay City or Receive 501(c)(3)," *Tombstone News*, 4 April 2014.

62. "Landmark Status No Longer Threatened: Tombstone Still Listed as Historic," *Tombstone Epitaph*, 3 April 2009.

63. Email correspondence with author, 19 February 2015.

64. John D. Dorst, *The Written Suburb: An American Site, an Ethnographic Dilemma* (Philadelphia: University of Pennsylvania Press, 1989), 182.

Chapter 2. Preservation and Performance

1. Douglas D. Martin, *Tombstone's Epitaph: The History of a Frontier Town as Chronicled in Its Newspaper* (Albuquerque: University of New Mexico Press, 1951), 16.

2. William M. Breakenridge, *Helldorado: Bringing the Law to the Mesquite*, ed. Richard Maxwell Brown (1928; reprint, Lincoln: University of Nebraska Press, 1992). Breakenridge was deputy sheriff under John Behan as well as a US deputy

marshal in the 1880s and knew all those involved in the shootout behind the OK Corral. His portrayal of Wyatt Earp in *Helldorado Days* is not a positive one.

3. For Helldorado Days and the birth of Tombstone tourism, see Kevin Britz, "'A True to Life Reproduction': The Origins of Tombstone's Helldorado Celebration," *Journal of Arizona History* 22 (Winter 2001): 369–408.

4. Mitchell Schwarzer, "Myths of Permanence and Transience in the Discourse on Historic Preservation in the United States," *Journal of Architectural Education* 48, no. 1 (1994): 2.

5. Barbara J. Howe, "Women in Historic Preservation: The Legacy of Ann Pamela Cunningham," *Public Historian* 12, no. 1 (Winter 1990): 31.

6. Judy Mattivi Morley, *Historic Preservation and the Imagined West: Albuquerque, Denver, and Seattle* (Lawrence: University Press of Kansas, 2006), 2, 3.

7. Pierre Bourdieu explores the connection between "taste" and the maintenance of class hierarchies and hegemonic power relations. He argues that the class distinctions of the economy produce the symbolic distinctions of culture, which in turn legitimate the class distinctions that produced them. He demonstrates how consumption of cultural objects—how "taste" for certain cultural practices and productions (such as going to museums or heritage sites)—reveals and reproduces the class system. His project is to show how taste and aesthetics, far from being innate to a particular object or a particular practice, are actually learned through the socializing institutions of the education system and social upbringing. Pierre Bourdieu, *Distinction: A Social Critique of the Judgment of Taste* (Cambridge, MA: Harvard University Press, 1984).

8. Randall Mason, "Economics and Heritage Conservation: Concepts, Values, and Agendas for Research," Economics and Heritage Conservation, a Meeting Organized by the Getty Conservation Institute, December 1998, Getty Center, Los Angeles, California, 2, 3.

9. Stuart Hall, "Whose Heritage?" in *The Politics of Heritage, the Legacies of Race*, ed. Jo Littler and Roshi Naidoo (New York: Routledge, 2005), 24.

10. National Park Service, http://www.nps.gov/nhl/; http://www.nps.gov/nhl/learn/intro.htm (accessed 23 November 2015).

11. Mike Wallace, *Mickey Mouse History and Other Essays on American Memory* (Philadelphia: Temple University Press, 1996), 4, 9.

12. Greenfield Village, http://www.thehenryford.org/village/ (accessed 28 November 2011).

13. Wallace, *Mickey Mouse History*, 12.

14. Ibid., 15.

15. Morley, *Historic Preservation and the Imagined West*, 2.

16. Colonial Williamsburg website, http://www.history.org/foundation/mission.cfm (accessed 28 November 2011).

17. Morley, *Historic Preservation and the Imagined West*, 2.

18. Wallace, *Mickey Mouse History*, 14, 15.

19. See Wallace, *Mickey Mouse History*, for an in-depth exploration into the ways history museums, especially "open air" history museums, Disneyland and EPCOT

Center, and Ronald Reagan's particular uses of historical narratives reveal the splice-and-dice approach to public history that has dominated discourses over what histories are worth preserving and telling and which ones do not fit as neatly within the metanarrative of the United States.

20. Michael G. Kammen, *Mystic Chords of Memory: The Transformation of Tradition in American Culture* (New York: Knopf, 1991), 626.

21. http://www.thehenryford.org/village/about.aspx (accessed 8 March 2015); http://www.colonialwilliamsburg.com/discover/ (accessed 10 May 2015).

22. Kammen, *Mystic Chords of Memory*, 13, 5.

23. Marita Sturken, *Tourists of History: Memory, Kitsch, and Consumerism from Oklahoma City to Ground Zero* (Durham, NC: Duke University Press, 2007), 10.

24. Richard R. Flores, *Remembering the Alamo: Memory, Modernity, and the Master Symbol* (Austin: University of Texas Press, 2002); Edward Tabor Linenthal, *Sacred Ground: Americans and Their Battlefields* (Urbana: University of Illinois Press, 1991).

25. Kammen, *Mystic Chords of Memory*, 626.

26. James Gilbert Ryan and Leonard C. Schlup, *Historical Dictionary of the 1940s* (Armonk, NY: M. E. Sharpe, 2006), 377.

27. Morley, *Historic Preservation and the Imagined West*, 10.

28. Johnson, *Hunger for the Wild*, 204.

29. Wrobel, *End of American Exceptionalism*. See also Johnson, *Hunger for the Wild*.

30. Schwarzer, "Myths of Permanence and Transience," 4; Morley, *Historic Preservation and the Imagined West*, 10.

31. Morley, *Historic Preservation and the Imagined West*, 10.

32. Billy G. Garrett and James W. Garrison, with the Tombstone Restoration Commission, *Plan for the Creation of a Historic Environment in Tombstone, Arizona* (Tombstone, AZ: Tombstone Restoration Commission, 1972), iii.

33. Ibid., 23.

34. "Here and There: Restoration of Tombstone Planned," *Desert*, March 1951, 31.

35. "Tombstone Historic District," National Historic Landmarks Program, National Park Service website: http://tps.cr.nps.gov/nhl/detail.cfm?ResourceId =88&ResourceType=District.

36. Faulk, *Tombstone*, 130.

37. Clarence Mortimer Palmer Jr. died in 1971. Elizabeth Palmer (his daughter-in-law), "Clarence Mortimer Palmer Jr. Life Story," 25 February 2014, https://family search.org/photos/stories/5507525 (accessed 3 September 2015).

38. Other inductees included Tombstone's founder, Ed Schieffelin, his brother Al Schieffelin, and their partner Richard Gird; Nellie Cashman, an Irish émigrée who was the driving force behind the founding of the Catholic church and the first hospital in Tombstone; Ethel Macia, an active member of the Arizona Pioneer Society, the Tombstone Women's Club, and a charter member of the Tombstone Restoration Commission, helping organize the first Helldorado Days in 1929; Harold O. Love, who bought and restored a number of historic buildings in Tombstone's historic district in the 1960s; and Ben Traywick, prolific researcher and writer of Tombstone history and recently retired Tombstone city historian. See

"First Annual Founder's Day Hall of Fame Induction Ceremony," *Tombstone News*, http://thetombstonenews.com/first-annual-founders-day-hall-of-fame-induction-ceremony-p2583-1.htm (accessed 23 November 2011).

39. Rothman, *Devil's Bargains*, 102.

40. Jane Tompkins, *West of Everything: The Inner Life of Westerns* (New York: Oxford University Press, 1992), 4.

41. Edna Landin, "Why Tombstone, Arizona Is Called the Town Too Tough to Die" (Tombstone, AZ: Tombstone Restoration Commission, 1950), "Tombstone Restoration Commission, 1959–1974," Sam V. Medigovich Collection, 1881–1974, MS 1077, RG 2, Arizona Historical Society, Tucson, Arizona (hereafter cited as Medigovich Collection).

42. Landin received a number of replies from studios. In response to one such plea by Landin to Wyatt Earp Enterprises, creators of the television show *The Life and Legend of Wyatt Earp* on ABC, the producers wrote a letter dated 16 March 1959:

> Dear Mrs. Landin:
> . . . I wish it were possible to shoot THE LIFE AND LEGEND OF WYATT EARP in Tombstone, with the main advantages you mentioned, but it is out of the question because of the very great expense it would entail on our part, and because the shows consist of interior and exterior shots. . . .
> I wish we might be of greater help in your fine project to restore Tombstone, but it is simply beyond our means. . . .
> Sincerely, Robert F. Sisk, s/lb

Edna Landin Papers, fol. 464, 1955–1963, Medigovich Collection.

43. See "Medicine: Revival in Tombstone," *Time*, 19 November 1945, http://content.time.com/time/subscriber/article/0,33009,886688,00.html (accessed 25 November 2015).

44. Edna Landin, "The Legend Lives," *Desert*, January 1965, 30–31.

45. "Tombstone Restoration Commission, 1959–1974," Medigovich Collection.

46. William S. Ellis, "The Scene: Bat, Wyatt, Doc, and Boot Hill to Boot," *Life*, 3 June 1966, R2.

47. Ibid., R6.

48. Dorothy C. Palmer, "Fly's Studio Next for Restoration," *Arizona Republic*, 26 October 1963, 21.

49. Ellis, "The Scene," R6.

50. "First Annual Founder's Day Hall of Fame Induction Ceremony."

51. Garrett and Garrison, *Historic Environment in Tombstone*, 28.

52. The materials they gathered are archived in the Medigovich Collection.

53. Garrett and Garrison, *Historic Environment in Tombstone*, 35.

54. Ibid., iii, v, 30, 25.

55. Ibid., iii, 30, v, E2.

56. Ibid., 44, 45.

57. "Tombstone Restoration Commission, 1959–1974," Medigovich Collection.

58. See, for example, "Wanted! For Crimes against American Heritage: The Town of Tombstone, Arizona," *The Independent* (UK), 23 July 2005; Andrew Pollack, "Wyatt Earp Fought Here, but the Corral Isn't O.K.," *New York Times*, 8 August 2005; Nicholas Riccardi, "Too Many Wyatt Earps Walking Tombstone's Streets," *Los Angeles Times*, 1 April 2009.

59. Tombstone Vigilantes, http://www.tombstonevigilantes.com/news.html (accessed 6 November 2011).

60. Helldorado Days had parades and reenactments but occurred only once a year, in October.

61. L. W. Michaelson, "Tombstone," *Prairie Schooner* 30, no. 1 (Spring 1956): 56, 57.

62. http://www.tombstonevigilantes.com/news.html.

63. Ibid.

64. Conversation with author, Tombstone, Arizona, February 2015.

65. Ibid.

66. Dana Cole, "Historian Ben Traywick Keeps Tombstone on the Map," *Auction Central News*, 11 September 2012, https://www.liveauctioneers.com/news/people/historian-ben-traywick-keeps-tombstone-on-the-map/ (accessed 25 November 2015).

67. Tombstone Wild Bunch and Hell's Belles website, http://www.tombstonewildbunch.com/ (accessed 5 September 2011).

68. Cole, "Historian Ben Traywick Keeps Tombstone on the Map."

69. Conversation with author, Lincoln, New Mexico, October 2011.

70. Dan Sorenson, "Historic Tombstone Lacks Means to Shore Up Image: Old West Town Depends on Tourism, Which Depends in Turn on Credibility," *Arizona Daily Star*, 2 September 2006.

71. Cole, "Historian Ben Traywick Keeps Tombstone on the Map."

72. Meredith Littlejohn, "Ben Traywick Retires as City Historian," *Tombstone News*, 15 October 2010, http://thetombstonenews.com/ben-traywick-retires-as-city-historian-p2837-1.htm (accessed 14 November 2011).

73. Anthony Victor Reyes, "Historian Concerned over Tombstone's History," *Arizona Sonora News*, 19 February 2014.

74. Don Dedera, "Coffee Break," *Arizona Republic*, 1955, Edna Landin Papers, folder 464, 1955–1963, Medigovich Collection.

75. "Magazine's Omission Irks Locals," *Tombstone Epitaph*, 28 January 2010. The towns that made it to *True West's* top ten in 2010 are, from last to first, The Dalles, Oregon; Dodge City, Kansas; Lincoln, New Mexico; Cherokee Nation; Fort Pierre, South Dakota; Glenwood Springs, Colorado; Dubois, Wyoming; Fort Davis, Texas; Florence, Arizona; and Virginia City, Nevada.

76. Pallock, "Wyatt Earp Fought Here, but the Corral Isn't O.K."

77. "Magazine's Omission Irks Locals," *Tombstone Epitaph*, 28 January 2010.

78. Mark Boardman, "Top Ten True Western Towns of 2011: Towns to Watch," *True West*, 11 January 2011, 27.

79. Kevin Nedakai, "City Snubbed in Top 10 Best Old West Towns," *Tombstone Epitaph*, 17 February 2012, 1.

80. John Stanley, "Top Ten True Western Towns of 2014," *True West*, 6 January 2014, http://www.truewestmagazine.com/top-10-true-western-towns-of-the-year-for-2014/ (accessed 3 September 2015).

81. See Chris Wilson, *The Myth of Santa Fe: Creating a Modern Regional Tradition* (Albuquerque: University of New Mexico Press, 1997); Hal Rothman, *The Culture of Tourism, the Tourism of Culture: Selling the Past to the Present in the American Southwest* (Albuquerque: University of New Mexico Press, 2003); Wallace, *Mickey Mouse History*; and Bonnie Christensen, *Red Lodge and the Mythic West: Coal Miners to Cowboys* (Lawrence: University Press of Kansas, 2002).

82. Meaghan Bayley, "Tombstone Park Puts the Park in Parking Lot," *Tombstone Epitaph*, 8 October 2009, 4, http://journalism.arizona.edu/sites/journalism.arizona.edu/files/files-page/epitaph_10-9-09.pdf (accessed 25 November 2015).

83. Tombstone Chamber of Commerce, tombstonechamber.com. See also Meredith Littlejohn, "Tombstone Named Preserve America Community," *Tombstone News*, 6 February 2009.

84. Sorenson, "Historic Tombstone."

Chapter 3. The Earp Legend in Film

1. Paul Andrew Hutton, "Showdown at the Hollywood Corral: Wyatt Earp and the Movies," *Montana: The Magazine of Western History* 45 (Summer 1995): 1.

2. Robert G. Athearn, *Westward the Briton* (New York: Charles Scribner's Sons, 1953).

3. Richard Aquila, ed., *Wanted Dead or Alive: The American West in Popular Culture* (Urbana: University of Illinois Press, 1998), 1.

4. Richard Brodhead, *Cultures of Letters: Scenes of Reading and Writing in Nineteenth-Century America* (Chicago: University of Chicago Press, 1995), 120, 121.

5. Bruner, *Culture on Tour*, 20.

6. John H. Lenihan, *Showdown: Confronting Modern America in the Western Film* (Urbana: University of Illinois Press, 1980), 4.

7. Stanley Corkin, *Cowboys as Cold Warriors: The Western and U.S. History* (Philadelphia: Temple University Press, 2004), 21.

8. Jim Kitses, "Introduction: Post-modernism and the Western," in *The Western Reader*, ed. Jim Kitses and Gregg Rickman (New York: Limelight, 1998), 21.

9. Aquila, *Wanted Dead or Alive*, 12.

10. Raymond Durgnat and Scott Simmon, "Six Creeds That Won the Western," in Kitses and Rickman, *Western Reader*, 70.

11. David Pierson, "Turner Network Television's Made-for-TV Western Films: Engaging Audiences through Genre and Themes," in *Hollywood's West: The American Frontier in Film, Television, and History*, ed. Peter C. Rollins and John E. O'Connor (Lexington: University Press of Kentucky, 2005), 286.

12. Slotkin, *Gunfighter Nation*, 237. For more on the function of repetition in popular culture, see Frederic Jameson's "Reification and Utopia in Mass Culture," in *Signatures of the Visible* (New York: Routledge, 1992).

13. Alexandra Keller, "Historical Discourse and American Identity in Westerns since the Reagan Era," in Rollins and O'Connor, *Hollywood's West*, 241.

14. Slotkin, *Gunfighter Nation*, 235.

15. See Aquila, *Wanted Dead or Alive*; Slotkin, *Gunfighter Nation*; Jon Tuska, *The Filming of the West* (New York: Doubleday, 1978); Will Wright, *Sixguns and Society: A Structural Study of the Western* (Berkeley: University of California Press, 1977).

16. Michael Coyne, *The Crowded Prairie: American National Identity in the Hollywood Western* (New York: Tauris, 1997), 15.

17. Lenihan, *Showdown*, 4.

18. Corkin, *Cowboys as Cold Warriors*, 3.

19. In *The Crowded Prairie*, Coyne states: "I take little account of the success of *Dances with Wolves* (1990) or *Unforgiven* (1992), both filmed long after the Western ceased to be a vital force in American culture" (6).

20. *Brokeback Mountain* (2005), which traces the complex romantic and sexual relationship of two men in the West from 1963 to 1983, is an example.

21. *No Country for Old Men* (2007), *Brokeback Mountain*, and *There Will Be Blood* (2007) are all set in the twentieth-century West.

22. *Unforgiven* (1992) and the remake of *3:10 to Yuma* (2007) are examples of films that critique the redemptive quality of violence that traditionally had been celebrated in earlier westerns.

23. Films about Tombstone or Wyatt Earp before 1946 include *Law and Order* (1932), *Frontier Marshal* (1934), *Frontier Marshal* (1939), *The Arizonian* (1935), *Law for Tombstone* (1937), and *Tombstone, the Town Too Tough to Die* (1942).

24. *My Darling Clementine*, DVD, directed by John Ford (1946; Los Angeles, CA: 20th Century Fox, 2004).

25. For more on Native American stereotypes in film, see Jacqueline Kilpatrick, *Celluloid Indians: Native Americans and Film* (Lincoln: University of Nebraska Press, 1999).

26. Charles Ramírez Berg says of Chihuahua that she "is an archetypal example" of the harlot stereotype explored in his study of Latino/a stereotypes in film:

> Without a man she is a leaf in the wind, so when Doc (Victor Mature) is out of town, she fixes her amorous attentions on Wyatt Earp (Henry Fonda). . . . Since the harlot is a slave to her passions, her conduct is simplistically attributed to her inherent nymphomania. In true stereotypical fashion we are never provided with any deeper motivation for her actions—she is basically a sex machine innately lusting for a white male. (71)

For further discussion of the trope of the Mexican woman as harlot in film, see Charles Ramírez Berg, *Latino Images in Film: Stereotypes, Subversion, and Resistance* (Austin: University of Texas Press, 2002).

27. "If justice and order did not continually demand his protection," Robert Warshow writes about the gunfighter in traditional westerns, "he [the Westerner] would be without a calling. Indeed, we come upon him often in just that situation, as the reign of law settles over the West and he is forced to see that his day is over; those are the pictures which end with his death or with his departure for some remote frontier." Robert Warshow, *Immediate Experience: Movies, Comics, Theatre, and Other Aspects of Popular Culture* (Garden City, NY: Doubleday, 1962), 140.

28. This is the third film to be based on Lake's *Wyatt Earp: Frontier Marshal*. The previous two were both titled *Frontier Marshal*, one produced in 1934, the other in 1939.

29. Stuart N. Lake, *Wyatt Earp: Frontier Marshal* (Boston: Houghton Mifflin, 1931), viii.

30. Casey Tefertiller, foreword to Walter Noble Burns, *Tombstone: An Iliad of the Southwest* (19127; reprint, Albuquerque: University of New Mexico Press, 1999), xvi.

31. Hutton, "Showdown," 13.

32. Barra, *Inventing Wyatt Earp*, 349; Lake, *Wyatt Earp*, 230.

33. John Mack Faragher, "The Tale of Wyatt Earp: Seven Films," in *Past Imperfect: History According to the Movies*, ed. Mark C. Carnes (New York: Henry Holt, 1995), 158.

34. Patricia Nelson Limerick, *The Legacy of Conquest: The Unbroken Past of the American West* (New York: W. W. Norton, 1987), 19.

35. Johnson, *Hunger for the Wild*.

36. Hutton, "Showdown," 13.

37. Keller, "Historical Discourse," 241.

38. Jean Baudrillard, "Simulacra and Simulations," from Jean Baudrillard, *Selected Writings*, ed. Mark Poster (Palo Alto, CA: Stanford University Press, 1988), http://topologicalmedialab.net/xinwei/classes/readings/Baudrillard/Simulacra+Simulations.pdf (accessed 25 November 2015).

39. Hutton, "Showdown," 14.

40. Faragher, "The Tale of Wyatt Earp," 154.

41. Hutton, "Showdown," 14.

42. The Ken Darby Singers, "The Legend of Wyatt Earp," lyrics by Harry Warren, music by Harold Adamson. This series, as the first about Wyatt Earp, became the foundational text for future television representations.

43. *The Life and Legend of Wyatt Earp*, "Wyatt Earp Becomes a Marshal," 6 September 1955.

44. Hutton, "Showdown," 14.

45. Cheyney Ryan, "Legal Outsiders in American Film: The Legal Nocturne," *Suffolk University Law Review* 42, no. 4 (2009): 870.

46. The films in this series are *Fistful of Dollars* (1964), *For a Few Dollars More* (1965), and *The Good, the Bad, and the Ugly* (1966). Perhaps Leone's film that is most critical of the western genre, *Once upon a Time in the West* (1968), though not as popular when released, has since developed a passionate cult following and is widely considered Leone's masterpiece.

47. This is the first time the now-famous street fight was dubbed the "Gunfight at the OK Corral."

48. Hutton, "Showdown," 24.

49. William H. Katerberg, *Future West: Utopia and Apocalypse in Frontier Science Fiction* (Lawrence: University Press of Kansas, 2008), 35.

50. See Limerick, *Legacy of Conquest*, 1987.

51. Barra, *Inventing Wyatt Earp*, 360.

52. *Star Trek*, "Spectre of the Gun," season 3, episode 1, first aired 25 October

1968 (one day before the eighty-seventh anniversary of the street fight behind the OK Corral).

53. Samuel Delany quoted in Carl Abbott, *Frontiers Past and Future: Science Fiction and the American West* (Lawrence: University Press of Kansas, 2006), 1.

54. Hutton, "Showdown," 24.

55. Faragher, "Tale of Wyatt Earp," 160.

56. *Westworld*, DVD, directed by Michael Crichton (1973; Burbank, CA: Warner Home Video, 2010).

57. A number of western films were released in the years since 1990's *Dances with Wolves*, many of which are among the top-grossing western films of all time. *Dances with Wolves* is at the top of that list. The next nine were all produced in 1990 or later: *True Grit* (2010), *Django Unchained* (2012), *Rango* (2011), *Wild Wild West* (1999), *Maverick* (1994), *Unforgiven* (1992), *Cowboys and Aliens* (2011), *The Lone Ranger* (2013), and *Back to the Future III* (1990). Box Office Mojo, http://www.boxofficemojo .com/genres/chart/?id=western.htm (accessed 25 November 2015).

58. *Tombstone*, DVD, directed by George P. Cosmatos (1993; Burbank, CA: Hollywood Pictures, 1997).

59. Hutton, "Showdown," 30.

60. For more on the Chinese population in Tombstone, see Benton-Cohen, *Borderline Americans*.

61. Slotkin, *Gunfighter Nation*, 154.

62. Faragher, "Tale of Wyatt Earp," 160.

63. Hutton, "Showdown," 30.

64. Philip J. Deloria, "Review of *Unforgiven, Posse, Bad Girls, The Ballad of Little Jo, Tombstone,* and *Geronimo: An American Legend,*" *American Historical Review* 100, no. 4 (1995): 1197.

65. In a survey conducted by the author on 10 May 2011, in answer to the question "When you hear the words 'Tombstone, Arizona,' what comes to mind?" 50 percent made reference to the 1993 film. (The other 50 percent were a combination of responses, including "headstones" and "the pizza.")

66. Conversations with author, Tombstone, Arizona, February 2015. Also, a travel blogger, writing about a visit to Tombstone, wrote, "We watched the DVD *Tombstone* (Kurt Russel [sic], Val Kilmer) before the trip to know about the story." See www.travelpod.com/travel-blog-entries/penguinx/sw-usa-2007/1191305700/tpod .html (accessed 10 May 2011).

67. Western television shows released since 1994 include *Dr. Quinn, Medicine Woman; Walker, Texas Ranger; Firefly; Deadwood; Justified; Hell on Wheels;* and *Longmire*.

Chapter 4. The Global Mythic West

1. "The New El Dorado: Tombstone in Arizona," *Leeds Mercury*, 22 May 1880, 1.

2. The facts surrounding Curly Bill's death are still debated among historians, as some reports indicate that he left Arizona in 1881. Wyatt Earp's assertion that he killed Brocius has never been verified.

3. "American Cow-boys," *Hadderfield Daily Chronicle*, 19 September 1883, 4.

4. "News of the Day," *Bristol Mercury and Daily Post*, 27 May 1882, 5.

5. "Hanging in Arizona," *Edinburgh Evening News*, 1 April 1884, 4; "Five Bandits Hanged in Tombstone," *Derby Daily Telegraph*, 31 March 1884, 4; *Yorkshire Post and Leeds Intelligencer*, 1 April 1884, 6, 7; "General News of the Week," *Stamford Mercury*, 4 April 1884, 3; *Aberdeen People's Journal*, 5 April 1884, 6. All of these are available on the British Newspaper Archive, http://www.britishnewspaperarchive.co.uk/.

6. Louis S. Warren, *Buffalo Bill's America: William Cody and the Wild West Show* (New York: Vintage, 2005), 284.

7. Robert W. Rydell and Rob Kroes, *Buffalo Bill in Bologna: The Americanization of the World, 1869–1922* (Chicago: University of Chicago Press, 2005), 4.

8. Warren, *Buffalo Bill's America*, 417. For more on Buffalo Bill both in America and abroad, see Paul Reddin, *Wild West Shows* (Champaign: University of Illinois Press, 1999); Frank Christianson, *The Life of Hon. William F. Cody, Known as Buffalo Bill* (Lincoln: University of Nebraska Press, 2011) and *The Wild West in England* (Lincoln: University of Nebraska Press, 2012). For Native Americans in Wild West shows, see Linda Scarangella McNenly, *Native Performers in Wild West Shows: From Buffalo Bill to Euro Disney* (Norman: University of Oklahoma Press, 2012); and F. G. Moses, *Wild West Shows and the Images of American Indians, 1883–1933* (Albuquerque: University of New Mexico Press, 1996).

9. "Ich bin ein Cowboy," *Economist*, 24 May 2001. http://www.economist.com /node/630986 (accessed 24 November 2015).

10. Susanne Zantop, "Close Encounters: Deutsch and Indianer," in Calloway et al., *Germans and Indians*, 4. Also see Julia Simone Stetler, *Buffalo Bill's Wild West in Germany: A Transnational History* (PhD diss., University of Nevada, Las Vegas, 2012).

11. Richard Slotkin, *Regeneration through Violence: The Mythology of the American Frontier, 1600–1860* (Norman: University of Oklahoma Press, 1973), 5.

12. See Frederick Jackson Turner, "The Significance of the Frontier in America," 1894, in *The Frontier in American History* (New York: Henry Holt, 1921), 1–38; and Ray Allen Billington, "How the Frontier Shaped the American Character," *American Heritage*, April 1958, 4.

13. Michael Steiner, "Frontierland as Tomorrowland: Walt Disney and the Architectural Packaging of the American West," *Montana, the Magazine of Western History* 48, no. 1 (Spring 1998): 5.

14. Patricia Nelson Limerick, *Something in the Soil: Legacies and Reckonings in the New West* (New York: W. W. Norton, 2000), 91.

15. Rob Kroes, "American Studies in Europe, or: Brother, Can You Paradigm?" *Transatlantica*, vol. 1, 2001, para. 16, https://transatlantica.revues.org/327 (accessed 25 November 2015).

16. Mary Yoko Brannen, "When Mickey Loses Face: Recontextualization, Semantic Fit, and the Semiotics of Foreignness," *Academy of Management Review* 29, no. 4 (2004): 595.

17. Tim Scheie, "Genre in Transitional Cinema: 'Arizona Bill' and the Silent French Western, 1912–1914," *French Forum* 36, no. 2 (2011): 201.

18. Lutz P. Koepnick, "Unsettling America: German Westerns and Modernity," *Modernism/Modernity* 2, no. 3 (1995): 1–22.

19. Christopher Frayling, *Spaghetti Westerns: Cowboys and Europeans from Karl May to Sergio Leone* (1981; reprint, London: Tauris, 1998), 10, 29, 65.

20. Ibid., 50.

21. Edward Buscombe, ed., *The BFI Companion to the Western* (New York: Atheneum, 1988), 48.

22. Ibid., 49. The use of the word "parodic" exposes Buscombe's tendency to privilege American westerns over those made internationally.

23. Coline Moire, Head of Communications, Icônes, email correspondence with author, 25 November 2015. See also Jean Thoren, "Gran Canaria's Grand Animation Event," *Animation Magazine*, 3 July 2012, http://www.animationmagazine.net /events/gran-canarias-grand-animation-event/ (accessed 24 November 2015); Stephen Price, "Little Tombstone Elevates ESMA," *Stash*, 31 January 2012, http:// www.stashmedia.tv/?p=8931 (accessed 25 November 2015). To watch the film, see https://vimeo.com/34655941.

24. The third in the *El Mariachi* series, *Once upon a Time in Mexico* is a clear nod to Sergio Leone and his film *Once upon a Time in the West* (1968) and is described by Rodriguez as the *The Good, the Bad, and the Ugly* of his trilogy. Roger Ebert, *Chicago Sun-Times*, 12 September 2003, http://rogerebert.suntimes.com/apps/pbcs.dll /article?AID=/20030912/REVIEWS/309120304/1023 (accessed 3 September 2015).

25. Well-known films directed by Takashi Miike include *Audition* (1999) and *Ichi the Killer* (2001) .

26. Frayling, *Spaghetti Westerns*, 105.

27. Hans-Michael Bock, "East Germany: The DEFA Story," in *The Oxford History of World Cinema*, ed. Geoffery Nowell-Smith (Oxford: Oxford University Press, 1996), 627, 628.

28. Ibid. Socialist realism was the style of art that depicted and glorified the proletariat's struggle toward socialist progress.

29. Thomas Paterson et al., *American Foreign Relations, a History,* vol. 2 (Boston: Wadsworth, 2010), 333.

30. Bock, "East Germany," 630; Gerd Gemünden, "Between Karl May and Karl Marx: The DEFA *Indianerfilme*," in Calloway et al., *Germans and Indians*, 244.

31. Gemünden, "Between Karl May and Karl Marx," 245.

32. Ibid., 249.

33. Steiner, "Frontierland as Tomorrowland," 9.

34. Disneyland Paris, http://www.welcometothemagic.com/disney-shows /buffalo-bill.htm (accessed 24 November 2015); and "Disneyland Paris Package and Extras Guide," http://www.welcometothemagic.com/images/docs/Disney Extras-Guide.pdf (accessed 24 November 2015), 4.

35. Steiner, "Frontierland as Tomorrowland," 1, 4.

36. Ibid., 4.

37. Masako Notoji, "Cultural Transformation of John Philip Sousa and Disneyland in Japan," in *Here, There, and Everywhere: The Foreign Politics of American Popular Culture*, ed. Reinhold Wagnleitner and Elaine Tyler May (Hanover, NH: University Press of New England, 2000), 224.

38. Kevin Mulroy, ed., *Western Amerykanski: Polish Poster Art and the Western* (Los

Angeles: Autry Museum of Western Heritage, and Seattle: University of Washington Press, 1999), 48.

39. Michael John Grist, "History of the Western Village Amusement Park, Japan," 12 July 2011, http://www.michaeljohngrist.com/2011/07/history-of-the-western-village-amusement-park-japan/ (accessed 5 March 2012).

40. Mulroy, *Western Amerykanski*, 48.

41. Michael John Grist, "Japan's Abandoned Animatronic John Wayne," 20 June 2011, http://www.michaeljohngrist.com/2011/06/japans-abandoned-animatronic-john-wayne/ (accessed 24 November 2015).

42. Florian/Abandoned Kansai, "Western Village—Japan's Abandoned Wild West Theme Park," http://abandonedkansai.com/2015/01/06/western-village-japans-abandoned-wild-west-theme-park/ (accessed 24 November 2015). To see photographs of the park's rusting façades, go to http://www.michaeljohngrist.com/2011/06/japans-abandoned-wild-west-town/. It is well worth the visit.

43. Laredo Western Town, http://www.laredo.org.uk/history.html (accessed 10 May 2012).

44. Deadwood Western Town, http://www.oldwest.org.uk/Deadwood/index.htm (accessed 24 November 2015).

45. Ibid.

46. One visitor attempted to distance himself from a typical, perhaps pedestrian, Disney experience, with the hashtag #pasdisneyland ("not Disneyland") on his Vine post. https://vine.co/tags/pasdisneyland, 11 July 2014 (accessed 3 September 2015).

47. French Property Guide to Themeparks, http://www.french-property.com/reference/theme_parks_france/ (accessed 24 November 2015). See also OK Corral, France, http://www.okcorral.fr/ (accessed 12 July 2012).

48. World Event Listings: Tourism Guides and Events Promotion, http://www.worldeventlistings.com/en/france/recommended-venues/ok-corral-park-p-26177 (accessed 24 November 2015).

49. French Property Guide to Themeparks, http://www.french-property.com/reference/theme_parks_france/ (accessed 24 November 2015).

50. Marvellous Provence, http://www.marvellous-provence.com/family-friendly/marseille-area/ok-corral (accessed 3 September 2015).

51. Pullman City, https://www.pullmancity.de/de_DE/home/ (accessed 3 September 2015).

52. Ruth Ellen Gruber, "Deep in the Heart of Bavaria," *New York Times*, 11 April 2004.

53. Ibid. Ruth Ellen Gruber visited Pullman City during a special Indian Week. Events included feathered performers presenting renditions of Plains Indian dances on Main Street. These were not Native Americans, however, but a group of Czech hobbyists. A visiting Cheyenne artist, Standing Elk, remarked on seeing the dancers that he could use this experience to encourage young people in his own community to study and maintain their traditions. "If Czechs can do it," he remarked, "so can they." The transnational journey of Native Americanness from Montana to Bavaria back to Montana is striking.

54. Rivka Galchen, "Wild West Germany: Why Do Cowboys and Indians So Captivate the Country?" *New Yorker*, 9 April 2012, http://www.newyorker.com /magazine/2012/04/09/wild-west-germany (accessed 24 November 2015).

55. Andrew Cockrum, "New Museum to Honor German 'Wild West' Author," *Tombstone Epitaph*, 17 April 2012.

56. Chris Wilson, *Myth of Santa Fe*, 304.

57. Steiner, "Frontierland as Tomorrowland," 6, emphasis in original.

58. Ibid.

59. Apache Spirit Ranch general introduction video, http://www.apachespirit ranch.com/impressions (accessed 18 June 2012). Because the ranch changed owners in 2014 and has been renamed, the original site with this video is no longer available.

60. Ibid.

61. Ibid., verbal emphasis in original.

62. Ibid.

63. Conversations with author, Tombstone Monument Ranch, February 2015.

64. Ibid.

65. Trip Advisor, http://www.tripadvisor.com/Hotel_Review-g31381-d2017550 -Reviews-Apache_Spirit_Ranch-Tombstone_Arizona.html (accessed 10 July 2012); http://www.tripadvisor.com/Hotel_Review-g31381-d2017550-Reviews-or10-Tomb stone_Monument_Ranch-Tombstone_Arizona.html#REVIEWS (accessed 17 May 2015).

66. Notoji, "Cultural Transformation," 225.

Chapter 5. Historians' Gunfight

1. Gary L. Roberts, "Trailing an American Mythmaker: History and Glenn G. Boyer's Tombstone Vendetta," 1998, http://home.earthlink.net/~knuthc01 /IMWEfiles/Mythmaker1source.htm (accessed 3 September 2015).

2. John P. Clum, "Yesterday's Tragedy: Three Men Hurled into Eternity in the Duration of a Moment," *Tombstone Epitaph*, 27 October 1881.

3. Harry Wood, "A Desperate Streetfight: Marshal Virgil Earp, Morgan and Wyatt Earp and Doc Holliday Meet the Cowboys—Three Men Killed and Two Wounded, One Seriously—Origins of the Trouble and Its Tragic Termination," *Tombstone Nugget*, 27 October 1881.

4. Wyatt S. Earp, "How Wyatt Earp Routed a Gang of Arizona Outlaws," *San Francisco Examiner*, 2 August 1896. This was the first of three articles in the series. Earp authority Gary Roberts says, "Despite its errors and some questions about the liberties taken by his ghost writer, the account attributed to Wyatt in the *San Francisco Examiner* in 1896 is perhaps the closest thing to an accurate account to be published before the 1920's. This conclusion is faint praise, but the *Examiner* articles at least described real events and got most of the names right." Gary L. Roberts, "The Real Tombstone Travesty: The Earp Controversy from Bechdolt to Boyer," *WOLA (Western Outlaw-Lawmen History Association) Journal* 8, no. 3 (Fall 1999), http://home.earthlink.net/~knuthc01/Travesty/realtravestysource.htm (accessed 25 November 2015).

5. "Fitz Gets an Injunction, the Courts Will Decide the Ownership of the Purse, Wyatt Earp Arrested Yesterday," *San Francisco Call*, 4 December 1896, 1.

6. "The Swindle Is Revealed," *San Francisco Call*, 10 December 1896. See also Isenberg, *Wyatt Earp*, 188–198.

7. "Look at His Phiz.: Wyatt Earp, a Bad Man and He Looks It," *Columbus (NE) Journal*, 27 January 1897, 1.

8. Andrew Isenberg posits that Wyatt had been confused with his brother Warren, who had indeed been shot and killed in a saloon in Wilcox, Arizona, in July 1900. It seems unlikely that he'd been confused with his brother Warren, however, since this article also mentions that Warren had been shot and killed. Isenberg, *Wyatt Earp*, 200.

9. "Murders Were Their Pastime," *Richmond (VA) Times*, 22 July 1900, 1.

10. J. M. Scanland, "Lurid Trails Are Left by Olden Day Bandits," *Los Angeles Sunday Times*, 12 March 1922.

11. Frederick R. Bechdolt, *When the West Was Young* (New York: Century, 1922), 103.

12. Mark J. Dworkin, *American Mythmaker: Walter Noble Burns and the Legends of Billy the Kid, Wyatt Earp, and Joaquin Murrieta* (Norman: University of Oklahoma Press, 2015), 84.

13. Breakenridge, *Helldorado*, 247–249. Breakenridge painted Wyatt Earp as a gambler, thief, and murderer, casting himself as the hero of Tombstone. Though Wyatt spent the rest of his days protesting his portrayal in the book, the work was a success and led to the annual celebration in Tombstone named for Breakenridge's tale.

14. Ibid., 256.

15. Dworkin, *American Mythmaker*, 91, 88.

16. Hutton, *Showdown*, 15.

17. Waters, *Earp Brothers of Tombstone*, 3.

18. Ed Bartholomew, *Wyatt Earp: The Untold Story 1848 to 1880* (Toyahvale, TX: Frontier, 1963), inside cover.

19. Tefertiller, *Wyatt Earp*, 333.

20. Ibid. Tefertiller argues that Lake's excessive use of the first person—not Wyatt Earp's own attempts at fame—are to blame for Earp's reputation for being a fanatical self-promoter.

21. Roberts, "Real Tombstone Travesty."

22. Waters, *Earp Brothers of Tombstone*, 6.

23. Roberts, "Real Tombstone Travesty."

24. Richard E. Erwin, *The Truth about Wyatt Earp* (Lincoln, NE: iUniverse, 2000), 6. Erwin, a former criminal defense attorney in California, is yet another grassroots historian who spent years unpacking the Earp story and attempting to understand the man behind the legend.

25. Janny Scott, "New Battleground of the Old West: Academia," *Arizona Republic*, 19 May 1993, A4.

26. Dick Kreck, "Showdown in the New West," *Denver Post Magazine*, 21 March 1993, 6–8.

27. Larry McMurtry, "How the West Was Won or Lost," *New Republic*, 22 October 1990, 33.

28. See Roberts, "Trailing an American Mythmaker"; Tony Ortega, "How the West Was Spun," *Phoenix New Times*, 24 December 1998; Jeff Sharlet, "Author's Methods Lead to Showdown over Much-Admired Book on Old West," *Chronicle of Higher Education*, 11 June 1999; Jefferson Decker, "Tombstone Blues," *Lingua Franca*, July/August 1999; Andrew Gumbel, "Historians Shoot It Out over Mrs. Earp's Fake Memoirs," *Independent* (UK), 13 February 2000; "History Exposé: The Façade behind the Front," *Tombstone Tumbleweed*, 16 March 2000; Billy Johnson, "Showdown at Schieffelin Hall," *Old West Chronicle*, November/December 2001.

29. Barra, *Inventing Wyatt Earp*, 384.

30. Erwin, *Truth*, 6.

31. Barra, *Inventing Wyatt Earp*, 386.

32. Jeffrey J. Morey, "The Curious Vendetta of Glenn G. Boyer," *Quarterly of the National Association for Outlaw and Lawman History* 17, no. 4 (1994): 22–28, http://home.earthlink.net/~knuthco1/IMWEfiles2/curiousvendettasource.htm (accessed 24 November 2015).

33. Interview with Casey Tefertiller, in Sierra Adare, "The Life and Legends of Wyatt Earp Have Led to a Verbal Shootout between Two 'Penslingers,'" *Wild West* 11, no. 3 (October 1998): 64. The interviews can be found at http://www.historynet.com/boyer-vs-tefertiller-penslingers-face-off-over-wyatt-earp.htm (accessed 24 November 2015). This is interesting as well because it seems incongruous that Boyer—a man who had been writing about Tombstone, Doc Holliday, and Wyatt Earp for decades—would not know anything about frontier journalism, either.

34. Morey, "Curious Vendetta."

35. Interview with Glenn G. Boyer, in Adare, "Verbal Shootout between Two 'Penslingers,'" http://www.historynet.com/boyer-vs-tefertiller-penslingers-face-off-over-wyatt-earp.htm (accessed 24 November 2015).

36. Morey, "Curious Vendetta."

37. Adare, "Verbal Shootout between Two 'Penslingers.'"

38. Morey, "Curious Vendetta."

39. Roberts, "Real Tombstone Travesty."

40. Tefertiller, "Trailing an American Mythmaker."

41. Ortega, "How the West Was Spun."

42. Adare, "Verbal Shootout between Two 'Penslingers.'"

43. Johnson, "Showdown at Schieffelin Hall," http://home.earthlink.net/~knuthco1/Itemsofinterest2/showdownathallsource.htm (accessed 24 November 2015).

44. Jeff Morey, 6 November 2000, "Schieffelin Hall—November 4, 2000, Eyewitness Accounts," from the Tombstone History Discussion Forum, http://home.earthlink.net/~knuthco1/IMWEfiles2/SchieffelinHall2000.htm (accessed 22 November 2015).

45. Ibid.

46. Johnson, "Showdown at Schieffelin Hall," including introduction by Mark Dworkin.

47. Casey Tefertiller, 7 November 2000, "Schieffelin Hall—November 4, 2000, Eyewitness Accounts," from the Tombstone History Discussion Forum, http://home.earthlink.net/~knuthco1/IMWEfiles2/SchieffelinHall2000.htm (accessed 22 November 2015).

48. Mark Boardman, "The 'Icon' Is Dead," *True West*, 16 April 2013, http://www.truewestmagazine.com/the-icon-is-dead/ (accessed 24 November 2015).

49. See "Tombstone's Truth Revealed in 'The Last Gunfight,'" *USA Today*, 14 July 2011; Glenn C. Alschuler, "Wild West Legends Take a Beating in Jeff Guinn's 'The Last Gunfight,'" *Tulsa World News*, 8 May 2011; Allen Barra, "O.K. Corral Is Less Than Meets the Hype," *Pittsburgh Post-Gazette*, 22 May 2011; Edward M. Edveld, "Legend Loses Its Allure in 'The Last Gunfight,'" *Kansas City (MO) Star*, 13 June 2011; Allen G. Breed, "Black-and-White View of O.K. Corral Gunfight Gets Grayer," *Denver Post*, 22 May 2011.

50. Email correspondence with author, 4 September 2014.

51. Allen Barra, "Book Review: Historian Calls Out the Big Guns, but Debunks Myths No One Has Believed in Decades," *Minneapolis Star Tribune*, 30 July 2013, http://www.startribune.com/review-wyatt-earp-a-vigilante-life-by-andrew-c-isenberg/217651621/ (accessed 1 November 2015).

52. James McGrath Morris, Review of *Wyatt Earp: A Vigilante Life, Santa Fe New Mexican*, 9 August 2013, http://www.santafenewmexican.com/pasatiempo/books/book_reviews/wyatt-earp-a-vigilante-life/article_32d7627a-007a-11e3-b8a1-001a4bcf6878.html (accessed 3 September 2015).

53. Barra, "Historian Calls Out the Big Guns." See also Allen Barra, "Attack on the Wyatt Earp Myth Lacks Ammunition," *Chicago Tribune*, 5 July 2013, http://articles.chicagotribune.com/2013-07-05/features/ct-prj-0707-wyatt-earp-andrew-isenberg-20130705_1_wyatt-earp-steven-lubet-frontier-marshal (accessed 1 November 2015).

54. Andrew Isenberg, "Author Responds to Wyatt Earp Review," *Chicago Tribune*, 19 July 2013, http://articles.chicagotribune.com/2013-07-19/features/ct-prj-0721-letter-to-editor-wyatt-earp-response-20130719_1_wyatt-earp-doc-holliday-con-man (accessed 1 November 2015).

Epilogue. Vigilantism and the Border

1. Ann O'Neill, "Showdown at the H$_2$O Corral," CNN, 10 May 2012, http://www.cnn.com/2012/05/10/us/tombstone-water-fight/index.html (accessed 3 September 2015).

2. Howard Fischer, "Federal Judge Rejects Tombstone's Water Lawsuit," *Sierra Vista Herald*, 13 March 2015.

3. Ann O'Neill, "Spotted Owl Could Be Game Changer in Tombstone Water War," CNN, 9 June 2012, http://www.cnn.com/2012/06/09/us/tombstone-shovel-brigade/index.html (accessed 3 September 2015). See also Meredith Stahler, "It Was Never about the Water," *Tombstone News*, 20 March 2015, http://thetombstonenews.com/it-was-never-about-the-water-p4552-1.htm (accessed 26 November 2015).

4. David Holthouse, "Minutemen, Other Anti-Immigrant Militia Groups Stake Out Arizona Border: High-powered Firearms, Militia Maneuvers and Racism at the

Minuteman Project," *Southern Poverty Law Center, Intelligence Report*, 27 June 2005, https://www.splcenter.org/fighting-hate/intelligence-report/2005/minute men-other-anti-immigrant-militia-groups-stake-out-arizona-border (accessed 3 September 2015).

5. Max Blumenthal, "Vigilante Injustice," *Salon*, 22 May 2003, http://www.salon .com/2003/05/22/vigilante_3/ (accessed 3 November 2015).

6. Susy Buchanan and David Holthouse, "Minuteman Civil Defense Corps Leader Chris Simcox Has Troubled Past," Southern Poverty Law Center, Intelligence Report, 31 January 2006, www.splcenter.org/get-informed/intelligence -report/browse-all-issues/2005/winter/the-little-prince (accessed 3 September 2015).

7. Simcox is now charged with child molestation and facing trial in Arizona. This, of course, is wildly ironic because he and his followers claimed that those attempting to cross the border from Mexico were criminals and a danger to the region. See David Neiwert, "Simcox's Child-Molestation Trial Only Latest Instance of Border-Watcher Criminality," Southern Poverty Law Center, HateWatch, 16 March 2015, https://www.splcenter.org/hatewatch/2015/03/16/simcox's-child-molestation -trial-only-latest-instance-border-watcher-criminality (accessed 3 September 2015).

8. Again we see the link between Tombstone and Germany.

9. Adam Lehrer, "Minuteman Work Continues in Southern Arizona," *Tucson Weekly*, 16 April 2010, http://www.tucsonweekly.com/TheRange/archives/2010 /04/16/minuteman-work-continues-in-southern-arizona (accessed 25 November 2015).

10. Top 100 Donations/Contributions to Simcox for Senate Campaign in the 2010 Election Cycle, http://www.campaignmoney.com/political/committees/sim cox-for-senate-inc.asp?cycle=10 (accessed 29 November 2015).

11. Carmen Mercer, *America: De-Fence-Less* (Tombstone, AZ: self-published, 2009), quotation in acknowledgments.

12. Stephen Lemons, "Minuteman CEO Carmen Mercer Named in Arizona Attorney General Lawsuit over Property Tax Scam," *Phoenix New Times*, http:// www.phoenixnewtimes.com/blogs/minuteman-ceo-carmen-mercer-named-in -arizona-attorney-general-lawsuit-over-property-tax-scam-6498819, 17 August 2009 (accessed 3 September 2015).

13. Sonia Scherr, "Armed MCDC to 'Forcefully Engage' Border 'Criminals,'" Southern Poverty Law Center, HateWatch, 19 March 2010, https://www.splcenter .org/hatewatch/2010/03/19/armed-mcdc-'forcefully-engage'-border-'criminals' (accessed 3 September 2015).

14. Sonia Scherr, "After Call to Arms, Nativist Extremist Leader Calls It Quits," Southern Poverty Law Center, HateWatch, 26 March 2010, https://www.splcenter .org/hatewatch/2010/03/26/after-call-arms-nativist-extremist-leader-calls-it-quits (accessed 3 September 2015).

15. Lehrer, "Minuteman Work Continues in Southern Arizona."

16. Benton-Cohen, *Borderline Americans*, 78.

17. Slotkin, *Regeneration through Violence*, 5.

Abbott, Carl. *Frontiers Past and Future: Science Fiction and the American West.* Lawrence: University Press of Kansas, 2006.

Adare, Sierra. "The Life and Legends of Wyatt Earp Have Led to a Verbal Shootout Between Two 'Penslingers.'" *Wild West* 11, no. 3 (October 1998): 64.

Apaches (Appachen). VHS. Directed by Gottfried Kolditz (1973; Berlin: Progress Film-Verleih, 1997).

Aquila, Richard, ed. *Wanted Dead or Alive: The American West in Popular Culture.* Urbana: University of Illinois Press, 1998.

Athearn, Robert G. *The Mythic West in Twentieth-Century America.* Lawrence: University Press of Kansas, 1986.

———. *Westward the Briton.* New York: Charles Scribner's Sons, 1953.

Barra, Allen. *Inventing Wyatt Earp: His Life and Many Legends.* New York: Carroll & Graf, 1998.

Bartholomew, Ed. *Wyatt Earp: The Man and the Myth.* Toyahvale, TX: Frontier, 1964.

———. *Wyatt Earp: The Untold Story 1848 to 1880.* Toyahvale, TX: Frontier, 1963.

Bechdolt, Frederick R. *When the West Was Young.* New York: Century, 1922.

Benton-Cohen, Katherine. *Borderline Americans: Racial Division and Labor War in the Arizona Borderlands.* Cambridge, MA: Harvard University Press, 2009.

Berg, Charles Ramírez. *Latino Images in Film: Stereotypes, Subversion, and Resistance.* Austin: University of Texas Press, 2002.

Billington, Ray Allen. "How the Frontier Shaped the American Character." *American Heritage,* April 1958, 4.

Boardman, Mark. "The 'Icon' Is Dead." *True West,* 16 April 2013, http://www.truewestmagazine.com/the-icon-is-dead/ (accessed 25 November 2015).

Bock, Hans-Michael. "East Germany: The DEFA Story." In *The Oxford History of World Cinema.* Edited by Geoffery Nowell-Smith. Oxford: Oxford University Press, 1996, 627–631.

Bourdieu, Pierre. *Distinction: A Social Critique of the Judgment of Taste.* Cambridge, MA: Harvard University Press, 1984.

Brannen, Mary Yoko. "When Mickey Loses Face: Recontextualization, Semantic Fit, and the Semiotics of Foreignness." *Academy of Management Review* 29, no. 4 (2004): 593–616.

Breakenridge, William M. *Helldorado: Bringing the Law to the Mesquite.* Edited by Richard Maxwell Brown. 1928. Reprint, Lincoln: University of Nebraska Press, 1992.

Britz, Kevin. "'A True to Life Reproduction': The Origins of Tombstone's Helldorado Celebration." *Journal of Arizona History* 22 (Winter 2001): 369–408.

Brodhead, Richard. *Cultures of Letters: Scenes of Reading and Writing in Nineteenth-Century America*. Chicago: University of Chicago Press, 1995.

Bruner, Edward M. "Abraham Lincoln as Authentic Reproduction: A Critique of Postmodernism." *American Anthropologist* 96, no. 2 (June 1994): 397–415.

———. *Culture on Tour: Ethnographies of Travel*. Chicago: University of Chicago Press, 2004.

Burns, Walter Noble. *Tombstone: An Iliad of the Southwest*. 1927. Reprint, Albuquerque: University of New Mexico Press, 1999.

Buscombe, Edward, ed. *The BFI Companion to the Western*. New York: Atheneum, 1988.

Buscombe, Edward, and Kevin Mulroy, "The Western Worldwide." In Mulroy, *Western Amerykanski: Polish Poster Art and the Western*, 3–67.

Calloway, Colin G., Gerd Gemünden, and Susanne Zantop, eds. *Germans and Indians: Fantasies, Encounters, Projections*. Lincoln: University of Nebraska Press, 2002.

Christensen, Bonnie. *Red Lodge and the Mythic West: Coal Miners to Cowboys*. Lawrence: University Press of Kansas, 2002.

Christianson, Frank. *The Life of Hon. William F. Cody, Known as Buffalo Bill*. Lincoln: University of Nebraska Press, 2011.

———. *The Wild West in England*. Lincoln: University of Nebraska Press, 2012.

Clements, Eric L. *After the Boom in Tombstone and Jerome: Decline in Western Resource Towns*. Reno: University of Nevada Press, 2003.

Cohen, Erik. "Authenticity and Commoditization in Tourism." *Annals of Tourism Research* 15 (1988): 371–386.

Corkin, Stanley. *Cowboys as Cold Warriors: The Western and U.S. History*. Philadelphia: Temple University Press, 2004.

Coyne, Michael. *The Crowded Prairie: American National Identity in the Hollywood Western*. New York: Tauris, 1997.

Deloria, Philip J. "Review of *Unforgiven, Posse, Bad Girls, The Ballad of Little Jo, Tombstone*, and *Geronimo: An American Legend*." *American Historical Review* 100, no. 4 (1995): 1194–1198.

DeLyser, Dydia. "Authenticity on the Ground: Engaging the Past in a California Ghost Town." *Annals of the Association of American Geographers* 89, no. 4 (December 1999): 602–632.

Dorst, John D. *The Written Suburb: An American Site, an Ethnographic Dilemma*. Philadelphia: University of Pennsylvania Press, 1989.

Durgnat, Raymond, and Scott Simmon. "Six Creeds That Won the Western." In Kitses and Rickman, *Western Reader*, 69–83.

Dworkin, Mark J. *American Mythmaker: Walter Noble Burns and the Legends of Billy the Kid, Wyatt Earp, and Joaquin Murrieta*. Norman: University of Oklahoma Press, 2015.

Eco, Umberto. *Travels in Hyperreality*. New York: Harcourt Brace, 1986.

Ellis, William S. "The Scene: Bat, Wyatt, Doc, and Boot Hill to Boot." *Life*, 3 June 1966, R2–R6.

Erwin, Robert E. *The Truth about Wyatt Earp.* Lincoln, NE: iUniverse, 2000.

Faragher, John Mack. *Rereading Frederick Jackson Turner: "The Significance of the Frontier in American History" and Other Essays.* New Haven, CT: Yale University Press, 1999.

———. "The Tale of Wyatt Earp: Seven Films." In *Past Imperfect: History According to the Movies.* Edited by Mark C. Carnes. New York: Henry Holt, 1995, 154–161.

Faulk, Odie B. *Tombstone, Arizona: Myth and Reality.* New York: Oxford University Press, 1972.

Flores, Richard R. *Remembering the Alamo: Memory, Modernity, and the Master Symbol.* Austin: University of Texas Press, 2002.

Frampton, Kenneth. "Prospects for a Critical Regionalism." In *Theorizing a New Agenda for Architecture: An Anthology of Architectural Theory, 1965–1995.* Edited by Kate Nesbitt. New York: Princeton Architectural Press, 1996, 468–483.

Franklin, Adrian. *Tourism: An Introduction.* London: Sage, 2003.

Frayling, Christopher. *Spaghetti Westerns: Cowboys and Europeans from Karl May to Sergio Leone.* 1981. Reprint, London: Tauris, 1998.

Frost, Warwick, and Jennifer Laing. *Imagining the American West through Film and Tourism.* New York: Routledge, 2015, 61–76.

Galchen, Rivka. "Wild West Germany: Why Do Cowboys and Indians So Captivate the Country?" *New Yorker,* 9 April 2012, 40–46.

Gemünden, Gerd. "Between Karl May and Karl Marx: The DEFA *Indianerfilme.*" In Calloway et al., *Germans and Indians,* 243–256.

Guinn, Jeff. *The Last Gunfight: The Real Story of the Shootout at the OK Corral—and How It Changed the American West.* New York: Simon & Schuster, 2011.

Hall, Stuart. "Encoding/Decoding." In *Media Studies: A Reader.* Edited by Paul Marris and Sue Thornham. New York: New York University Press, 2000, 51–61.

———. "Notes on Deconstructing the Popular." In *Cultural Theory and Popular Culture: A Reader,* 4th ed. Edited by John Storey. Essex, UK: Pearson, 2009, 508–518.

———. "Whose Heritage?" In *The Politics of Heritage, the Legacies of Race.* Edited by Jo Littler and Roshi Naidoo. New York: Routledge, 2005, 23–35.

"Here and There on the Desert: Restoration of Tombstone Planned." *Desert,* March 1951, 31.

Hobsbawm, Eric, and Terrance Ranger. *The Invention of Tradition.* New York: Cambridge University Press, 1983.

Howe, Barbara J. "Women in Historic Preservation: The Legacy of Ann Pamela Cunningham." *Public Historian* 12, no. 1 (Winter 1990): 31–61.

Hutton, Paul Andrew. "Showdown at the Hollywood Corral: Wyatt Earp and the Movies." *Montana: The Magazine of Western History* 45 (Summer 1995): 1–31.

Isenberg, Andrew C. *Wyatt Earp: A Vigilante Life.* New York: Hill & Wang, 2013.

Jameson, Fredric. "Reification and Utopia in Mass Culture." *Signatures of the Visible.* New York: Routledge, 1992.

Johnson, Michael L. *Hunger for the Wild: America's Obsession with the Untamed West.* Lawrence: University Press of Kansas, 2007.

Johnson, Paul Lee. *The McLaury Brothers of Arizona: An OK Corral Obituary.* Denton: University of North Texas Press, 2012.

Kammen, Michael G. *Mystic Chords of Memory: The Transformation of Tradition in American Culture.* New York: Knopf, 1991.

Katerberg, William H. *Future West: Utopia and Apocalypse in Frontier Science Fiction.* Lawrence: University Press of Kansas, 2008.

Keller, Alexandra. "Historical Discourse and American Identity in Westerns since the Reagan Era." In Rollins and O'Connor, *Hollywood's West*, 239–260.

Kilpatrick, Jacqueline. *Celluloid Indians: Native Americans and Film.* Lincoln: University of Nebraska Press, 1999.

Kitses, Jim, and Gregg Rickman, eds. *The Western Reader.* New York: Limelight, 1998.

Koepnick, Lutz P. "Unsettling America: German Westerns and Modernity." *Modernism/Modernity* 2, no. 3 (1995): 1–22.

Kroes, Rob. "American Studies in Europe, or: Brother, Can You Paradigm?" *Transatlantica*, vol. 1, 2001, https://transatlantica.revues.org/327 (accessed 25 November 2015).

Lake, Stuart N. *Wyatt Earp: Frontier Marshal.* Boston: Houghton Mifflin, 1931.

Landin, Edna. "The Legend Lives." *Desert*, January 1965, 30–31.

Larson, Al. "Mountain Justice: An Examination of Three Mountainous West County Courthouses." *Material Culture* 31, no. 1 (Spring 1999): 21–31.

Lenihan, John H. *Showdown: Confronting Modern America in the Western Film.* Urbana: University of Illinois Press, 1980.

The Life and Legend of Wyatt Earp. Online. Directed by Frederick Hazlitt Brennan. 1955–1961; Los Angeles, CA: CBS Television Distribution, 2007.

Limerick, Patricia Nelson. *The Legacy of Conquest: The Unbroken Past of the American West.* New York: W. W. Norton, 1987.

———. *Something in the Soil: Legacies and Reckonings in the New West.* New York: W. W. Norton, 2000.

Linenthal, Edward Tabor. *Sacred Ground: Americans and Their Battlefields.* Urbana: University of Illinois Press, 1991.

Little Tombstone, http://little-tombstone.com/. Dir. Frédéric Azais, Théo Di Malta, Benjamin Leymonerie, and Adrien Quillet; music by Alexandre Scuri. 2011. ESMA (Ecole Superieure des Metiers Aristiques), Toulouse. Film.

Lutz, Hartmut. "German Indianthusiasm: A Socially Constructed German National(ist) Myth." In Calloway et al., *Germans and Indians*, 167–184.

MacCannell, Dean. *The Tourist: A New Theory of the Leisure Class.* Berkeley: University of California Press, 1976.

Martin, Douglas D. *Tombstone's Epitaph: The History of a Frontier Town as Chronicled in Its Newspaper.* Albuquerque: University of New Mexico Press, 1951.

Mason, Randall. "Economics and Heritage Conservation: Concepts, Values, and Agendas for Research." Economics and Heritage Conservation, a Meeting Organized by the Getty Conservation Institute. Getty Center, Los Angeles, California, December 1998.

McMurtry, Larry. "How the West Was Won or Lost," *New Republic*, 22 October 1990: 32–38.

McNenly, Linda Scarangella. *Native Performers in Wild West Shows: From Buffalo Bill to Euro Disney.* Norman: University of Oklahoma Press, 2012.

Mercer, Carmen. *America: De-Fence-Less.* Tombstone, AZ: self-published, 2009.

Michaelson, L. W. "Tombstone." *Prairie Schooner* 30, no. 1 (Spring 1956): 56–57.

Morey, Jeffrey J. "The Curious Vendetta of Glenn G. Boyer." *Quarterly of the National Association for Outlaw and Lawman History* 17, no. 4 (1994): 22–28.

Morley, Judy Mattivi. *Historic Preservation and the Imagined West: Albuquerque, Denver, and Seattle.* Lawrence: University Press of Kansas, 2006.

Moses, F. G. *Wild West Shows and the Images of American Indians, 1883–1933.* Albuquerque: University of New Mexico Press, 1996.

Mulroy, Kevin, ed. *Western Amerykanski: Polish Poster Art and the Western.* Los Angeles: Autry Museum of Western Heritage, and Seattle: University of Washington Press, 1999.

My Darling Clementine. Dir. John Ford. 1946. Twentieth Century Fox. Film.

Nicholas, Liza, Elaine M. Bapis, and Thomas J. Harvey, eds. *Imagining the Big Open: Nature, Identity, and Play in the New West.* Salt Lake City: University of Utah Press, 2003.

Notoji, Masako. "Cultural Transformation of John Philip Sousa and Disneyland in Japan." In *Here, There, and Everywhere: The Foreign Politics of American Popular Culture.* Edited by Reinhold Wagnleitner and Elaine Tyler May. Hanover, NH: University Press of New England, 2000, 219–226.

Paterson, Thomas, et al. *American Foreign Relations, a History.* Vol. 2. Boston: Wadsworth, 2010.

Pierson, David. "Turner Network Television's Made-for-TV Western Films: Engaging Audiences through Genre and Themes." In Rollins and O'Connor, *Hollywood's West*, 281–299.

Ramírez Berg, Charles. *Latino Images in Film: Stereotypes, Subversion, and Resistance.* Austin: University of Texas Press, 2002.

Reddin, Paul. *Wild West Shows.* Champaign: University of Illinois Press, 1999.

Roberts, Gary L. "The Real Tombstone Travesty: The Earp Controversy from Bechdolt to Boyer." *WOLA (Western Outlaw-Lawmen History Association) Journal* 8, no. 3 (Fall 1999), http://home.earthlink.net/~knuthco1/Travesty/realtravestysource.htm (accessed 25 November 2015).

Rollins, Peter C., and John E. O'Connor. *Hollywood's West: The American Frontier in Film, Television, and History.* Lexington: University Press of Kentucky, 2005.

Rosebrook, J. Stuart. "The Best of Heritage Travel 2014." *True West*, 9 December 2013, http://www.truewestmagazine.com/the-best-of-heritage-travel-2014-2/ (accessed 25 November 2015).

Rothman, Hal. *The Culture of Tourism, the Tourism of Culture: Selling the Past to the Present in the American Southwest.* Albuquerque: University of New Mexico Press, 2003.

———. *Devil's Bargains: Tourism in the Twentieth-Century American West.* Lawrence: University Press of Kansas, 1998.

Ryan, Cheyney. "Legal Outsiders in American Film: The Legal Nocturne." *Suffolk University Law Review* 42, no. 4 (2009): 869–98.

Ryan, James Gilbert, and Leonard C. Schlup. *Historical Dictionary of the 1940s.* Armonk, NY: M. E. Sharpe, 2006.

Rydell, Robert W., and Rob Kroes. *Buffalo Bill in Bologna: The Americanization of the World, 1869–1922.* Chicago: University of Chicago Press, 2005.

Scheie, Tim. "Genre in Transitional Cinema: 'Arizona Bill' and the Silent French Western, 1912–1914." *French Forum* 36, no. 2 (2011): 201–219.

Schwarzer, Mitchell. "Myths of Permanence and Transience in the Discourse on Historic Preservation in the United States." *Journal of Architectural Education* 48, no. 1 (1994): 2–11.

Sharlet, Jeff. "Author's Methods Lead to Showdown over Much-Admired Book on Old West." *Chronicle of Higher Education,* 11 June 1999, http://chronicle.com /article/Author-s-Methods-Lead-to/33543 (accessed 25 November 2015).

Shillingberg, William B. *Tombstone, A.T.: A History of Early Mining, Milling, and Mayhem.* Spokane, WA: Arthur H. Clark, 1999.

Sieg, Katrin. "Indian Impersonation as Historical Surrogation." In Calloway et al., *Germans and Indians,* 217–242.

Simmon, Scott. *The Invention of the Western: A Cultural History of the Genre's First Half-Century.* Cambridge: Cambridge University Press, 2003.

Slotkin, Richard. *Fatal Environment: The Myth of the Frontier in the Age of Industrialization, 1800–1890.* 1985. Reprint, Norman: University of Oklahoma Press, 1998.

———. *Gunfighter Nation: The Myth of the Frontier in Twentieth-Century America.* 1992. Reprint, Norman: University of Oklahoma Press, 1998.

———. *Regeneration through Violence: The Mythology of the American Frontier, 1600–1860.* Norman: University of Oklahoma Press, 1973.

Smith, Henry Nash. *Virgin Land: The American West as Symbol and Myth.* 1950. Reprint, Cambridge, MA: Harvard University Press, 1978.

Stanley, John. "Top Ten True Western Towns of 2014." *True West* magazine, 6 January 2014, http://www.truewestmagazine.com/top-10-true-western-towns -of-the-year-for-2014/ (accessed 25 November 2015).

Steiner, Michael. "Frontierland as Tomorrowland: Walt Disney and the Architectural Packaging of the American West." *Montana, the Magazine of Western History* 48, no. 1 (Spring 1998): 2–17.

Stetler, Julia Simone. *Buffalo Bill's Wild West in Germany: A Transnational History.* PhD dissertation, University of Nevada, Las Vegas, 2012.

Sturken, Marita. *Tourists of History: Memory, Kitsch, and Consumerism from Oklahoma City to Ground Zero.* Durham, NC: Duke University Press, 2007.

Sukiyaki Western Django. Dir. Takashi Miike. Sony Pictures Entertainment Japan. September 2007. Film.

Tefertiller, Casey. Foreword to Walter Noble Burns, *Tombstone: An Iliad of the Southwest.* 1927. Reprint, Albuquerque: University of New Mexico Press, 1999.

———. *Wyatt Earp: The Life behind the Legend.* New York: Wiley, 1997.

Tombstone. Dir. George P. Cosmatos. 1993. Cinergi Pictures. Film.

Tompkins, Jane. *West of Everything: The Inner Life of Westerns.* New York: Oxford University Press, 1992.

"Top Ten True Western Towns of 2011: Towns to Watch." *True West*, 11 January 2011.

Traywick, Ben. "Tombstone's Cemetery: Boothill." *Wild West,* 12 June 2006, http://www.historynet.com/tombstones-cemetery-boothill.htm (25 November 2015).

Turner, Frederick Jackson. "The Significance of the Frontier in America." 1894. *The Frontier in American History* (New York: Henry Holt, 1921), 1–38.

Turner, Victor. "Liminality and Communitas." In *The Ritual Process: Structure and Anti-Structure.* Chicago: Aldine, 1969, 94–130.

Tuska, Jon. *The Filming of the West.* New York: Doubleday, 1978.

Urry, John. *The Tourist Gaze.* London: Sage, 2002.

Wallace, Mike. *Mickey Mouse History and Other Essays on American Memory.* Philadelphia: Temple University Press, 1996.

Warren, Louis S. *Buffalo Bill's America: William Cody and the Wild West Show.* New York: Vintage, 2005.

Warshow, Robert. *Immediate Experience: Movies, Comics, Theatre, and Other Aspects of Popular Culture.* Garden City, NY: Doubleday, 1962.

Waters, Frank L. *The Earp Brothers of Tombstone: The Story of Mrs. Virgil Earp.* New York: C. N. Potter, 1960.

Westworld, DVD, directed by Michael Crichton. 1973. Burbank, CA: Warner Home Video, 2010.

Wilson, Chris. *The Myth of Santa Fe: Creating a Modern Regional Tradition.* Albuquerque: University of New Mexico Press, 1997.

Wilson, R. Michael. *Legal Executions in the Western Territories, 1847–1911.* Jefferson, NC: McFarland, 2010.

Wright, Will. *Sixguns and Society: A Structural Study of the Western.* Berkeley: University of California Press, 1977.

Wrobel, David M. *The End of American Exceptionalism: Frontier Anxiety from the Old West to the New Deal.* Lawrence: University Press of Kansas, 1993.

Wrobel, David, and Patrick Long, eds. *Seeing and Being Seen: Tourism and the American West.* Lawrence: University Press of Kansas, 2001.

Wyatt Earp. DVD. Directed by Lawrence Kasdan. 1994. Burbank, CA: Warner Brothers, 2004.

Zantop, Susanne. "Introduction: Close Encounters: Deutsch and Indianer." In Calloway et al., *Germans and Indians*, 3–14.

INDEX